SAP BusinessObjects Dashboards 4.1 Cookbook

Over 100 simple and incredibly effective recipes to help transform your static business data into exciting dashboards filled with dynamic charts and graphics

David Lai

Xavier Hacking

PUBLISHING

enterprise

professional expertise distilled

BIRMINGHAM - MUMBAI

SAP BusinessObjects Dashboards 4.1 Cookbook

First published: May 2011

Second edition: March 2015

Production reference: 1250315

Published by Packt Publishing Ltd.
Livery Place
35 Livery Street
Birmingham B3 2PB, UK.

ISBN 978-1-78439-195-9

www.packtpub.com

Credits

Authors
David Lai

Xavier Hacking

Reviewers
Darren Barber

Atul Bhimrao Divekar

Femke Kooij

Bernard Timbal Duclaux de Martin

Commissioning Editor
Dipika Gaonkar

Acquisition Editor
Llewellyn Rozario

Content Development Editor
Samantha Gonzalves

Technical Editors
Ruchi Desai

Pramod Kumavat

Copy Editors
Puja Lalwani

Adithi Shetty

Project Coordinator
Sanchita Mandal

Proofreaders
Simran Bhogal

Maria Gould

Paul Hindle

Jonathan Todd

Indexer
Mariammal Chettiyar

Graphics
Sheetal Aute

Jason Monteiro

Production Coordinator
Aparna Bhagat

Cover Work
Aparna Bhagat

Foreword

For the last decade, Xavier and David have authored several books and articles on SAP BusinessObjects products, including Design Studio and Dashboards. I have personally known Xavier for many years, and his approach to Business Intelligence, with practical advice and real, step-by-step development support, has been invaluable for thousands of developers and business people struggling to keep up with this rapidly changing technology.

Currently, there is no other guide that is more comprehensive than the cookbook you are now holding. It covers all the new capabilities within SAP BusinessObjects Dashboards 4.1. I particularly like the way Xavier and David continue to write using *recipes*. This approach quickly allows you to find the functionality you need, and then get the step-by-step advice on how to do it. This is very unlike some other books on the market that only tell you *what* to do, but really do not show you *how* to do it.

In this updated and expanded edition, you will appreciate the new chapters on performance tuning and how to get maximum developer performance through shortcuts, tips, and tricks. You will also find an updated section on dashboards based on mobile and HTML and an introduction to Design Studio.

In addition to these new sections, you will still find in-depth information on all aspects of Dashboards 4.1, including spreadsheet customization options, the manipulation of worksheets and canvas components, and data visualization, including the numerous charts and associated components that can be implemented as extensions. By following the advice in this book, your dashboards can cease to be static presentations of data and take on a new form of interactivity, where you can save scenarios and interact with the data in ways not done before.

In this book, you will also find recommendations on key concepts that are taught in classes but are seldom used by beginner developers, including how to hide graphs and call them through dynamic visibility and how to tailor the look and feel of a dashboard using templates and standards.

You will also appreciate that all of the dashboard connectivity options are explained, including connections to Excel XML Maps, SAP HANA, Live Office, Query as a Web Service, SAP BW, ODBC, and others. David and Xavier also cover how to integrate third-party add-ons such as Google Maps and Salesforce.com. Any developer, whether a senior or beginner, will significantly benefit from this latest cookbook. Frankly, all my developers use the previous cookbook as a reference when they are stuck on certain tasks, and I, personally, have been using the cookbook in my lectures at the SAP University Alliance over the last few years. It is with great anticipation that we can now welcome another updated version into our development labs, training classes, and forums. I hope you will enjoy this book as much as I have.

Dr. Bjarne Berg

CIO, Comerit Inc. and professor, SAP University Alliance at Lenoir-Rhyne University.

About the Author

David Lai is a SAP BusinessObjects consultant and specializes in data visualization and data warehousing. He graduated with a degree in computer engineering from the University of Toronto. He has a passion for providing organizations with smart Business Intelligence solutions that encompass best practices and techniques. In addition, he is an active contributor to the community and provides his knowledge in best practices and solutions.

He started his Business Intelligence blog (`http://www.davidlai101.com/blog`) in 2008, where he provides tips, tricks, and best practices for Xcelsius and BusinessObjects-related material. He is a bronze-level contributor to the SAP community network, has presented at SAP InsideTrack, and provides BusinessObjects training to students.

Aside from work, David enjoys physical activities such as weight training, basketball, volleyball, and skiing. He also has a strong passion for Latin dance.

David is the owner of Xinfinity Solutions, where he provides consulting services as a SAP BusinessObjects consultant. He has worked for a long list of satisfied clients in various industries.

Acknowledgments

Writing this book has been a long journey, and it would not have been possible without the guidance, inspiration, and mentorship provided by many others along the way. I'd like to show appreciation to all those who have assisted me along the path.

First of all, I would like to thank the Xcelsius developers for their efforts in bringing us new features and fixes with every new version of Xcelsius.

I would like to thank everyone in the Xcelsius community for their contributions on SDN, LinkedIn, and blogs. Without the community, we wouldn't have anywhere to look for help when we come across a problem. In addition, thoughts and ideas are taken into account by the development team to create a better product in the long run. A big thank you goes to Kalyan Verma for giving me the opportunity to contribute to his blog, `http://myxcelsius.com`, and really getting me kick-started with community participation (an excellent job on getting myxcelsius.com to where it is today!). Another big thanks to Mico Yuk of Everything Xcelsius for her past advice and really getting the community involved with Xcelsius.

I'd like to thank Xavier Hacking for coauthoring the book. Without Xavier's teamwork, knowledge, and expertise, this book would not have been a success. I would also like to commend his great work on his blog at `http://www.hackingsap.com`.

A big thanks to the Packt Publishing team (Stephanie Moss, Leena Purkait, Reshma Sundaresan, and Samantha Gonsalves) for providing all the necessary guidance in our writing process. Without the Packt Publishing team, this book would not have been possible.

Finally, I'd like to acknowledge Ryan Goodman for inspiring me to participate in blogging and assisting the community on Business Intelligence best practices and solutions.

About the Author

Xavier Hacking is an SAP BI specialist from Eindhoven, the Netherlands, and works as a consultant for Interdobs. He has a master's degree in industrial engineering and management science from the Eindhoven University of Technology. He has worked with a wide range of products from the SAP Business Intelligence portfolio, including SAP BW, SAP BusinessObjects Dashboards, Design Studio, Web Intelligence, Crystal Reports, and the SAP BusinessObjects BI Platform. His main focus is dashboard development within the various SAP environments.

Xavier is the coauthor of the first edition of this book and the book *Getting Started with SAP BusinessObjects Design Studio, SAP Press*. He writes for the SAP Experts BI Hub and has his own blog related to Business Intelligence at HackingSAP.com (http://HackingSAP.com/). You can follow Xavier on Twitter (http://twitter.com/xjhacking).

Acknowledgments

I want to thank the readers of the first edition of this book for making it such a success. The response to the book has been absolutely great since its release back in 2011. The online SAP BI community on Twitter, the SAP Community Network, the LinkedIn groups, and all the blogs form a great platform, where problems are solved and new ideas are started. A book like this wouldn't be possible without you all. Thanks.

Next, I want to thank the coauthor, David Lai, for another great run we had with this project. Also, a big thank you goes out to Samantha Gonsalves from Packt Publishing for coordinating this project.

Writing a book such as this needs a supportive environment to succeed. I want to thank Leon Huijsmans and Rob Huisman of Interdobs and my girlfriend, Marieke, for their unlimited help, advice, and support.

About the Reviewers

Darren Barber is a freelance consultant with over a decade of experience in the field of Business Intelligence. He has worked on every phase of the BI process, from data warehousing, ETL, and data modeling to reporting, dashboarding, and analytics. Working and living out of downtown Toronto, Darren helps companies realize the full potential value of their data.

Atul Bhimrao Divekar has worked with Business Intelligence applications for over 5 years, focusing primarily on the SAP BusinessObjects toolset. He is a SAP BO, SAP HANA 1.0, ITIL 2011, and Linux administrator certified consultant.

He holds a BSc degree in computer science from the University of Mumbai. Apart from being a SAP BO and SAP HANA mentor, he is an ardent follower of recent technologies. So, if he is not working, then you are sure to find him on the Web learning and getting updated about the recent gadgets, mobile applications, and four wheelers on the international market.

I would like to thank my brother, Vikram Divekar, for always supporting me. I would also like to thank my sister, Poonam Hadke, Aai (mother) Ranjana Divekar, and friends for all that they do to help me.

I would like to thank all the people behind this project who trusted me and made this book possible.

Femke Kooij is a dashboard and report designer and developer specializing in SAP BusinessObjects Dashboards (better known as Xcelsius) and Crystal Reports. She started developing with Xcelsius 3.0 in 2004 when it was still owned by Infomersion and has since worked with the product up till the current version, SAP BusinessObjects Dashboards 4.1. She has shared her knowledge and experience with others through her own blog (www.femkekooij.com).

She also has a lot of experience with other SAP BusinessObjects tools, such as Web Intelligence, Information Design Tool (universes), BusinessObjects Data Services (ETL), and the overall server platform (Launchpad, CMC). Her latest project focuses mainly on the integration between BusinessObjects and SAP.

Lately, she has been exploring other visualization tools such as QlikView and the Tableau software.

Bernard Timbal Duclaux de Martin is a Business Intelligence architect and technical expert with 15 years of experience. He has taken part in several large Business Intelligence system deployments and administration in banking and insurance companies. In addition, he is proficient in modeling, data extraction, transformation, loading, and reporting design. He has written four books, including two regarding SAP BusinessObjects Enterprise administration.

www.PacktPub.com

Support files, eBooks, discount offers, and more

For support files and downloads related to your book, please visit www.PacktPub.com.

Did you know that Packt offers eBook versions of every book published, with PDF and ePub files available? You can upgrade to the eBook version at www.PacktPub.com and as a print book customer, you are entitled to a discount on the eBook copy. Get in touch with us at service@packtpub.com for more details.

At www.PacktPub.com, you can also read a collection of free technical articles, sign up for a range of free newsletters and receive exclusive discounts and offers on Packt books and eBooks.

https://www2.packtpub.com/books/subscription/packtlib

Do you need instant solutions to your IT questions? PacktLib is Packt's online digital book library. Here, you can search, access, and read Packt's entire library of books.

Why subscribe?

- ▸ Fully searchable across every book published by Packt
- ▸ Copy and paste, print, and bookmark content
- ▸ On demand and accessible via a web browser

Free access for Packt account holders

If you have an account with Packt at www.PacktPub.com, you can use this to access PacktLib today and view 9 entirely free books. Simply use your login credentials for immediate access.

Instant updates on new Packt books

Get notified! Find out when new books are published by following @PacktEnterprise on Twitter or the *Packt Enterprise* Facebook page.

Table of Contents

Preface

SAP BusinessObjects Dashboards 4.1 (formerly known as Xcelsius) is a desktop dashboard and visualization solution that is a core part of SAP BusinessObjects BI 4.1. Once a user creates a dashboard model, it can be deployed in Flash format to web portals, SAP environments, the SAP BusinessObjects BI Platform, and desktop applications such as PowerPoint, Word, or PDF.

For dashboard designers/developers, SAP BusinessObjects Dashboards allows for rapid development of data visualizations through a flexible and easy-to-use graphical user interface.

Using SAP BusinessObjects Dashboards, we can accomplish the following:

- Create interactive dashboards that have a wow factor unlike other dashboard tool competitors.
- Connect dashboards to over 10 different types of data connections.
- Integration and interoperability with existing SAP BusinessObjects BI content.
- We can embed our dashboards into a variety of different formats to allow for convenient sharing between users.
- Ability to create custom add-on components using the SAP BusinessObjects Dashboards SDK.

SAP BusinessObjects Dashboards in its original conception was a way to build visualizations and dashboards using Excel data. That is also where the original name Xcelsius comes from. Over the past decade, BusinessObjects has enhanced Xcelsius into a fully featured enterprise-ready dashboard solution that works with any data source.

After the acquisition of BusinessObjects by SAP, the mission to make Xcelsius a dashboard product to serve all its customers (beyond being just a personal productivity tool) continued. The BI market and SAP customers were also demanding an enterprise dashboard solution for the types of projects they were using Xcelsius for, for example, dashboards for thousands of users using large data warehouses as a datasource. The name Xcelsius was no longer meaningful or relevant.

By changing the name Xcelsius to SAP BusinessObjects Dashboards, SAP is showing its commitment to delivering a solution that serves the needs of all BI customers as well as aligning the name to the product's growing capabilities and roadmap.

The SAP BusinessObjects Dashboards portfolio consists of several different packages (see the edition comparison later in the preface). In this book, we use SAP BusinessObjects Dashboards to refer to the tool itself.

What this book covers

Chapter 1, Staying in Control, presents you with best practices for using the SAP BusinessObjects Dashboards spreadsheet, the data model, and connections with the components on the canvas.

Chapter 2, Data Visualization, presents you with recipes on how to use different components such as charts, tables, and graphs to visualize data on the dashboard.

Chapter 3, From a Static to an Interactive Dashboard, shows you how to add interactivity to your dashboards by adding selectors, maps, buttons, drilldowns, and so on.

Chapter 4, Dynamic Visibility, shows you how to make components visible/invisible and provides scenarios where dynamic visibility becomes useful.

Chapter 5, Using Alerts, contains examples of different ways of showing alerts on a dashboard.

Chapter 6, Advanced Components, provides recipes on SAP BusinessObjects Dashboards' more advanced components.

Chapter 7, Dashboard Look and Feel, teaches you how to tweak the visuals and user experience of the dashboard by customizing the look of components.

Chapter 8, Dashboard Data Connectivity, talks about the various options to connect a dashboard to external data sources.

Chapter 9, Exporting and Publishing, contains recipes on how to export SAP BusinessObjects Dashboards into different environments.

Chapter 10, Top Third-party Add-ons, contains an introduction to some of the most useful third-party add-ons for SAP BusinessObjects Dashboards.

Chapter 11, Performance Tuning, teaches you how to improve the performance of your dashboards by tweaking the spreadsheet and optimizing the data sources' connection setup.

Chapter 12, Increasing Productivity, discusses various development best practices and tips to save precious development time.

Appendix A, Real-world Dashboard Case Studies, demonstrates how to implement various techniques covered in this book by creating two applications: a calculator that displays monthly payments of a mortgage and a sales/profit dashboard that displays the sales or profit of each state on a map.

Appendix B, Additional Resources – Supported Excel Functions and System/Software Requirements, lists some helpful online resources for further reference and some useful Microsoft Excel functions supported by SAP BusinessObjects Dashboards.

Appendix C, The Future of Dashboarding with SAP Design Studio, introduces you to a new SAP tool: Design Studio. A comparison with SAP BusinessObjects Dashboards is made and the future roadmap for this tool is shared.

What you need for this book

The following tables provide a comparison of the four different SAP BusinessObjects Dashboards packages offered by SAP. You will need to install one of these packages in order to use this book, preferably the SAP BusinessObjects Dashboards package as it has the most features enabled.

The first table summarizes the components available in each version:

Component	SAP Crystal Presentation Design	SAP Crystal Dashboards, personal edition	SAP Crystal Dashboards, departmental edition	SAP BusinessObjects Dashboards
Basic data presentation components	✔	✔	✔	✔
Themes and color schemes	✔	✔	✔	✔
Play Control, Play Selector, and Accordion Menu		✔	✔	✔
Calendar, Panel Set, History, and Trend Analyzer		✔	✔	✔
Reporting Services Button			✔	✔
Slide Show, Connection Refresh Button, and SWF Loader		✔	✔	✔
Query Refresh Button and Query Prompt Selector			✔	✔

The second table summarizes the external connections available in each version:

Component	SAP Crystal Presentation Design	SAP Crystal Dashboards, personal edition	SAP Crystal Dashboards, departmental edition	SAP BusinessObjects Dashboards
Data connectivity	None	Web Service (2 connections maximum) XML Data (2 connections maximum) Flash Variables Crystal Reports FS Command External Interface	All the personal edition connections Web Service (unlimited) XML Data (unlimited) Portal Data LCDS connections Live Office	All the departmental edition connections Query as a Web Service SAP BW
BI platform connectivity	Not available	Not available	SAP Crystal Reports Server 2011	SAP BusinessObjects Business Intelligence Platform 4.0
Viewing license required for connected dashboards	Not available	Not available	SAP Crystal Dashboard Viewing option	Xcelsius Interactive viewing license
Limitations	Does not support external data connections	Maximum of 2 Web Service or XML Data connections in any one model	Maximum of 100 named users can view a given dashboard SAP BusinessOne is the only supported SAP application Cannot be used with SAP BusinessObjects Business Intelligence Platform or SAP Edge BI	None

Who this book is for

If you are a developer with a good command and knowledge of creating dashboards, but are not yet an advanced SAP BusinessObjects Dashboards user, then this is the perfect book for you. You should have a good working knowledge of Microsoft Excel, as well as knowledge of basic dashboard practices, though experience of SAP BusinessObjects Dashboards as a specific dashboard tool is not essential.

This book provides an interactive hands-on approach to SAP BusinessObjects Dashboards education by allowing you to work with components, learn best practices, and practice troubleshooting techniques.

Conventions

In this book, you will find a number of styles of text that distinguish between different kinds of information. Here are some examples of these styles, and an explanation of their meaning.

Code words in text, database table names, folder names, filenames, file extensions, pathnames, dummy URLs, user input, and Twitter handles are shown as follows: "You must be able to view hidden files and folders in the `C:\Documents and Settings\your_user_id` folder."

A block of code is set as follows:

```
final String BO_CMS_NAME = "server";
final String BO_AUTH_TYPE = "secEnterprise";
```

When we wish to draw your attention to a particular part of a code block, the relevant lines or items are set in bold:

```
final String BO_CMS_NAME = "server";
final String BO_AUTH_TYPE = "secEnterprise";
```

New terms and **important words** are shown in bold. Words that you see on the screen, in menus or dialog boxes for example, appear in the text like this: "Double-click the group or right-click and select **Rename** from the context menu."

> Warnings or important notes appear in a box like this.

> Tips and tricks appear like this.

Reader feedback

Feedback from our readers is always welcome. Let us know what you think about this book—what you liked or may have disliked. Reader feedback is important for us to develop titles that you really get the most out of.

To send us general feedback, simply send an e-mail to feedback@packtpub.com, and mention the book title via the subject of your message.

If there is a topic that you have expertise in and you are interested in either writing or contributing to a book, see our author guide on www.packtpub.com/authors.

Customer support

Now that you are the proud owner of a Packt book, we have a number of things to help you to get the most from your purchase.

Downloading the example code

You can download the example code files for all Packt books you have purchased from your account at http://www.packtpub.com. If you purchased this book elsewhere, you can visit http://www.packtpub.com/support and register to have the files e-mailed directly to you.

Some of the code files (XLF files) for this book may be created in an older version of SAP BusinessObjects Dashboards than you are using. The following message will appear when this is the case, but you can use these files without a problem:

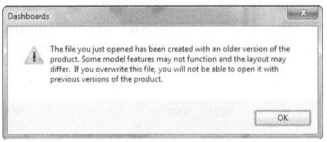

The only remark here is that if you overwrite the file, it can not be opened again in the version of SAP BusinessObjects Dashboards it was originally created with.

Downloading the color images of this book

We also provide you with a PDF file that has color images of the screenshots/diagrams used in this book. The color images will help you better understand the changes in the output. You can download this file from `http://www.packtpub.com/sites/default/files/downloads/B03491_ColoredImages.pdf`.

Errata

Although we have taken every care to ensure the accuracy of our content, mistakes do happen. If you find a mistake in one of our books—maybe a mistake in the text or the code—we would be grateful if you would report this to us. By doing so, you can save other readers from frustration and help us improve subsequent versions of this book. If you find any errata, please report them by visiting `http://www.packtpub.com/submit-errata`, selecting your book, clicking on the **errata submission form** link, and entering the details of your errata. Once your errata are verified, your submission will be accepted and the errata will be uploaded on our website, or added to any list of existing errata, under the Errata section of that title. Any existing errata can be viewed by selecting your title from `http://www.packtpub.com/support`.

Piracy

Piracy of copyright material on the Internet is an ongoing problem across all media. At Packt, we take the protection of our copyright and licenses very seriously. If you come across any illegal copies of our works, in any form, on the Internet, please provide us with the location address or website name immediately so that we can pursue a remedy.

Please contact us at `copyright@packtpub.com` with a link to the suspected pirated material.

We appreciate your help in protecting our authors, and our ability to bring you valuable content.

Questions

You can contact us at `questions@packtpub.com` if you are having a problem with any aspect of the book, and we will do our best to address it.

1
Staying in Control

In this chapter, we will begin with the introduction of SAP BusinessObjects Dashboards and understanding the dashboard workspace.

In this chapter, we will cover the following recipes:

- Using the Object Browser
- Searching for components
- Grouping the canvas components
- Making the spreadsheet more readable with colors
- Making the spreadsheet more readable with comments
- Making the spreadsheet more readable with borders
- Using named ranges
- Copying the format of one cell to another cell or range
- Debugging the spreadsheets
- Navigating between worksheets

Introduction

During the development of a typical **SAP BusinessObjects** dashboard, the number of components as well as the Excel spreadsheet data bindings can become quite complex. To prevent us from getting lost in an unmanageable chaos of components, interactions, bindings, and several different Excel functionalities, a structured approach should be followed right from the start of dashboard development. Also, we should use the advantages Excel gives us to build an optimal data model that is easy to read and maintain.

Understanding the dashboard workspace

Before you begin designing dashboards, it is important that you understand the workspace. The workspace area is illustrated as follows:

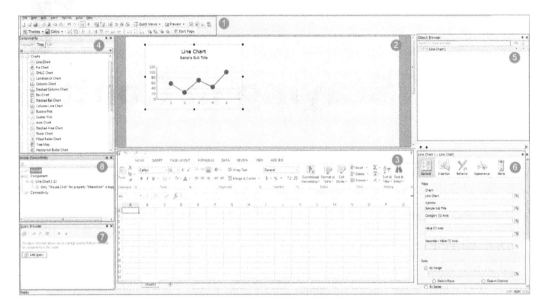

Let's have a look at some of the important sections of the dashboard workspace as depicted in the preceding screenshot:

- ▶ Menu bar and toolbar (**1**): SAP BusinessObjects Dashboards consists of a menu bar as well as five toolbars that are used to help develop dashboards.

- ▶ Dashboard canvas (**2**): This is where the dashboard presentation is built. Users drag and drop dashboard objects here.

- ▶ Embedded spreadsheet (**3**): This embedded spreadsheet is used to associate the dashboard objects with data. More information on tips and best practices when building your spreadsheet models can be found later in this chapter.

- ▶ The **Components** window (**4**): Users can drag and drop dashboard components from the **Components** window onto the dashboard canvas.

- ▶ The **Object Browser** (**5**): All objects existing in the dashboard model can be found in the **Object Browser**. It provides a way to easily access your dashboard objects. For more instructions on using the object browser, please refer to the following recipe, *Using the Object Browser*.

- ▶ The **Properties** window (**6**): This contains settings and formatting options for a selected component.

- The **Query Browser** (**7**): This allows users to create and manage dashboard queries. For more information, please refer to the recipe *Using the Query Browser* in *Chapter 8, Dashboard Data Connectivity*.

- The **Mobile Compatibility** window (**8**): This provides mobile compatibility information on all the objects found in the dashboard model. For more information, please refer to the recipe *Going mobile* in *Chapter 9, Exporting and Publishing*.

Using the Object Browser

The **Object Browser** has a number of features which come in very handy during the development of a complex dashboard. In this section, we will discuss hiding, locking, and ordering of components.

Getting ready

Drag several components to the canvas.

How to do it...

1. Go to the **Object Browser**.

2. Click on the dot in the first of the two columns on the right side of the **Object Browser** for the component that you want to hide. The dot turns into a checkmark. As you can see, the component now disappears from the canvas.

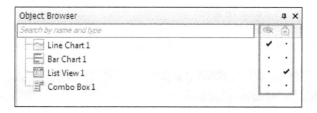

3. Now click on the dot on the right for any of the components.

4. Try to move the component or make any other change to it.

5. As you'll see, the component is completely locked and doesn't change.

6. Make sure some of your components are on top of each other in the canvas. We now want to use the **Object Browser** to rearrange these overlapping components.

7. Select the component in the **Object Browser** that is on top of the list.

8. Click the arrow down button in the **Object Browser** multiple times until the component is on top of all the other components.

9. As you can see, the component shifts all the way to the top.

How it works...

As we have seen in this recipe, we can hide components and/or groups of components, which will make your life easier if you are using a lot of overlapping components. By checking **Hide** for some components, you won't be bothered by these and you can work with the others that are unhidden. ·

 There is one thing you should keep in mind. If you hide a component that is part of a group but the group itself is unhidden, the complete group will still be movable and its properties will be changeable.

Also, we saw that we can lock one or more components or groups of components. Doing this makes it impossible to select these components, so it won't be possible to move, change, or do anything else with them. In this way you can be sure you won't accidentally alter these components.

 Hiding and/or locking a component from the **Object Browser** only hides and/ or locks that component during the development of a dashboard. When you preview or execute the dashboard, the component will appear again and function normally.

Finally, we changed the order of components on the canvas. This is an important feature when we are using overlaying components in our dashboard.

To move a component on top of all other components, you can also right-click on it and select the **Bring To Front** option. **Send To Back** will move the component all the way down. The options **Bring Forward** and **Send Back** do the same as the arrows in the **Object Browser**: they move the component one step up or down at a time.

Searching for components

The ability to do a search for components from the **Object Browser** is a helpful feature new to SAP BusinessObjects Dashboards 4.1. You can perform a search by either name or component type. This comes in handy when you have a lot of objects on the dashboard that are inside groups or canvas containers.

Getting ready

Make sure you have a dashboard that contains a set of components.

How to do it...

1. Open up the **Object Browser** window.

2. In the top-left input box, type in the object name or component type that you are searching for. You will see that your search will filter the objects accordingly.

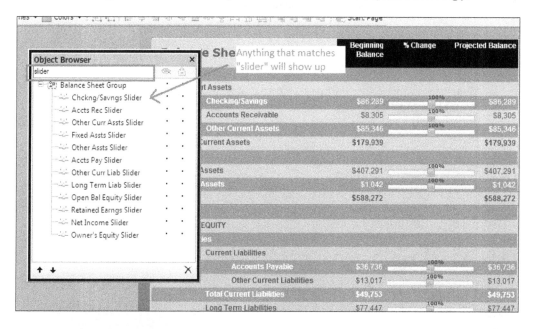

How it works...

As you can see, the search functionality is a useful feature as you can easily find objects by their name.

 The search functionality works best when you have named all your objects properly.

Grouping the canvas components

Canvas components can be grouped with one or more other components.

Getting ready

Drag several components to the canvas.

How to do it...

1. Select the components that you want to group. You can do this by either selecting multiple components from the dashboard canvas by dragging the mouse over them, or clicking the components one-by-one while holding the *Ctrl* button on your keyboard.

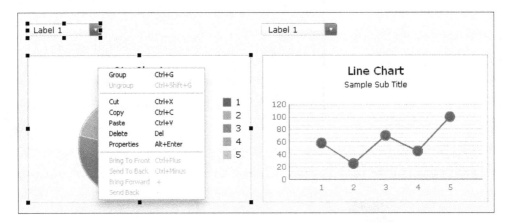

2. Right-click anywhere on the canvas and select **Group** from the context menu. You can also use the shortcut *Ctrl + G* to group these components. As you can see, the components are now a group with a common border.

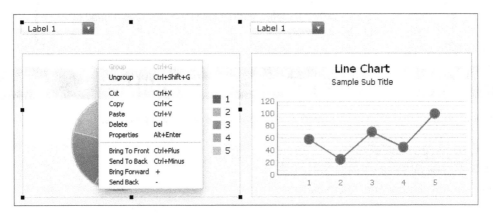

If you double-click on the grouped object you will see a **Common** tab where you can set the **Dynamic Visibility** and **Entry Effect**.

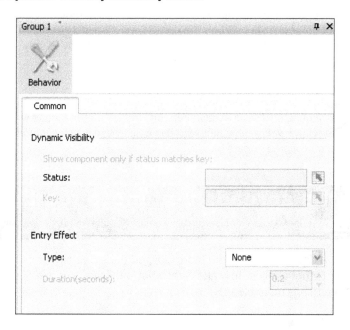

3. If you create a lot of groups of components, we advise that you name these groups to prevent you from getting lost and confused during the dashboard development. First go to the **Object Browser**.

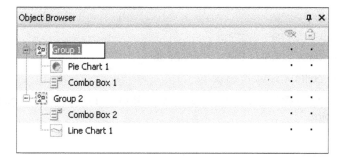

4. Select the group you want to rename.

5. Double-click the group or right-click and select **Rename** from the context menu.

6. Type in the new name for this group.

How it works...

When your dashboard gets more complex, not only will the data model in the spreadsheet grow, the number of components used on the canvas will also increase. Using groups to differentiate the canvas components from each other is a great way to stay in control of your dashboard.

 Name the groups as something that can be visually matched to your dashboard, such as a section heading. In that way, someone who did not originally develop the dashboard can quickly see which set of components the object group refers to.

Making the spreadsheet more readable with colors

The more complex a dashboard gets, the more clogged the spreadsheet might get with data, Excel formulas, and other usages. To make clear what the exact purpose of a cell is, we color code them to make things more clear.

Getting ready

You need a basic SAP BusinessObjects Dashboards file containing a few components in the canvas with some bindings to the data model in the spreadsheet.

How to do it...

1. Go to your data model in the spreadsheet.
2. Select the cell(s) you want to color.
3. Click on the **Fill Color** button in the **Font** section of the **Home** tab and select the desired color.

4. Color the cells that have dynamic visibility values in orange.

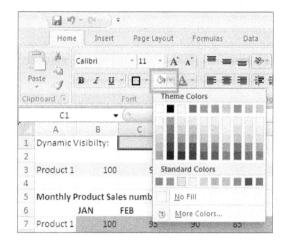

5. Color the cells with input values from canvas components in yellow. In the following screenshot, row **A3:N3** is used as the destination range for a drill down from a chart.

6. Color the cells that will be filled with data from an external data source in blue.

7. Color the cells with Excel formulas in green.

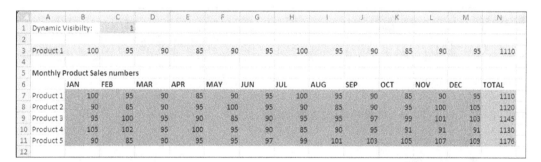

<table>
<tr><th></th><th>A</th><th>B</th><th>C</th><th>D</th><th>E</th><th>F</th><th>G</th><th>H</th><th>I</th><th>J</th><th>K</th><th>L</th><th>M</th><th>N</th></tr>
<tr><td>1</td><td colspan="2">Dynamic Visibilty:</td><td>1</td><td></td><td></td><td></td><td></td><td></td><td></td><td></td><td></td><td></td><td></td><td></td></tr>
<tr><td>2</td><td></td><td></td><td></td><td></td><td></td><td></td><td></td><td></td><td></td><td></td><td></td><td></td><td></td><td></td></tr>
<tr><td>3</td><td>Product 1</td><td>100</td><td>95</td><td>90</td><td>85</td><td>90</td><td>95</td><td>100</td><td>95</td><td>90</td><td>85</td><td>90</td><td>95</td><td>1110</td></tr>
<tr><td>4</td><td></td><td></td><td></td><td></td><td></td><td></td><td></td><td></td><td></td><td></td><td></td><td></td><td></td><td></td></tr>
<tr><td>5</td><td colspan="3">Monthly Product Sales numbers</td><td></td><td></td><td></td><td></td><td></td><td></td><td></td><td></td><td></td><td></td></tr>
<tr><td>6</td><td></td><td>JAN</td><td>FEB</td><td>MAR</td><td>APR</td><td>MAY</td><td>JUN</td><td>JUL</td><td>AUG</td><td>SEP</td><td>OCT</td><td>NOV</td><td>DEC</td><td>TOTAL</td></tr>
<tr><td>7</td><td>Product 1</td><td>100</td><td>95</td><td>90</td><td>85</td><td>90</td><td>95</td><td>100</td><td>95</td><td>90</td><td>85</td><td>90</td><td>95</td><td>1110</td></tr>
<tr><td>8</td><td>Product 2</td><td>90</td><td>85</td><td>90</td><td>95</td><td>100</td><td>95</td><td>90</td><td>85</td><td>90</td><td>95</td><td>100</td><td>105</td><td>1120</td></tr>
<tr><td>9</td><td>Product 3</td><td>95</td><td>100</td><td>95</td><td>90</td><td>85</td><td>90</td><td>95</td><td>95</td><td>97</td><td>99</td><td>101</td><td>103</td><td>1145</td></tr>
<tr><td>10</td><td>Product 4</td><td>105</td><td>102</td><td>95</td><td>100</td><td>95</td><td>90</td><td>85</td><td>90</td><td>95</td><td>91</td><td>91</td><td>91</td><td>1130</td></tr>
<tr><td>11</td><td>Product 5</td><td>90</td><td>85</td><td>90</td><td>95</td><td>95</td><td>97</td><td>99</td><td>101</td><td>103</td><td>105</td><td>107</td><td>109</td><td>1176</td></tr>
<tr><td>12</td><td></td><td></td><td></td><td></td><td></td><td></td><td></td><td></td><td></td><td></td><td></td><td></td><td></td><td></td></tr>
</table>

How it works...

As you can see, there are many roles that cells in the spreadsheet can play. If these were not color coded, you would be faced with a daunting task when updating the Excel model in the future. In our example, we colored calculations in green, external data input in blue, and component input data in yellow.

There's more...

To make the data model readable, not only for yourself but also for others, it is helpful to create a **legend** in your spreadsheet that explains what each color represents. Any color scheme can be used, but it is important that you stick to the chosen scheme and use it consistently throughout the development of your dashboard.

It is important to create a separate worksheet that houses the legend, as seen in the following screenshot. You can also use this overall summary worksheet to include the information such as project name, description, usage, version (history), and so on.

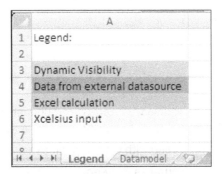

Making the spreadsheet more readable with comments

Sometimes, cells need additional information to explain how they are used. You can create comment text on an adjacent cell. Or, if you do not want to fill up other cells, you can right-click on the same cell and select **Insert Comment**.

Getting ready

You need a basic dashboard containing a few components in the canvas with some bindings to the data model in the spreadsheet. You can also just reuse the dashboard from the previous recipe.

How to do it...

1. Right-click on the cell to which you want to add the extra information.
2. Choose **Insert Comment**.

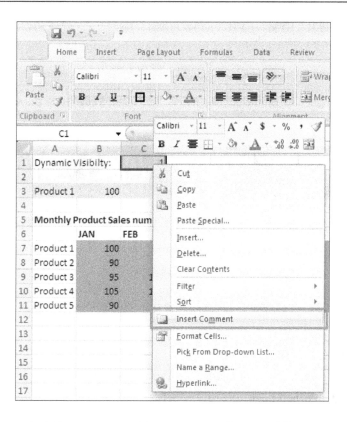

3. Add your text. A small red triangle will appear in the upper-right corner of the cell.

4. Now hover your mouse over the cell and the comment you just entered will appear.

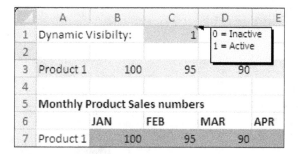

How it works...

Comments are related to one spreadsheet cell only and are shown if you hover over the cell. This is a great way to document information that you do not need to see all the time, and keeps your data model clean.

A little remark about the usage of comments: they increase the size of the SAP BusinessObjects Dashboards file a bit.

 If you want the comment to always show up without hovering over the cell, you can right-click on the comment and then select **Show/Hide Comments**.

Making the spreadsheet more readable with borders

To separate cells from each other and create different areas within a spreadsheet, you can use cell borders.

Getting ready

You can use the same basic dashboard as in the previous examples.

How to do it...

1. Select the cell(s) you want to add a border to and right-click on it.

2. Now select **Format cells...**.

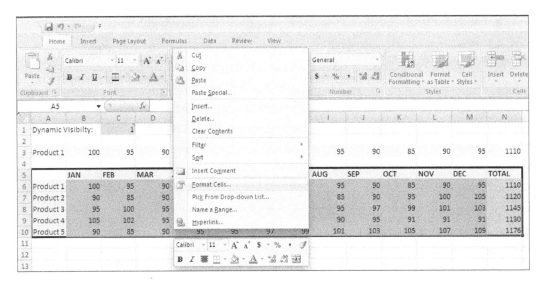

3. Go to the **Border** tab.

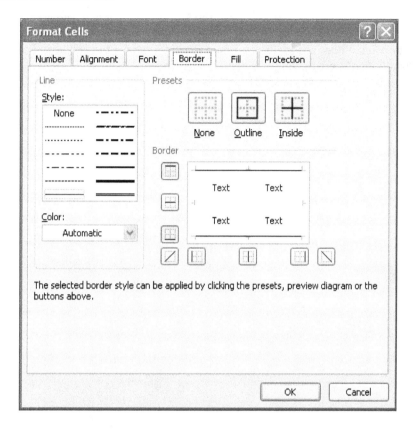

4. Select the desired style of the border line.
5. Select on which side(s) of the cell(s) the border should appear.
6. Click on **OK**.

There's more...

We will now discuss three more topics regarding spreadsheet borders: using the toolbar border button, using multiple worksheets, and placing Excel logic within the spreadsheet.

Using the toolbar border button

Instead of right-clicking on the cells and using the **Format Cells** option, you can also use the **Border** button on the toolbar to adjust the border styles for a cell or a group of cells. You can find this button in the **Font** section of the **Home** tab. If you select the cell(s) and click on this button, a list of options will be shown, which you can choose from.

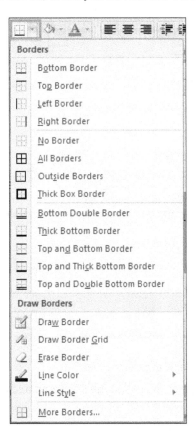

Using multiple worksheets

You can use borders to split data within a spreadsheet. But if your dashboard contains data from a lot of different (functional) areas, it is recommended that you split your spreadsheet into several worksheets. This will help you to keep your dashboard maintainable.

A good strategy to split up the spreadsheet is to divide your data in different areas that correspond to certain layers or tabs that you created on the dashboard canvas. You can also use separate sheets for each external data connection. Give each worksheet a meaningful name.

Placing your Excel logic wisely

Another general guideline is to place as many cells with Excel logic and SAP BusinessObjects Dashboards interactivity functionality at the top left of the spreadsheet. This place is easy to reach without a lot of annoying scrolling and searching. Even more importantly, your dataset may grow (vertically and/or horizontally) over time. This can be a risk especially when you are using an external data connection and you don't want your logic to be overwritten. For example, if you use a column summation, place it at the top of the column instead of the bottom. This way, if you need to add another value to the list of cells to be summed, you can add it to the bottom without having to shift down the formula cell.

Using named ranges

With **named ranges**, it is possible to define a worksheet cell or a range of cells with a logical name.

Getting ready

You can use one of the dashboards from the previous recipes, or just create a new blank dashboard.

How to do it...

1. Select a range of cells (for example, **B1:B12**).

2. Insert a description (for example, `Total_Sales`) for this range in the **Name Box** in the upper left-hand side of the worksheet.

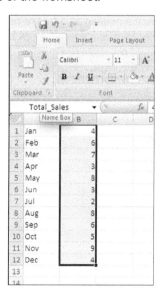

3. Now, this named range can be used in formulas in other worksheet cells. Type the formula =SUM(Total_Sales) in cell **B13**.

	A	B	C	D	E	
	B13		▼		f_x =SUM(Total_Sales)	
1	Jan	4				
2	Feb	6				
3	Mar	7				
4	Apr	3				
5	May	8				
6	Jun	3				
7	Jul	2				
8	Aug	8				
9	Sep	6				
10	Oct	5				
11	Nov	9				
12	Dec	4				
13		65				
14						

How it works...

Using named ranges makes your formulas more readable, especially when you are working with multiple worksheets and using formulas that refer to cells in other worksheets.

There is a restriction to using named ranges in SAP BusinessObjects Dashboards: the defined named range must refer to a single cell or must use formulas that return a single value from a range of cells. For example, let's say we have two named ranges: Sales (**A1:A12**) and Cost (**B1:B12**). A supported formula would be =SUM(Sales)-SUM(Cost). An unsupported formula would be =Sales-Cost.

There's more...

In this section, we will discuss two ways to select and manage your named ranges.

Defined named ranges

Clicking on the little triangle in the Name Box will show a list of all your defined named ranges in all your worksheets.

The Name Manager

If you use a lot of named ranges, the **Name Manager** can be a helpful tool to manage your named ranges. Here, you can also edit and delete the existing named ranges. You can find the **Name Manager** under the **Defined Names** section of the **Formulas** tab or by using the shortcut *Ctrl + F3*.

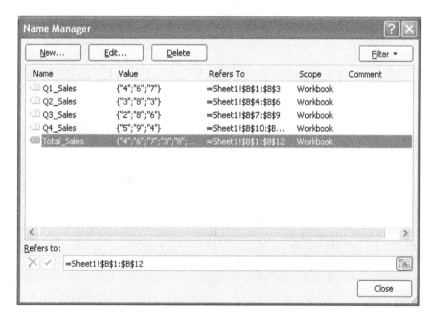

Copying the format of one cell to another cell or range

This recipe shows you how to copy the formatting of one cell to another cell or range. For example, we can copy a yellow background and Calibri font from cell **A1** to cell **A2**.

How to do it...

1. Click on the source cell that you want to copy the formatting from.
2. Click on the **Format Painter** icon, which you can find in the **Clipboard** section of the **Home** tab.

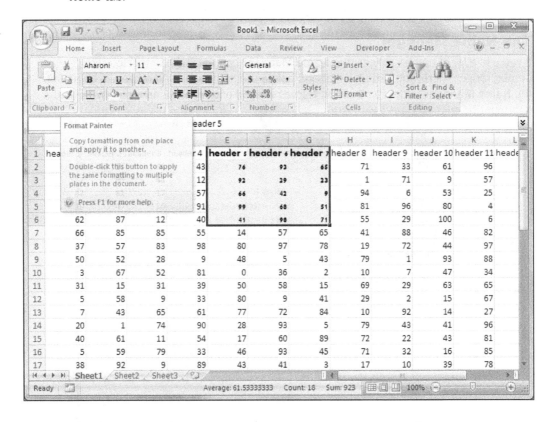

3. Click on the cell or range that you want to copy the source cell's formatting to.

How it works...

For SAP BusinessObjects Dashboards developers, it happens very often when they have to copy colored cells that represent different types of logic such as dynamic visibility cells, insertion cells, and so on.

The **Format Painter** tool works by taking the source cell that you have selected and applying the formatting to the cell(s) that you paint to. This is very useful because we can copy cell formats without having to perform a **Copy** and **Paste Special** action every time.

There's more...

An alternative to accomplishing the same task is to copy a cell and then click **Paste Special...** and choose the **Formats** option from **Paste**.

Debugging the spreadsheets

It is common that SAP BusinessObjects Dashboards developers may accidently put in the incorrect formula when developing logic on their spreadsheets. Using the *Ctrl +* ` hotkey will make things much easier.

How to do it...

1. Select the worksheet you want to see formulas for.
2. Hit the *Ctrl +* ` (grave accent) hotkey.
3. You will see the value in the cell change to the formula.

How it works...

The *Ctrl +* ` hotkey works by showing the underlying formula of a cell. This is extremely useful if you are comparing formulas from multiple cells, as the developer does not have to flip between formulas in order to see what they are doing wrong when comparing multiple cells. Developers can quickly analyze their worksheet and find the cause of their problem.

The following screenshot shows the results of two Excel formulas in cells **A1** and **A2**:

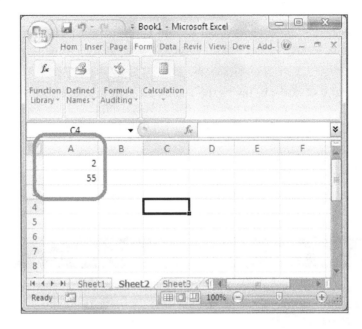

After using the *Ctrl + `* hotkey, the formulas of both cells are displayed, as you can see in the next screenshot:

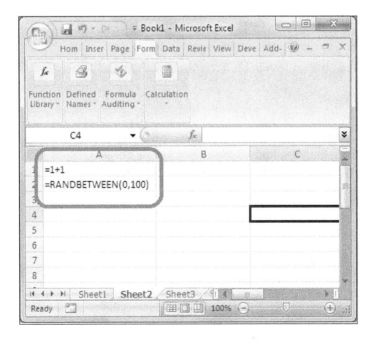

There's more...

An alternative way to accomplish the same task is to go to the **Formula Auditing** section of the **Formulas** tab and then click on **Show Formulas**. Refer to the following screenshot:

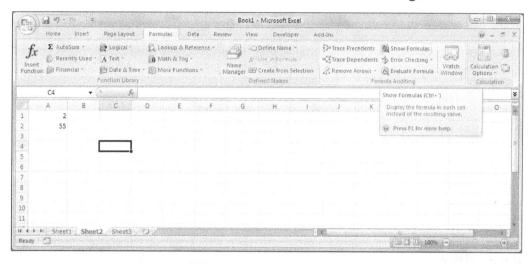

Navigating between worksheets

When developing dashboards it is a common problem to have to manually scroll through tabs when there are too many worksheets. To access tabs that are not visible, we are used to pressing the arrow keys to move to the desired tab.

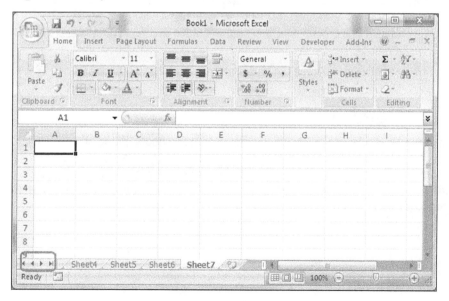

How to do it...

1. To have all tabs displayed in one menu, right-click on any of the arrow keys at the bottom, in the left-hand side navigation area. You will then see the list of tabs that you can choose from.

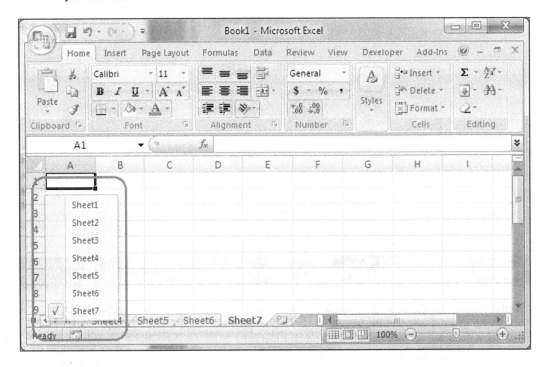

2. You can also use *Ctrl + PageUp*, which will move to the previous sheet in your workbook.

3. *Ctrl + PageDown* will navigate to the next sheet in the workbook.

How it works...

This tip allows developers to quickly toggle between worksheets. Being able to quickly right-click and view a menu of all available tabs is faster than scrolling through each tab in order to reach tabs that are not visible. In addition, the ability to use a hotkey to cycle through each tab brings some time-saving benefits to those who are comfortable with using the keyboard to perform all their actions.

2
Data Visualization

In this chapter, we will cover the following recipes:

- ▸ Adding a line chart to your dashboard
- ▸ Using a bullet chart
- ▸ Using sparklines
- ▸ Using a combination chart
- ▸ Using a waterfall chart
- ▸ Using a pie chart
- ▸ Using a scatter plot chart
- ▸ Using a bubble plot chart
- ▸ Using a radar chart
- ▸ Using an OHLC chart and a candlestick chart
- ▸ Sorting series
- ▸ Zooming in on charts
- ▸ Scaling the *y*-axis
- ▸ Using a tree map
- ▸ Showing a trend without a chart
- ▸ Displaying raw data
- ▸ Illustrating single values

Introduction

Data visualization may be the most important topic when we are talking about dashboard creation. It enables us to view data, compare values, and make analyses in a clear and effective way. A dashboard is the ideal platform to present these visualizations.

Data can be presented in a graphical way; for example, with lines, bars, colored areas, gauges, or just with a simple red/green indicator. But on the other hand, in some cases, it may be more effective to use a simple list of values instead of these graphs. This totally depends on the purpose of the dashboard.

SAP BusinessObjects Dashboards provides a great toolkit with lots of visualization components. This chapter will discuss these components and show you how to use them.

Adding a line chart to your dashboard

A **line chart** is very useful to visualize data that changes over time. It consists of a set of data points that are connected by a line. The horizontal *x*-axis typically shows the categories in which the data is divided. The vertical *y*-axis shows us the values.

This recipe shows how to add a line chart to a dashboard and how to link it to the data in the spreadsheet. We will also discuss the components that are similar to the line chart component: bar chart, column chart, area chart, stacked chart, and the Marimekko chart.

Getting ready

Open a new file in SAP BusinessObjects Dashboards and enter the data into the spreadsheet, as shown in the following screenshot:

	A	B	C	D	E	F
1						
2						
3						
4		Q1	Q2	Q3	Q4	
5	Apple	500	750	600	350	
6	Banana	1000	650	850	750	
7	Cherry	400	500	600	300	
8						

 You can also click on the **Line Chart** component in the **Components** browser, move your cursor to the canvas area (the arrow will now change into a cross), and click again. You can use whatever method you prefer.

How to do it...

1. Drag a **Line Chart** component from the **Components** browser into the canvas:

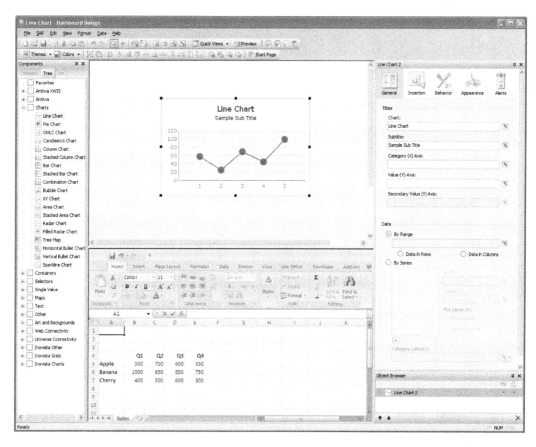

2. Select the **Line Chart** component you just added to the canvas by clicking on it. Now, the component is surrounded by eight blocks that enable you to adjust the size of the component.

3. The properties pane for this component is also visible now. By default, the **General** tab is selected. In the **Data** section we can bind the data we entered earlier in the spreadsheet to this component. Click on the button on the right-hand side of the **By Range** field:

> If the properties pane isn't present on your screen, you can activate it from the menu under **View | Properties**. You can also right-click the component and select **Properties**.

4. In the spreadsheet, select the range from **A4** to **E7** and click on **OK**. The data is now bound to the component:

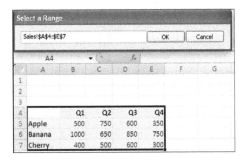

5. The **Data** section of the properties pane now looks like what is shown in the following screenshot. The chart will show the data series we just bound.

6. In the same way, we can add titles to this chart. Select spreadsheet cell **A1** and enter `Sales_data`; also, enter `2011` in cell **A2**.

7. Bind the **Chart** field in the properties pane with spreadsheet cell **A1** and bind the **Subtitle** field with cell A2.

 You can also enter a value in these title fields directly.

8. In the **Category (Y) Axis** field, enter `Tonne`.

9. Your setup should now look like what is shown in the following screenshot. Click on the **Preview** button to try the dashboard.

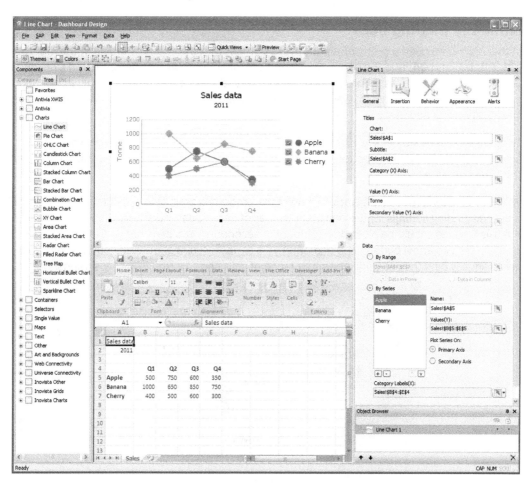

How it works...

The preceding section showed how to connect data in one or more spreadsheet cells to the **Line Chart** component through several options in its properties pane. This is how we bind data and you will be using this a lot during the development of dashboards with SAP BusinessObjects Dashboards.

There's more...

In this section we will discuss manually binding data to charts and how to hide and show data series in a chart. We will also go through some other chart components that work in a similar way to the **Line Chart** component.

Manually binding data

In this recipe, we used a pretty straightforward dataset with the category labels in the first row (**Q1**, **Q2**, **Q3**, and **Q4**) and the series names in the first column (**Apple**, **Banana**, and **Cherry**). SAP BusinessObjects Dashboards is able to understand this dataset and bind this information automatically. However, this may not always be the case, and therefore, not always lead to the visualization you had in mind.

To change the direction of the visualization of the spreadsheet data in the chart, you can select the **Data in Columns** option in the **Data** section of the properties pane. This will switch the series and the labels.

By clicking on **By Series** in the **Data** section of the properties pane, it is possible to manually adjust all binding settings for the name and values of each series. Additionally, you can select the axis a series should be plotted on (primary or secondary). You can change the series order by using the two arrow buttons and add or remove series by using the **+** and **-** buttons. Also, you can manually bind the category labels to a range of cells shown in the following screenshot:

Hide/show series

Series in a chart can be hidden or shown by the user when using the dashboard by following these steps:

1. Go to the **Appearance** tab and select the sub-tab **Layout**.
2. Make sure that **Enable Legend** is selected.
3. Select **Enable Hide/Show Chart Series at Run-Time**.
4. Set **Interaction** to **Check Box**.
5. Click on the **Preview** button to try this feature.

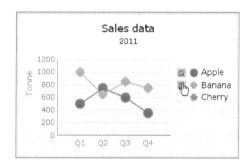

Other charts

In the following sections, several other chart types will be introduced. These charts work roughly in the same way as the line chart component.

Bar chart and column chart

The bar chart and column chart components can be configured in exactly the same way as a **Line Chart** component. A bar chart presents values in horizontal bars while the column chart uses vertical bars. These types of charts are typically not used to present data over a long time period, but to show data from different categories that need to be compared. The following screenshot shows the bar chart and column chart representation:

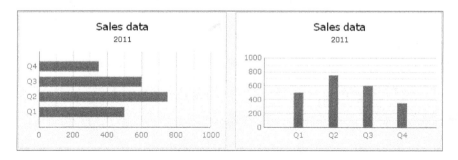

Area chart

The area chart component is a line chart with a filled area beneath the line. Another difference between these two types of charts is that in an area chart, the first value (**Q1**) is plotted on the far left-hand side and the last value (**Q4**) on the far right-hand side of the chart. An area chart is used to visualize the cumulated total value of the series over a period of time. This component can be configured in the same way as the line chart component. The following screenshot displays an area chart:

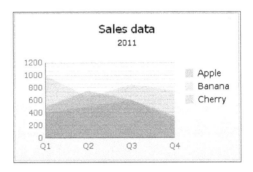

Stacked charts

The bar chart, column chart, and area chart components all have a stacked versions: stacked bar chart, stacked column chart, and stacked area chart. These stacked chart components show the values of the series on top of each other in the same column. You can use stacked charts if the dashboard user wants to compare totals, as shown in the following screenshot:

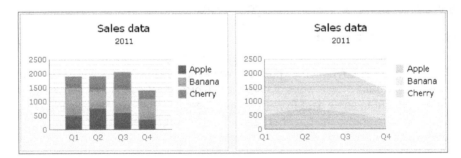

Marimekko chart

The Marimekko chart is a special type of stacked chart. Instead of displaying absolute values, the bars now have the same height and the segments of each bar represent a percentage of the total. The same principle counts for the width of each bar. The following screenshot displays a Marimekko chart:

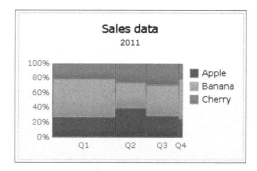

The setup of the Marimekko chart component is similar to the other stacked chart components, with only one addition. In the **Data** section of the **General** tab of the properties pane, we will now find the option to bind category values, which will determine the width of the bars as seen in the following screenshot:

Using a bullet chart

A **bullet chart** is in fact a bar or column chart with a lot of extra options. It can serve as a replacement for gauges and meters. Besides visualizing a data point as bar and column charts do, a bullet chart is able to show a target and two or more qualitative ranges. These ranges can indicate whether a value can be considered bad, satisfactory, good, and so on.

This recipe will show you how to configure a bullet chart. SAP BusinessObjects Dashboards has two bullet chart components: horizontal and vertical. Both components have exactly the same configuration options and work in the same manner. This recipe will use the horizontal bullet chart.

Getting ready

Open a new file in SAP BusinessObjects Dashboards and enter the data into the spreadsheet, as shown in the following screenshot:

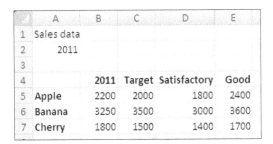

How to do it...

1. Drag a **Horizontal Bullet Chart** component into the canvas.

2. Bind the **By Range** field to the spreadsheet range from **A4** to **E7**:

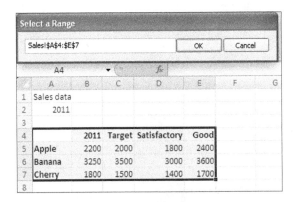

3. Also bind the **Chart** field in the **Titles** section to spreadsheet cell **A1** and bind the **Subtitle** field to cell **A2**.

4. Hit the **Preview** button and hover on the different sections of the bars. The dashboard now shows the detailed information we just bound:

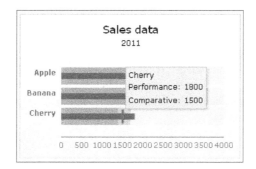

How it works...

The bullet chart components can show a result value, a target, and qualitative ranges. Furthermore, each series can have its own label and sub-label. Let's have a look at exactly how these variables are configured in the preceding _How to do it..._ section.

First, select **By Series** in the **Data** section of the properties pane for the **Horizontal Bullet Chart** component; then, select the **Apple** series. You can now see the detailed bindings SAP BusinessObjects Dashboards made for this series as shown in the following screenshot:

The **Label** field is bound to spreadsheet cell **A5** (**Apple**). We did not edit the **Sub-Label** field so this remains empty, but you can bind it to a cell with a certain value or enter a value in this field directly. The result value, cell **B5** (2200), is bound to the **Performance Value** field, which is represented in the chart by a small horizontal bar. Next, the target value of cell **C5** (2000) is bound to the **Comparative Value** field. This value is visualized by a vertical dash. There are two cells that are bound as **Scale Values**: **D5** (1800) and **E5** (2400). Using two values means that the chart will show three areas: 0-1800, 1800-2400, and 2400-max. You can use as many values as you need. These areas are shown in the chart as three colored blocks in the background. If you don't use scale values, there won't be a colored block in the chart. Take a look at the following screenshot:

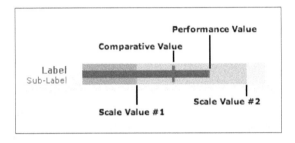

There's more...

The bullet chart in the recipe uses the same x-axis for all three series. It is also possible to configure separate x axes as done in the following steps:

1. Select the **Bullet Chart** component and go to the **Behavior** tab. Select the **Scale** sub-tab.

2. Select **Configure scale by series**. Now you can edit the scaling settings for each series separately.

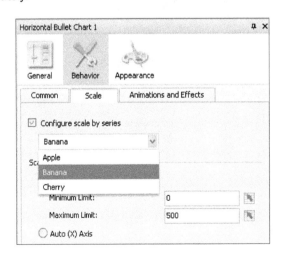

3. Go to the **Appearance** tab and select the **Text** sub-tab.

4. Here, you can select which **Horizontal Axis Labels** should be shown:

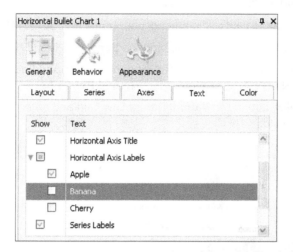

Using sparklines

Sparklines are typically small graphics, showing a horizontal line connecting several data points without labeling the values on their axes. The purpose of a sparkline is to show the movement of a trend over a certain period. Since its details are not available, the context of a sparkline must be clear to the dashboard user to interpret its meaning properly. This recipe will show you how to configure a sparkline.

Getting ready

Open a new file in SAP BusinessObjects Dashboards and enter the data into the spreadsheet, as shown in the following screenshot:

	A	B	C	D	E	F	G	H	I	J	K	L	M
1	Sales data												
2	2011												
3													
4		Jan	Feb	Mar	Apr	May	Jun	Jul	Aug	Sep	Oct	Nov	Dec
5	Apple	800	750	600	500	450	550	650	800	1000	1200	1100	900

How to do it...

1. Drag a **Sparkline Chart** component into the canvas.

2. Bind the **By Range** field to the spreadsheet range from **A4** to **M5**.

3. Bind the **Chart** field to cell **A1** and bind the **Subtitle** field to cell **A2**.

4. Go to the **Behavior** tab of the properties pane of the **Sparkline Chart** component. In the **Normal Range Area** section, select **Normal Range Area**.

5. Enter the value 600 in the **Normal Range Low** field and enter 1000 in the **Normal Range High** field:

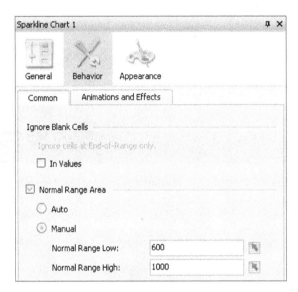

6. Go to the **Appearance** tab and select the **Text** sub-tab.

7. Select **Show** for **Start Value**.

8. Set the **Position** for this **Start Value** text to **Left**.

9. Select **Show** for the **End Value** option.

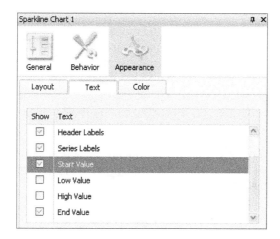

10. Now go to the **Color** tab and select all markers:

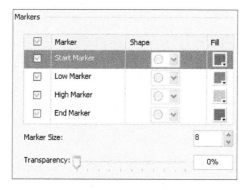

11. Your dashboard should look like what is shown in the following screenshot:

How it works...

The configuration of the **General** tab within the properties pane of a sparkline chart component looks like the configuration of a line chart component. But, a sparkline chart component has fewer options here: no axis and no category labels can be defined. From a dashboard user's perspective, this also means that the user has to know and understand the context of the presented data. When multiple sparklines are displayed and they all have different bands without axes, it is very difficult to compare the values. The user needs to be aware of this.

With the **Normal Range Area** section in the **Behavior** tab, it is possible to illustrate the range of the values of this series. Also, the start and end and the highest and lowest values of the presented series can be emphasized.

There's more...

In this section, we will discuss some specific labels for the sparkline component: header labels and low and high values.

Header labels

Header labels can label two parts of the sparkline chart component: the series name(s) and the sparkline(s). To activate these labels follow the given steps:

1. Bind the **Header Labels** field in the **General** tab to two spreadsheet cells.

2. Enter the value of the series name(s) header in the first cell, and the value of the sparkline(s) header in the second cell.

3. Now go to the **Appearance** tab and select the **Text** sub-tab.

4. Select **Header Labels**. The labels will now appear in the component, as shown in the following screenshot:

Low and high values

Besides the start and end values of a sparkline, you can also show the lowest and highest values. In the **Text** sub-tab of the **Appearance** tab, you can select them to be visible as shown in the following screenshot:

Using a combination chart

With the **combination chart** you can use both columns and lines to visualize data in one single chart.

Getting ready

Open a new file in SAP BusinessObjects Dashboards and enter the data, as shown in the following screenshot, into the spreadsheet:

	A	B	C	D	E
1	Marketing				
2		2011			
3					
4		Q1	Q2	Q3	Q4
5	Marketing budget	100000	70000	150000	150000
6	Market share	5%	4%	8%	12%

In the **Number** section of the **Home** tab of the toolbar, use the % option to convert the market share values into percentages:

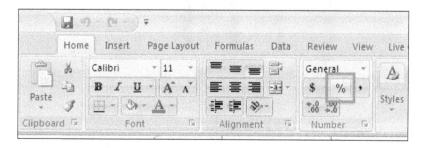

How to do it...

1. Drag a **Combination Chart** component to the canvas.

2. Bind the **Chart** field to cell **A1** and the **Subtitle** field to cell **B2**.

3. Bind the **By Range** field to the spreadsheet range from **A4** to **E6**.

4. Select **By Series** and select the **Market share** series. Select the option to **Plot Series On**: **Secondary Axis**:

5. As you can see now, both axes are populated with values:

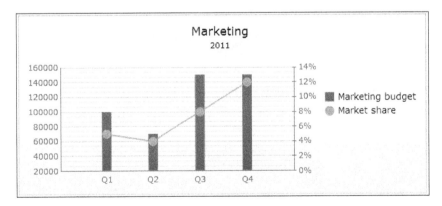

How it works...

After binding the data to the component, we adjusted the **Market share** series to plot its data on the secondary axis. After doing this, a second *y*-axis appeared on the right-hand side of the chart, labeled with percentages.

There's more...

In the **Series** sub-tab within the **Appearance** tab of the properties pane, you can determine how each series will appear: either as a column or a line. Here, you can also set the series colors and marker **Shape**, **Marker Size**, and **Transparency** as shown in the following screenshot:

Using a waterfall chart

A **waterfall chart** is useful to visualize the fluctuation of a value in positive and negative values. The first and final values are displayed as full columns (starting at 0). The values in between represent the positive and negative fluctuations. A good example is the stock level of goods in a warehouse. A waterfall chart can show how it changes over time.

This recipe shows you how to set up such a waterfall chart.

Getting ready

Open a new SAP BusinessObjects Dashboards file and enter data in the spreadsheet as shown in the following screenshot. As you can see in row **3**, the first and final value (January and December) show the total stock level, instead of the change relative to the previous period, as is shown in the other months:

	A	B	C	D	E	F	G	H	I	J	K	L	M
1		Jan	Feb	Mar	Apr	May	Jun	Jul	Aug	Sep	Oct	Nov	Dec
2	Stock level	500	600	900	350	800	1200	1400	1100	900	1200	700	800
3	Change	500	100	300	-550	450	400	200	-300	-200	300	-500	800

How to do it...

1. Drag a **Waterfall Chart** component into the canvas.
2. Bind the **Values** field to the spreadsheet range from **B3** to **M3**.
3. Bind the **Labels** field to the spreadsheet range from **B1** to **M1**.

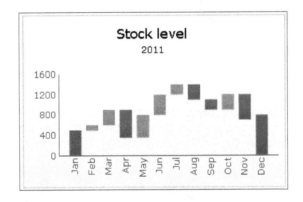

How it works...

Instead of showing the total value for each category, the waterfall chart shows how an initial value (January) changes over time until it ends in the final value (December). To make this work, you have to make sure that the first and final values of your dataset represent the actual initial and final value. The other values that are in between should only represent the amount of increase or decrease of a value.

There's more...

There are four categories of values in a waterfall chart: initial value, final value, positive value, and negative value. These values all have their own color. Initially, the positive values are green and the negative ones are red. In the **Series** sub-tab within the **Appearance** tab of the properties pane, you can change the color of each type of value:

Using a pie chart

A **pie chart** is circular chart divided into one or more slices. Each **slice** represents the proportion of a value to the total of all values. Pie charts can be used to show the share of a value in contrast to other values or the grand total. However, it may be hard to compare the size of slices within a pie chart when there are more than three slices, or across other pie charts. Therefore, if you need to compare data, we recommend using a bar chart instead.

Getting ready

Open a new file in SAP BusinessObjects Dashboards and enter the data, as shown in the following screenshot, into the spreadsheet:

How to do it...

1. Drag a **Pie Chart** component onto the canvas.
2. Bind the **Values** field to spreadsheet cells **B5** through **B7**.
3. Bind the **Labels** field to cells **A5** through **A7**.
4. Bind the **Chart** field to cell **A1** and the **Subtitle** field to cell **B2**:

5. **Preview** the dashboard:

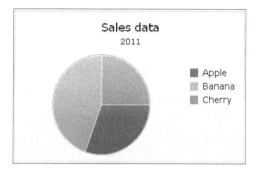

How it works...

We bound the fields from the **General** tab to the data in the spreadsheet, making this chart show the three labels and the associated portions of the total in a pie. Obviously, the pie chart component cannot use multiple series of data like the line chart and other chart components.

Using a scatter plot chart

A **scatter plot chart** can display values that consist of two variables. The chart shows a set of points, each of which refer to a combination of a value on the *x*-axis and a value on the *y*-axis.

 In previous versions of SAP BusinessObjects Dashboards (before 4.1) the scatter plot chart component was called XY-chart component.

Getting ready

Open a new file in SAP BusinessObjects Dashboards and enter the data, as shown in the following screenshot, into the spreadsheet:

	A	B	C
1	House price vs. Weeks until sale		
2			
3			
4		House price	Weeks until sale
5	Cat 1	100000	4
6	Cat 2	200000	20
7	Cat 3	300000	32
8	Cat 4	400000	18
9	Cat 5	500000	22

How to do it...

1. Drag a **Scatter Plot** chart component into the canvas.

2. Bind the data **By Range** to spreadsheet cells **B5** until **C9**.

3. Bind the **Chart** field to cell **A1** and delete the subtitle.

4. Bind the **Value (X) Axis** field to cell **B4** and the **Value (Y) Axis** field to cell **C4**. Now it is clear what the implication of each axis is.

5. Go to the **Behavior** tab and select the **Scale** sub-tab. Now select **Fixed Label Size**.

6. Click on the **Preview** button to try the dashboard.

How it works...

In this example, we created a dashboard that compares the price of a house (variable 1) with the number of weeks until it is sold (variable 2). It shows us that cheap houses are sold very quickly; houses priced between cheap and expensive (mid-range) take a very long time to sell; while expensive houses are somewhat in between.

By using the **Fixed Label Size** option, the values of the x-axis are shortened for better readability. As we saw in the recipe, thousands (100,000) become K (100K). In addition, millions turn into M, billions into B, and trillions into T.

Using a bubble plot chart

A **bubble plot chart** is essentially the same as a scatter plot chart, except that it has a third variable that determines the size of each point. The following screenshot represents a bubble plot chart:

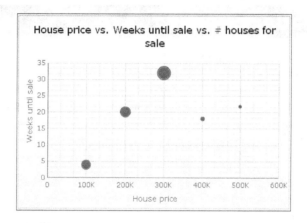

Getting ready

You can reuse the dashboard from the *Using a scatter plot chart* recipe and add the values in column **D**, as shown in the following screenshot:

	A	B	C	D
1	House price vs. Weeks until sale vs. # houses for sale			
2				
3				
4		House price	Weeks until sale	# houses for sale
5	Cat 1	100000	4	560
6	Cat 2	200000	20	680
7	Cat 3	300000	32	1130
8	Cat 4	400000	18	120
9	Cat 5	500000	22	70

How to do it...

1. Drag a **Bubble Plot Chart** component into the canvas.
2. Bind the data **By Range** to spreadsheet cells **B5** through **D9**.
3. Bind the **Chart** field to cell **A1** and delete the subtitle.
4. Bind the **Value (X) Axis** field to cell **B4** and the **Value (Y) Axis** field to cell **C4**.
5. Go to the **Behavior** tab and select the **Scale** sub-tab. Now select **Fixed Label Size**.

How it works...

In addition to the analysis we made in the *Using a scatter plot chart* recipe, we can now also see that the number of houses for sale in the mid-range market is very high, while the availability in the expensive market is very low.

Using a radar chart

The **radar chart** is able to represent more than two variables in a single chart. In this chart, the multiple axes all start at the same point. The radar chart can be used to make comparisons between series based on their score on a set of variables. In this way outliers can be quickly discovered and analyzed. The following screenshot represents a radar chart:

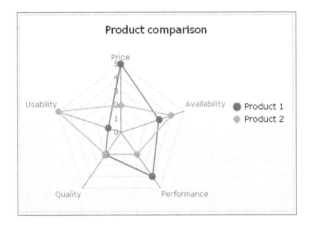

Getting ready

Open a new file in SAP BusinessObjects Dashboards and enter the data, as shown in the following screenshot, into the spreadsheet:

	A	B	C	D	E	F
1						
2						
3						
4		Price	Availability	Performance	Quality	Usability
5	Product 1	5	3	4	2	1
6	Product 2	2	4	2	2	5
7						

How to do it...

1. Drag a **Radar Chart** component to the canvas.
2. Enter a name and subtitle for the chart.
3. Bind the cell range **A4** to **F6** to the **By Range** field.

How it works...

Our dataset has two series and five categories. The chart has an axis for each category, and on these axes, the accompanying values are plotted for each series. The values of a series are connected with a line.

There's more...

The filled radar chart component does the same job as the radar chart component and has the same configuration options. The only difference in the filled radar chart component is that the area between the connected value points is filled with a color. As the following figure shows, the overlap area stands out as it is darker:

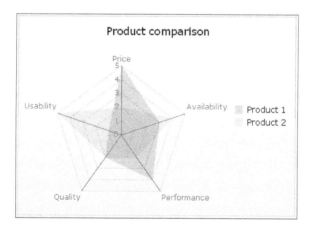

Using an OHLC chart and a candlestick chart

The **OHLC chart** and **candlestick chart** are both designed to show the movement of a stock price over time. OHLC stands for Open, High, Low, and Close. These four stock price values are illustrated for each time unit.

Both components work in exactly the same way, so you can use both the OHLC chart component and the candlestick chart component for this recipe. The only difference between them is the graphical visualization. The following screenshot displays an OHLC chart:

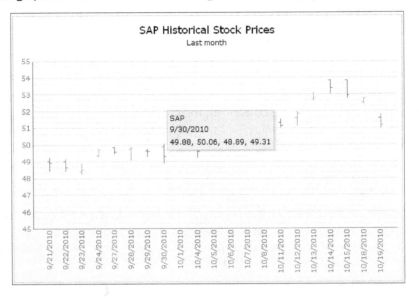

Getting ready

For this recipe, we need some historical stock data. Open your browser and go to http://www.nasdaq.com/ and look for historical quotes on the SAP AG stock as shown in the following screenshot:

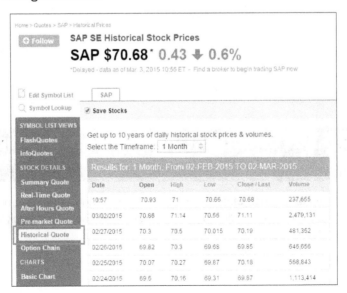

Select a timeframe of one month and copy and paste the quotes to the spreadsheet of a new SAP BusinessObjects Dashboards file, as shown in the following screenshot:

	A	B	C	D	E	F
1	SAP Historical Stock Prices					
2	Last Month					
3						
4	date	close	volume	open	high	low
5	3/2/2015	71.11	2479131	70.86	71.14	70.56
6	2/27/2015	70.19	481352	70.3	70.5	70.015
7	2/26/2015	69.85	646656	69.82	70.3	69.68
8	2/25/2015	70.18	568843	70.07	70.27	69.87
9	2/24/2015	69.87	1113414	69.6	70.16	69.31
10	2/23/2015	69.68	563082	69.71	70.01	69.52
11	2/20/2015	69.63	813047	68.48	69.95	68.31
12	2/19/2015	68.88	432577	68.51	69.25	68.34
13	2/18/2015	68.96	600888	68.24	69.15	68.16

How to do it...

1. First, prepare the data in the spreadsheet. It is now sorted from new to old quotes. As the **OHLC Chart** component does not enable sorting (see the recipe, *Sorting series*, later in this chapter) we have to sort the data ourselves in the spreadsheet. Start by selecting all the cells you just pasted into the spreadsheet.

2. Sort this selection by using the **Sort & Filter** function in the **Editing** section of the **Home** tab of the spreadsheet toolbar. Choose the **Sort Oldest to Newest** option:

3. Add an **OHLC Chart** component to the canvas.

4. Enter a chart title and subtitle, or bind these fields to cells in the spreadsheet.

5. Bind the data **By Range** to the range of cells that include all values in the **Open**, **High**, **Low**, and **Close** columns.

6. Select **By Series** and enter SAP in the **Series Name** field.

7. In the dataset we copied from the NASDAQ website and pasted to the spreadsheet, the dates are in the first column. Bind the **Category Labels** field to the cells in the **Date** column:

How it works...

▶ The OHLC chart we just created works as follows: the vertical lines show the price range (from the highest to the lowest value) of a stock for each day. The little mark on the left of these vertical lines indicates the opening price. The little mark on the right indicates the closing price. In addition to this, a line with a set of marks has a dark color if the closing price is lower than the opening price and a light color if the closing price is higher than the opening price as seen in the following screenshot:

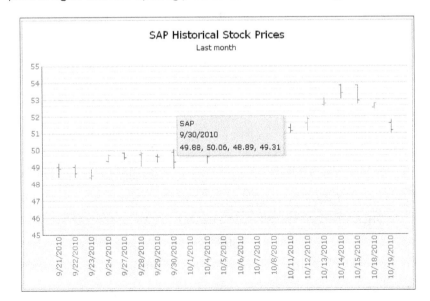

▸ The candlestick chart shows exactly the same data as the OHLC chart. In the candlestick chart a rectangle is used to illustrate the opening and closing prices. If this rectangle is transparent, the closing price is higher than the opening price, and if it's filled the closing price is lower as seen in the following screenshot:

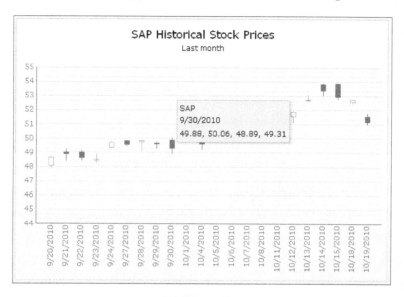

Sorting series

A chart does not always look like what you had in mind. In some cases, you may want to see data sorted from high to low values, while in other situations, you want to see the categories displayed in a more logical order. For example, in the following bar chart, the quarters are sorted from last (Q4) to first (Q1). To change this, you can of course adjust the data model in the spreadsheet, like we did in the *Using an OHLC chart and a candlestick chart* recipe. An easier and better way is to use the sorting settings for the bar chart component.

Sorting is available in the following components: line chart, pie chart, column chart, stacked column chart, bar chart, stacked bar chart, combination chart, area chart, stacked area chart, radar chart, and filled radar chart.

Getting ready

You can reuse any of the dashboards you created earlier, as long as they contain one of the previously mentioned components.

How to do it...

1. Select the component, go to the **Behavior** tab, and select the **Common** sub-tab.

2. Select **Enable Sorting**.

3. Select **By Category Labels**.

4. Select **Reverse Order**.

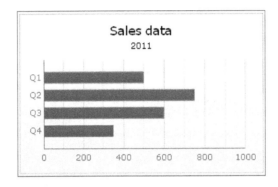

How it works...

As you can see in the preceding screenshot, the order of the quarters has changed. In SAP BusinessObjects Dashboards, the first category is by default the lowest category on its axis. With the reverse order setting, this can be changed.

There's more...

Besides sorting by category labels, it is also possible to sort by data. If you have more than one series, you have to choose one of these series to base the sorting order on, as shown in the following screenshot:

The following chart shows the data in ascending order:

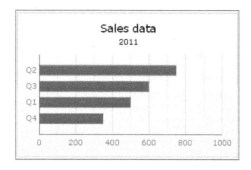

Zooming in on charts

If you are visualizing a dataset with a large number of values on the x-axis (the category axis), the chart might be a bit hard to use. To see a section of such a chart in more detail, we can use the range slider to zoom in on the data.

 The range slider option is available in the following chart components: line chart, OHLC chart, candlestick chart, column chart, bar chart, stacked column chart, stacked bar chart, combination chart, area chart, stacked area chart, and waterfall chart.

Getting ready

You can reuse any of the dashboards you have already made, which include one of the components mentioned previously. In this recipe, we will use the dashboard created in the _Adding a line chart to your dashboard_ recipe.

How to do it...

1. Select the chart then go to the **Behavior** tab and select the **Common** sub-tab.
2. Select **Enable Range Slider**.
3. Under **Beginning Range Value** select **Category Label** and enter value Q1.
4. Under **End Range Value** also select **Category Label** and enter value Q3.

5. Bind the **Range Labels** field to cells **B4** until **E4**.

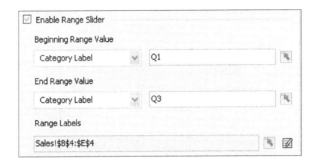

6. Go to the **Appearance** tab and select the **Text** sub-tab. Select **Range Labels** and set the text size to 8.

7. Run the dashboard by hitting the **Preview** button and try the functionality of the range slider.

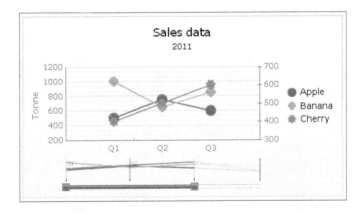

How it works...

The range slider option makes it possible to select a section of the chart by sliding the beginning and end values of this range. In this recipe, we used category labels to define the initial range values. You can also choose to use the **Position** field and enter the position of the desired value in its series. Q1 would be position 1 and Q3 would be position 3.

Scaling the y-axis

After binding a chart to a dataset in the spreadsheet, SAP BusinessObjects Dashboards makes up a scale on the *y* axis by default, based on the lowest and highest values in the visualized dataset. The problem with this auto-scaling is that it creates a *y*-axis that doesn't start with 0, which may cause a bad interpretation of the data.

In the following screenshot, the same results are presented in two bar charts. The chart on the left-hand side gives the indication that **Product B** has performed a lot better than **Product A**; the bar is more than two times larger! This is, of course, wrong, as the *y*-axis starts at **$470,000**. The chart on the right-hand side shows a version that is much more useful for analysis.

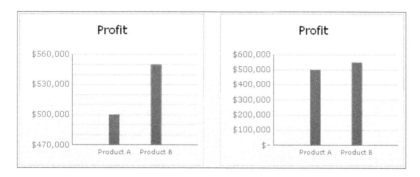

Getting ready

You can reuse any of the dashboards you have already made with chart components. In this recipe, we will use the dashboard created in the *Adding a line chart to your dashboard* recipe.

How to do it...

1. Select the chart, go to the **Behavior** tab, and select the **Scale** sub-tab. If your chart has a secondary axis, there will be two sub-tabs: **Primary Scale** and **Secondary Scale**.

2. Select **Manual (Y) Axis**.

3. Enter 0 under **Minimum Limit** and 1000 under **Maximum Limit**.

4. Select **Fixed Label Size**.

5. Set the **Size of Divisions** to 200 and **Minor Divisions** to 1:

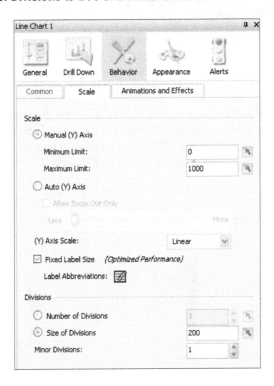

How it works...

The y-axis of the chart will now have a fixed minimum and maximum limit. Remember that this also means that values higher than 1000 won't be displayed correctly with these settings. They will be placed on the maximum value (1000) of this chart.

The **Fixed Label Size** option keeps the labels on the y-axis readable. 1,000 is 1K, 1,000,000 is 1M, a billion is 1B, and a trillion is 1T.

There's more...

We conclude this recipe with two additional options regarding scaling the y-axis: variable maximum limits and **Allow Zoom Out Only**.

Variable maximum limits

To make sure that values in the dataset never pass the maximum limit, we can use a variable maximum limit by following these steps:

1. Go to the spreadsheet and enter this formula in cell **D1**: =MAX(B5:E7). This will result in the maximum value of the range **B5** through **E7**.

2. Bind the **Maximum Limit** to cell **D1**. The y-axis will now display the exact maximum value that resulted from the formula.

3. To make this value a more rounded number we have to adjust the formula. Change the formula to =ROUNDUP((MAX(B5:E7)),-3). The -3 indicates that the value will be rounded up to the nearest thousand. So if the maximum value is 1978, the maximum limit on the y-axis will be 2000. -1 rounds to the nearest tens, -2 to the nearest hundred, and so on.

Allow Zoom Out Only

If you do want to use an automatic axis, SAP BusinessObjects Dashboards offers the **Allow Zoom Out Only** option. This option is only useful if a dataset that is presented in a chart is variable (for example, by switching with a selector; see *Chapter 3, From a Static to an Interactive Dashboard*). By selecting this option, the y-axis will only scale to larger values when a dataset with higher values is presented. If the values are lower, the scale will not change. With the slider, you can set the sensitivity of the growth factor.

Using a tree map

The **tree map**, also known as a **heat map**, visualizes values by dividing an area into a set of rectangles. The following screenshot shows an example of a tree map:

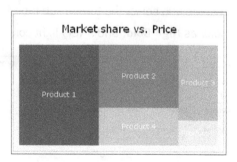

As you can see, two variables are used in this chart: one variable expressed by the relative size of each rectangle and another one illustrated by the color intensity. Instead of using the tree map, you can also choose the scatter plot chart to display two variables in one chart.

Getting ready

For this recipe, we can reuse the file we created in the *Using a scatter plot chart* recipe.

How to do it...

1. Drag a **Tree Map** component to the canvas.

2. Enter a name for the chart.

3. Bind the cell range **A4** to **C9** to the **By Range** field.

4. Select **Data in Columns**.

5. Select **By Series** and bind the **Name** field to cell **A1**:

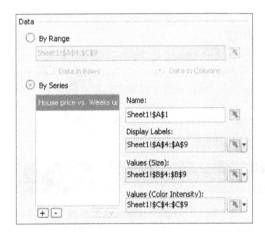

6. Go to the **Appearance** tab and select the **Series** sub-tab.

7. Select a very dark color as **High Color** and a very light color as **Low Color**:

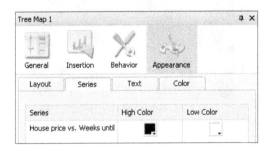

8. **Preview** the dashboard to check the result:

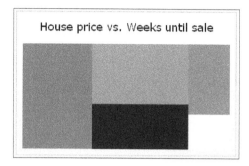

How it works...

The tree map arranges the rectangles from big to small. The Cat 5 data (most expensive houses) is presented on the far left-hand side, while Cat 1 (cheapest houses) is illustrated by the block on the lower right-hand side. This rectangle also has the lightest color, indicating the lowest **Weeks until sale** value. In the recipe, we changed the colors to a more extreme range so that the differences between the rectangles are clearer.

Showing a trend without a chart

Showing a trend with a line chart is very useful if you want to show data over more than two periods. In some cases, all this historical information is unnecessary and you only want to display the direction of the trend—up, down, or no change. The **trend** icon component delivers this functionality. This recipe will show you how to use it.

Getting ready

Open a new SAP BusinessObjects Dashboards file and enter the data, as shown in the following screenshot, into the spreadsheet:

	A	B
1	Value A	1000
2	Value B	250

How to do it...

1. Drag a **Trend Icon** component into the canvas.
2. Enter this formula in spreadsheet cell **B3**: =B2-B1.

3. Now bind the **Data** field of the **Trend Icon** component to cell **B3**. The **Trend Icon** component will now turn red and show a downward arrow:

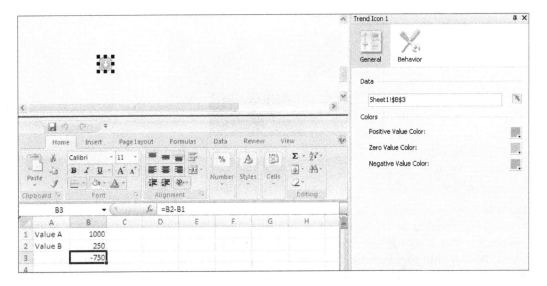

How it works...

The trend icon component can only be bound to a single cell. If this cell has a positive value, the component will be shown in positive state (arrow up). If the value is negative, the component will turn into its negative state (arrow down). If the value is zero, a neutral state is shown (flat line icon):

We used the formula to calculate whether the change in trend is positive, negative, or neutral.

Displaying raw data

If you want to display numbers and text without a chart, but just in a table, you can use the Spreadsheet Table component.

Getting ready

Open a new SAP BusinessObjects Dashboards file and enter the data, as shown in the following screenshot, into the spreadsheet:

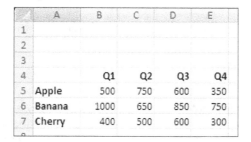

How to do it...

1. In the spreadsheet, select cells **A4** through **E4**.

2. Add a **Bottom Border** by using the **Borders** menu in the **Font** section of the **Home** tab in the spreadsheet:

3. Select cells **A4** through **A7** and add a **Right Border**.

4. Drag a **Spreadsheet Table** component into the canvas.

5. Bind the **Display Data** field with the spreadsheet range from **A4** to **E7**.

6. Go to the **Behavior** tab and deselect **Row** in the **Row Selectability** section.

7. Go to the **Appearance** tab and deselect **Show Gridlines** in the **Layout** sub-tab.

8. The dashboard should now look like what is shown in the following screenshot:

	Q1	Q2	Q3	Q4
Apple	500	750	600	350
Banana	1000	650	850	750
Cherry	400	500	600	300

How it works...

The Spreadsheet Table component shows a range of cells exactly as they are formatted in the spreadsheet. You can add borders and colors, change fonts and alignments, and so on. If you make any changes to the formatting, you have to bind the cells again to the component to make the new formatting visible.

The data insertion options as well as the selectable options, are not used in this recipe, but will be explained in *Chapter 3, From a Static to an Interactive Dashboard*.

There's more...

The **List View** component and the **Scorecard** component are also able to show spreadsheet data. The main difference is that these two components don't respect any formatting used in the spreadsheet. The Scorecard component has a lot of alerting options (not only colors but also icons) and is covered in the *Using alerts in a Scorecard* recipe in *Chapter 5, Using Alerts*.

Illustrating single values

SAP BusinessObjects Dashboards offers three component types to display single values: gauges, progress bars, and value components. A gauge and progress bar shows data on a scale, while the value component only shows a value in numbers. The **gauge** is the only component of these three types that has the ability to show more than one value. There are a number of different gauge versions available, where the progress bar has only a horizontal and vertical version. All these components are ideally used in combination with Alerts. Alerts will be discussed in *Chapter 5, Using Alerts*.

This recipe will show you how to set up a gauge. The other two component types work in the same way.

Getting ready

No preparation is needed; just open a new SAP BusinessObjects Dashboards file.

How to do it...

1. Add a **Gauge** component to the canvas.

2. Enter 75 in spreadsheet cell **A1** and bind this cell to the **By Range** field.

3. Select **By Indicators** and rename **Indicator 1** to **Result**.

4. Add a second indicator by clicking on the plus button.

5. Rename this indicator to **Target**, enter 90 in the **Value** field, and select **Type** as **Outside Marker**:

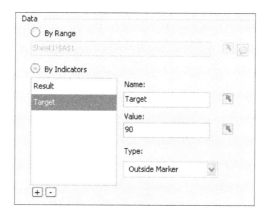

6. Go to the **Appearance** tab and select the **Text** sub-tab. Select **Show Limits** and set size to 8.

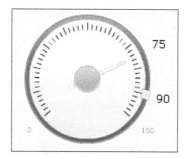

How it works...

As you can see, binding single values works in the same way as binding data series for charts. The gauge component can show more than one indicator and has the option to enter fixed values.

There's more...

Single-value components can be manually scaled or auto-scaled. There are four options for auto-scaling:

- ▸ **Value-based**: The limits cover a range around the value
- ▸ **Zero-based**: The higher limit is equal to the bound value, while the lower limit is zero
- ▸ **Zero-centered**: The limits cover a range that includes the value and its negative/positive with zero in the middle
- ▸ **Alert-based**: The limits are based on the selected alert method (see *Chapter 5, Using Alerts* for more on using alerts)

3
From a Static to an Interactive Dashboard

In this chapter, we will cover the following recipes:

- ▶ Selecting your data from a list
- ▶ Drilling down from a chart
- ▶ Using the Filter selector component for hierarchies
- ▶ An alternative hierarchy selection method
- ▶ Using the Hierarchical Table
- ▶ Using Filtered Rows
- ▶ Using maps to select data of an area or country
- ▶ Adding a Mac OS X-looking dock to your dashboard
- ▶ Resetting your data (the reset button)
- ▶ Making selections from a custom image (the push button and image component)
- ▶ Inputting data values
- ▶ Using the Play Selector / Play Control component
- ▶ Opening up a Web Intelligence report using dashboard parameters
- ▶ Selecting calendar dates
- ▶ Using sliders to create a what-if scenario

Introduction

An important strength that SAP BusinessObjects Dashboards has is the amount of control it allows a developer to provide the user with. This leads to totally customized dashboards, which give users the interactivity that guides them to make the right business decisions. It is important that developers know what type of interactive tools are available so that they can utilize the power of these tools.

With the right interactivity, users can retrieve information more quickly and efficiently. This chapter will provide developers with recipes on interactivity, which will improve the dashboard user experience.

Selecting your data from a list

Filtering data into a smaller dataset is a very important feature to implement when building dashboards. The reason is that people want to have a large amount of data available to them, but they do not want to have to see all of it at once; otherwise, it will become overwhelming for the users. It will require the users to hunt for data, which is not the purpose of a dashboard.

In our example, we will be selecting from a list of regions that will populate a gauge value appropriately:

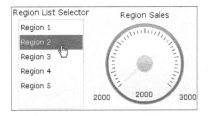

Getting ready

Have your data list ready. In our example, we will show a simple list of five elements with their corresponding values, as shown in the following screenshot:

How to do it...

1. Select a **List Box** selector from the **Selectors** section of the **Components** window and drag it onto the canvas.

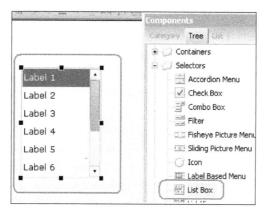

2. In the general section of the **List Box** selector, bind the labels to **A2:A6**, source data to **B2:B6**, and destination to **D2**, as shown in the following screenshot. Select **Row** as the **Insertion Type**. The destination cell **D2** will be the cell to which the gauge will be bound.

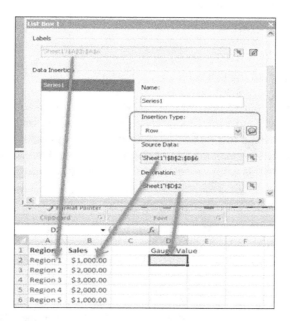

3.   Drag a gauge onto the canvas from the **Single Value | Gauge** section of the **Components** window. Bind the gauge data to cell **D2**.

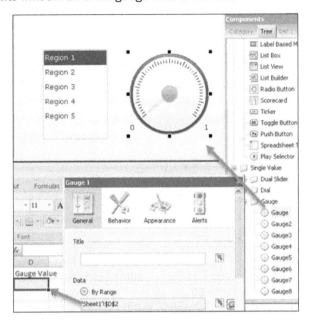

4.   Click on **Preview** and test your result.

How it works...

Selecting from a list of data using a selector is quite easy, as you have seen in this recipe. Basically, you'll need to have a set of labels to identify the list of items that you are selecting from. You will then need your source data which relates back to the list of items being selected from. In our example, we used a row one cell wide as the selected item type. If we wanted to, we could have even chosen a row that's 100 cells wide. Just try not to go over a width of 512 cells, otherwise you may start running into performance issues. Finally, the destination in our example is one row as that is what we selected as our **Insertion Type**.

There's more...

We just showed you how to use the **List Box** selector. However, we could have used other selector components to accomplish the same task, such as a combobox dropdown, list view, label-based menu, spreadsheet table selector, and so on. It is important to choose the selectors that best fit your dashboard visually.

SAP BusinessObjects Dashboards provides great flexibility by offering many different methods for **Insertion Type**, such as filtered rows, by row, by column, by label, by position number, and so on.

See also

For more detailed information on using **Filtered Rows**, which is an advanced insertion type, please refer to the recipe *Using Filtered Rows* later on in this chapter.

Drilling down from a chart

Being able to drill down from higher-level data to more granular data is a very important feature in SAP BusinessObjects Dashboards. We want to be able to retrieve high-level and granular-level data easily without hunting for it. By using drilldowns, users can easily navigate through the different levels of data.

Getting ready

Insert two charts into the canvas (Parent = Column Chart; Child = Line Chart). Data in the child chart is driven from the parent chart.

 Please refer to the example `Drilling down from a chart.xlf` from the code bundle on how to set up and bind data appropriately to the charts.

How to do it...

1. In our example, the parent chart contains **Regional Sales** information. The child chart contains a drilldown of a monthly trend.

2. Turn on the drilldown capability from the parent chart by clicking on the **Insertion** icon and then on the **Enable Data Insertion** checkbox.

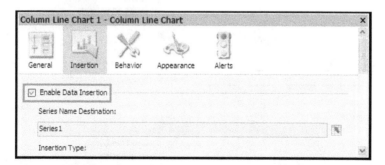

3. Select the **Insertion Type** that you will use for the drilldown bars. In our case, we will drill down based on **Row** and bind to the line chart data in cells **D6:I9**. Then, select the destination of the drilldown value. We have selected cells **D3:I3** in our case.

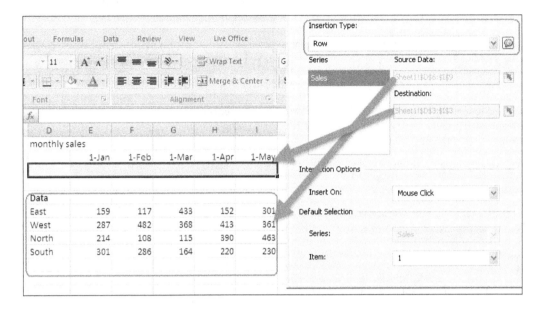

4. The destination cells **D3:I3** control the chart data for our monthly trend dataset as shown in the following screenshot:

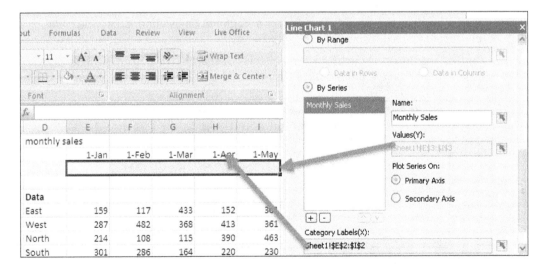

5. Preview the finished example and verify that the drilldown works by clicking on each bar of the **Regional Sales** chart.

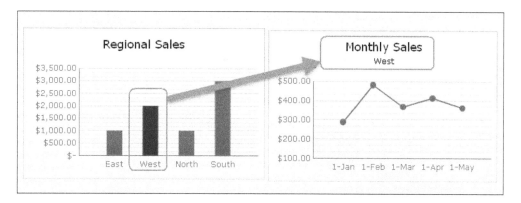

How it works...

In our example, we showed how to drill down from a set of regional sales to a monthly trend for a selected region. In the drilldown properties screen, the source rows **D6:I9** from step 3 are linked to each bar. When a user clicks on the bar, it will select the appropriate row from **D6:I9** and transfer it to the destination at **D3:I3**, to which the child chart will bind its data.

There's more...

In our example, we had all the data available to us on the spreadsheet. We can also accomplish drilldown capability on a query by sending in the drilldown parameter when clicking on a bar and then retrieving the appropriate child data by calling the child query.

Using the Filter selector component for hierarchies

SAP BusinessObjects Dashboards provides an easy-to-use selector component for hierarchical data. For example, we may have a hierarchy that consists of a **Region**, **Sales District**, and **Sales Office**. We can easily create this with the **Filter** component.

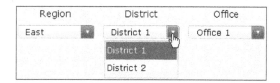

Getting ready

It is important to set up the data as shown in the following screenshot so that the Filter component can consume it properly. Every row has to have values for the Region, Sales District, and Sales Office as well as the metric value(s) that you want populated on your destination. We have highlighted the destination in **F3** and the filter-related stuff in **A3:C6** and **D3:D6**. Information on how everything works can be found in the *How it works...* section.

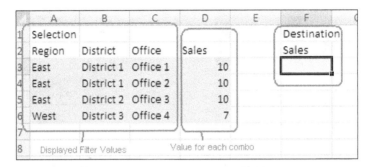

How to do it...

1. Add a **Filter** component from the **Selectors** category onto the canvas. In the **Properties** window, set **Number of Filters** to **3** since our hierarchy has three levels.

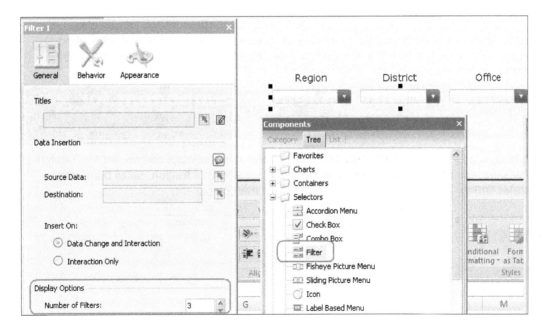

2. Bind the **Source Data** to the area in green (**A3:D6**) from the data setup in the *Getting ready* section.

3. Bind the **Titles** section to cells **A2:C2**.

4. Bind the **Destination** to the cell **F3**.

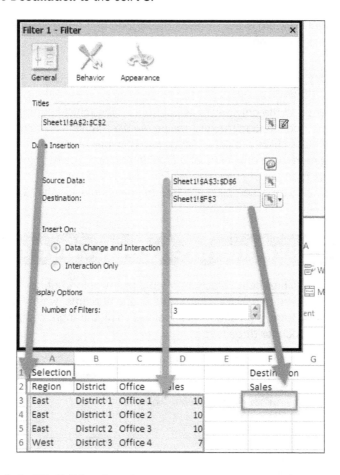

5. Insert a **Label Text** object into the canvas and bind it to destination cell **F3**.

6. Preview and make sure the Filter component works.

How it works...

The **Filter** selector component works by grouping values in each column of the source data. In our example, we selected three filters, so the first three columns of the source data will consist of the three hierarchies. The main parent is **Region**, which then branches down to **District**, and finally **Office**.

Now that we are familiar with the cells colored in blue from the image in the *Getting ready* section of this recipe, we'll explain what the cell in yellow is. The destination cell **F3** can be of arbitrary width and will consist of metrics or values associated with the chosen hierarchy combination. For example, if we select **East | District 1 | Office 1**, it will retrieve the values corresponding to that combination row.

Note that the destination width is the same as the second part of the source data (**D3:D6**), which in our case is one column.

There's more...

The **Filter** component isn't the only way to select from a hierarchical approach. We can also try a more advanced method found in the next recipe, *An alternative hierarchy selection method*, which will show the hierarchies in a set of list boxes. This may be the preferred approach if a user wants to see more than one value at a time. In addition, the recipe *Presenting micro charts in a Tree Grid*, found in *Chapter 10, Top Third-party Add-ons*, will show users how a third-party component can accomplish a hierarchy selection using the familiar Windows tree explorer.

An alternative hierarchy selection method

When navigating through hierarchy selection, often a user would want to see a list of available parents or children, instead of only being able to see one at a time, when looking at a set of drop-down filters. Here is an alternative method using the more complex list box breadcrumb-type approach for three levels.

Getting ready

Set up the data as shown in the following screenshot. Columns A to C contain the initial full hierarchical data. The sections **E** to **G**, **I** to **J**, and **L** each contain a breadcrumb trail whose source is one column less than the parent. More about how everything works will be explained in the *How it works...* section.

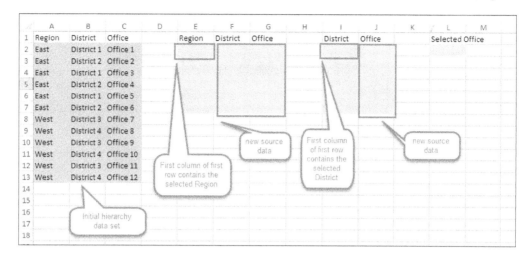

How to do it...

1. Insert three **List Box** selectors onto the canvas. On the first **List Box** selector, which belongs to **Region**, set the **Labels** to the values of column **A** (**A2:A13**).

2. Select **Filtered Rows** as the **Insertion Type** and set the **Source Data** to columns **A** to **C**. Set the **Destination** to columns **E** to **G**. Notice that we select all three source columns because the first column of the first row of the destination contains the selected region.

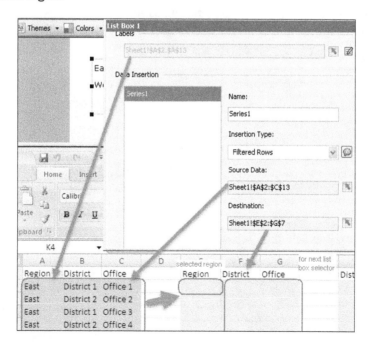

3. Do the same with the next list box (**District**); select the labels and filtered rows from columns **F** to **G**.

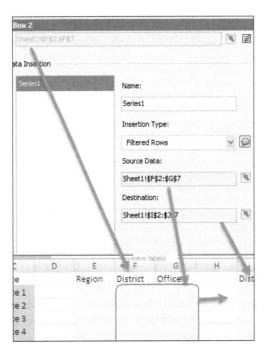

4. Finally, the **Office** list box will be getting its **Labels** value from the column **J**. You can either use **Label** or **Row** as the **Insertion Type** as we are only down to one selection column.

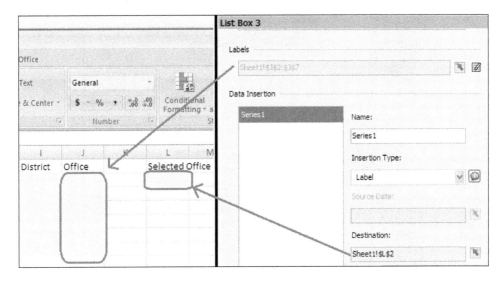

How it works...

In this example, each list box is a hierarchical level. In order to transfer all the appropriate values from one parent to the next data source, we must use the Filtered Rows method to grab all the parent's children, until the last child, where we can use label or row for the insertion type.

See also

For more detailed information on using Filtered Rows, read the *Using Filtered Rows* recipe later in this chapter.

Using the Hierarchical Table

The Hierarchical Table is a powerful component that was introduced in SAP BusinessObjects Dashboards 4.0 FP3. It allows users to connect to either a BEx query connection or an OLAP universe and take advantage of its hierarchical display and multi-selection capability.

Before the Hierarchical Table was introduced, there was no way to accomplish native hierarchical display and selection without significant workarounds.

Calendar	Amount	Fact Finance Count
▼ ☐ All	$1,358,640,412.70	39,409
► ☐ 2001	$146,821,471.40	6,740
▼ ☐ 2002	$422,713,118.86	12,840
► ☑ 1	$80,509,026.95	3,358
► ☑ 2	$85,304,627.25	3,392
► ☐ 3	$136,436,173.26	3,025
► ☐ 4	$120,463,291.40	3,065

 Although the Hierarchical Table component is extremely powerful, please note that it can only be used with either a BEx query or an OLAP universe. It will not work on a universe based on a relational database.

Getting ready

Before you can take advantage of the Hierarchical Table component, you must have an OLAP universe or a BEx query connection available. In our example, we create a simple cube from the Adventureworks data warehouse, which is easily accessible from MSDN.

You can download the Adventureworks data warehouse available at `http://msftdbprodsamples.codeplex.com/releases/view/105902`.

To set up a simple cube, please follow the instructions available at `http://www.accelebrate.com/library/tutorials/ssas-2008`.

To set up an OLAP connection to the cube, please follow the instructions available at `http://wiki.scn.sap.com/wiki/display/BOBJ/Setting+up+OLAP+Microsoft+Analysis+Service+through+an+XMLA+connection+with+SSO`.

Finally, you will have to set up an OLAP universe that connects to the OLAP connection. Instructions for this can be found at `http://scn.sap.com/docs/DOC-22026`.

How to do it...

1. Create an OLAP universe query / BEx query from the Query Browser.

 For instructions on how to create a query from the Query Browser, please refer to the *Using the Query Browser* recipe in *Chapter 8, Dashboard Data Connectivity*.

2. From the **Components** window, go to the **Selectors** category and drag a **Hierarchical Table** component onto the dashboard canvas.

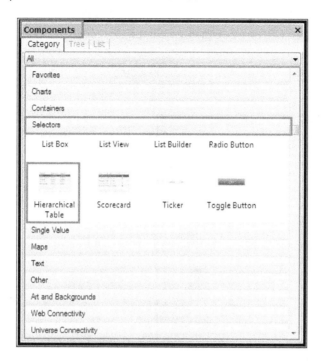

3. Click on the **Bind to Query Data** button and choose the query that you created in step 1. Next, choose the dimensions and measures that you want displayed on the Hierarchical Table. By default, you must select at least one hierarchy dimension.

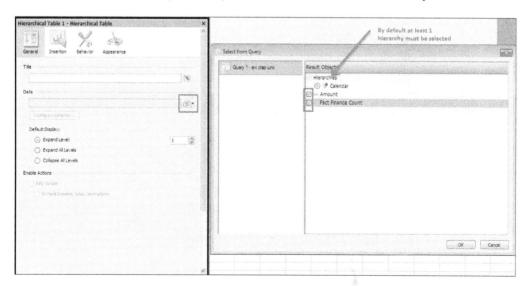

4. Click on the **Configure Columns** button below the data binding to adjust the column widths on the Hierarchical Table. We do this because by default, SAP BusinessObjects Dashboards does not set the column widths very well when we first bind the data.

5. On the **Appearance** tab, edit the number formats for each measure appropriately. For example, you can set dollar amounts as the currency with two decimal places.

6. Next, we want to capture rows that are selected during runtime. To do this, click on the **Insertion** tab. For the **Insertion Type**, you have the option of **Value** or **Row**.

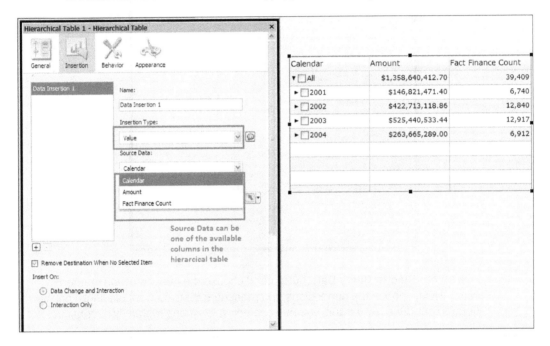

7. For the **Value** insertion option, you must choose an option for **Source Data**, which is one of the columns in the Hierarchical Table.

8. In our example, we will choose the **Insertion Type** as **Row**, which grabs values from all the columns. We'll need to bind the output destination. We will assume that a user can select a maximum of 30 rows. So we'll bind the output to a 30 x 3 destination range.

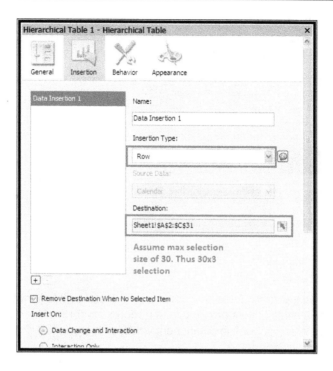

9. Bind a spreadsheet table object to the destination output from step 8 to prove that our selection works.

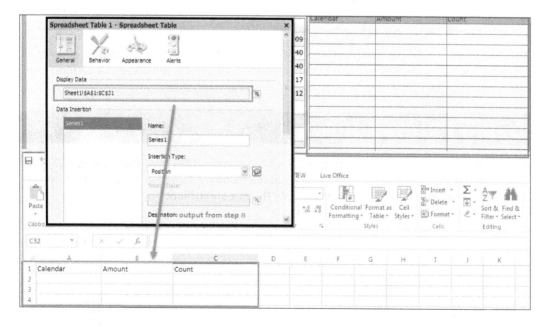

10. Finally, test the Hierarchical Table by entering preview mode. In the following screenshot, you can see that we can expand/collapse our Hierarchical Table, as well as make multiple selections!

Calendar	Amount	Fact Finance Count
▼ ☐ All	$1,358,640,412.70	39,409
► ☐ 2001	$146,821,471.40	6,740
▼ ☐ 2002	$422,713,118.86	12,840
► ☑ 1	$80,509,026.95	3,358
▼ ☑ 2	$85,304,627.25	3,392
☐ 4	$22,079,552.50	1,118
☑ 5	$36,873,652.21	1,126
☐ 6	$26,351,422.54	1,148
► ☐ 2	$126,426,172.26	3,035

Calendar	Amount	Count
1	80509026.95000002	3358
2	85304627.25	3392
5	36873652.209999986	1126

How it works...

As you can see, the Hierarchical Table selector is a very useful component because before this component was available, we were unable to perform any form of hierarchical analysis as well as simple multi-selection. The component achieves hierarchical capabilities by taking advantage of the OLAP cube engine.

There's more...

Unfortunately, the Hierarchical Table selector is only available from cube sources and not a traditional data warehouse table, because it uses the OLAP cube engine to do the processing.

The hierarchical capability, in our opinion, is doable with data warehouse tables as other tools allow this. So hopefully, SAP will one day upgrade the Hierarchical Table selector so that it works with your traditional data warehouse universe based on tables.

Using Filtered Rows

Filtered Rows was one of the greatest additions to Xcelsius 2008 (now SAP BusinessObjects Dashboards 4.1) from Xcelsius 4.5. If we look at the following screenshot, we see that we have a set of **Sales** metrics that are grouped by **Region** and **Office**:

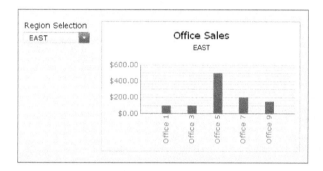

Let's say we want to be able to select a region and show a sales comparison chart between the different sales offices of that region. Before the advent of Filtered Rows, we would have had to perform a complex VLOOKUP or have the result come back through a query every time a region was selected. Both methods are very time consuming.

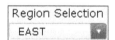

How to do it...

1. We will use a **Combo Box** selector to choose the desired region.

2. In the **Combo Box** selector properties, bind the **Labels** to the **Region** column.

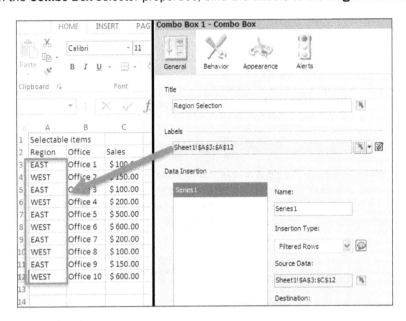

3. Select **Filtered Rows** as the **Insertion Type**. Bind **Source Data** to cells **A3:C12**. The **Destination** will contain the chart values as well as the selected region.

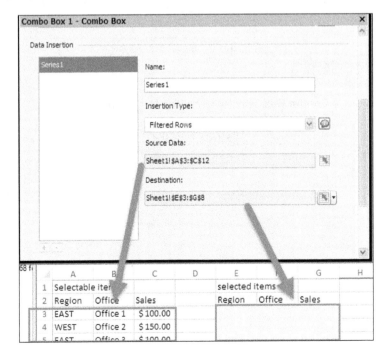

4. Bind the chart values to the **Destination** section from step 3.

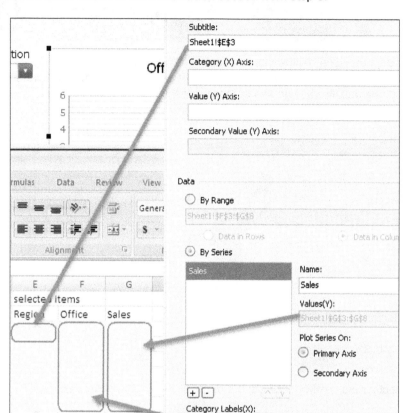

How it works...

The Filtered Rows insertion type allows users to select groupings of data easily without having to implement complex VLOOKUP logic or database querying. It allows for performance gains and eases future maintenance.

Using maps to select data of an area or country

Using maps on a dashboard allows us to visually identify data using a picture instead of a table/chart, for example to analyze which regions of an area are doing poorly versus which regions are doing well. As you can see by looking at the following map of Canada, users are able to visually distinguish between each province:

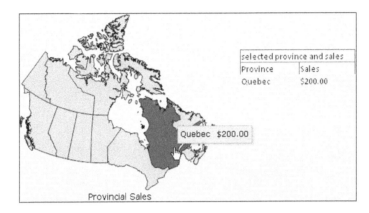

How to do it...

1. Select a map component from the **Maps** section. In our example, we will use Canada.

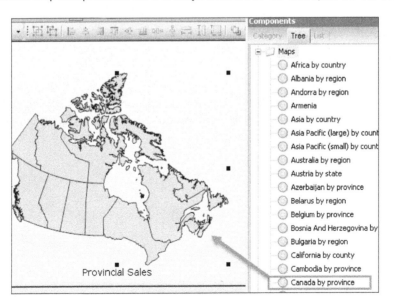

2. In the map's properties, bind the region keys as shown in the following screenshot.

Tip to find map regions:

A full list of the region keys for each map included in SAP BusinessObjects Dashboards can be found in the `MapRegions.xls` spreadsheet in the `<install path>\Xcelsius 4.0\assets\samples\User Guide Samples\` directory.

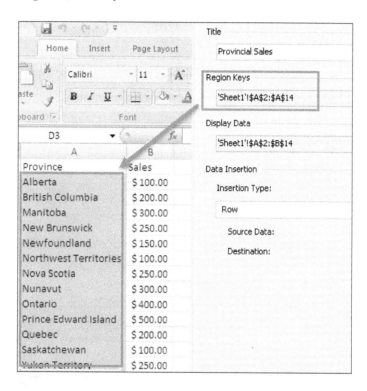

3. Next, bind the **Display Data**, which will be the key/value pair. The key comes from the key that you used in step 2 and the value can be any value associated with that key.

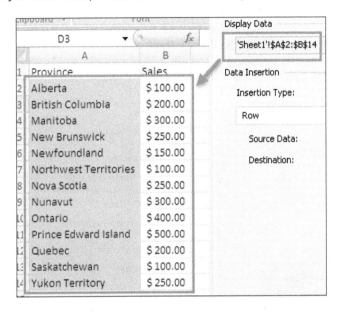

4. Now bind the **Source Data**. Make sure that the first column of the **Source Data** contains the matching key value from step 2.

5. Bind the **Destination** to the cells **D3:E3**.

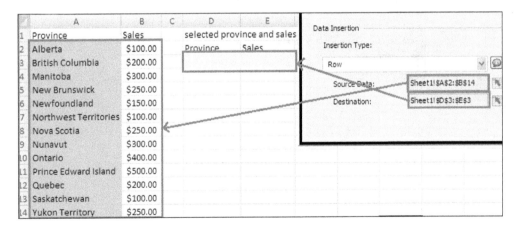

6. Now, drag a **Spreadsheet Table** component onto the canvas and bind the **Display Data** to cells **D3:E3**. This will change according to the province you click on during runtime.

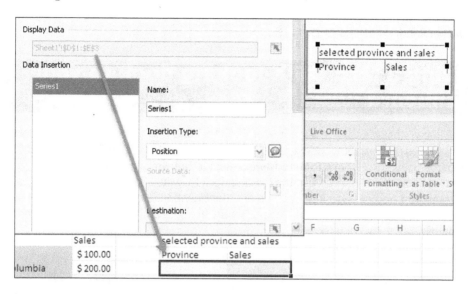

How it works...

The map component works by using a key/value pair that is assigned to each map section. It is important that the order of items bound to the **Region** section is in alphabetical order. Otherwise, the wrong keys will be bound. For example, in the following screenshot, Yukon and Nova Scotia are in the wrong alphabetical order. Thus, the key/value pair will be incorrect.

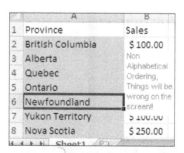

The **Display Data** section in step 3 is used to show what will be displayed as a user hovers the mouse over a region. There are two columns that can be shown (key/value). The key must match the key that was bound to the **Region** data; otherwise it, will not show up.

Finally, we have our **Source Data**, and again we must have a matching key in the first column in order to match the correct row.

There's more...

To make the visualization even better for a map component, it is common to use alert coloring to show how the provinces are doing. To accomplish this, please read the *Displaying alerts on a map* recipe in *Chapter 5, Using Alerts*.

Adding a Mac OS X-looking dock to your dashboard

It is well known that Macs have a great user interface, and one of the great things about this interface is the program loading dock. We can emulate this in SAP BusinessObjects Dashboards using the **Fisheye Picture Menu** selector. But why would someone want to use the loading dock? Well, you can use the loading dock to switch between dashboards on the main dashboard. You can use it to open up another dashboard, or you can use it as a selector to change your charts or data. In this recipe, we are going to emulate swapping between dashboards.

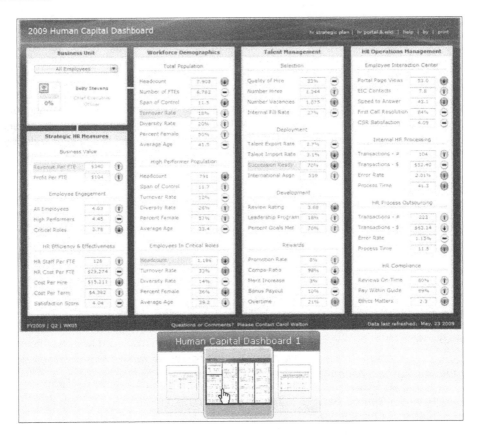

How to do it...

1. Select the **Fisheye Picture Menu** selector.

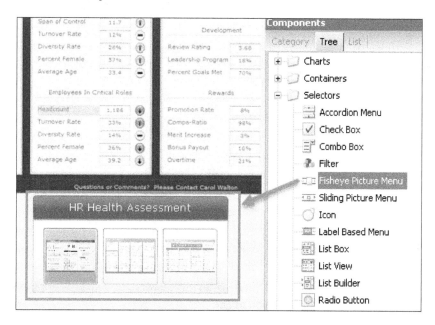

2. We'll need to link an image of each dashboard to the fisheye menu. To do this, press the **Import** button on the **Images Embedded** section of the fisheye menu properties. In our example, we are using three dashboards. So click on the **Click to Add Images** button to load each of the three dashboard images.

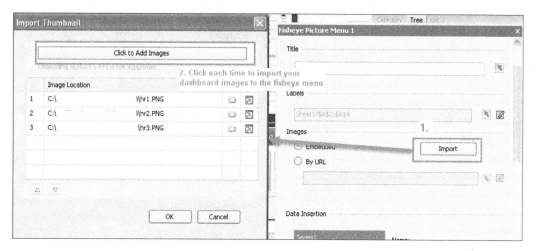

3. Bind the **Labels** to the spreadsheet as shown so that the user knows the name of the dashboard when they hover over any of the icons:

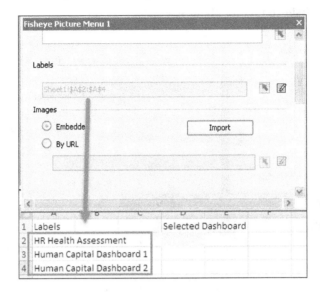

4. Bind the **Source Data** and **Destination**. In this case, we are just using **Position** for the source. Bind the **Destination** to cell **D2**.

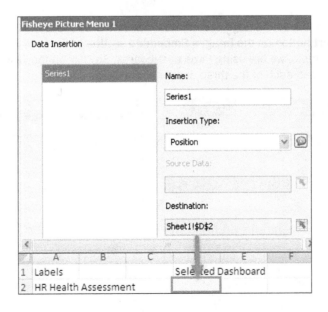

5. Set the dynamic visibility of each dashboard to the corresponding position of the fisheye menu selector. For example, the **HR Health Assessment** dashboard has `position 1`, so in the dashboard properties, the dynamic visibility should be set to `1` for cell **D2**.

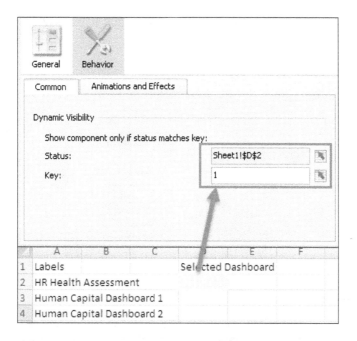

How it works...

The **Fisheye Picture Menu** is a very simple component similar to the Mac OS X loading dock. It allows users to scroll through icons that will zoom in as you hover over them. As outlined in step 2, we can see that we have to bind images that are similar to program icons. Those icons are linked to the **Source Data** in step 4.

There's more...

There is another component called the **Sliding Picture Menu** that acts the same way and is set up the same way as the **Fisheye Picture Menu**, except that you don't get the zoom upon mouseover feature.

Resetting your data (the reset button)

It is common that a user may want to go back to their default or starting view. Let's say I have five selectors and I have modified all five of them. To get back to the starting point would be a pain. Thus, having a one-click approach to go back to default is useful.

How to do it...

Select the **Reset Button** option from the **Other** components section and drag it onto the canvas.

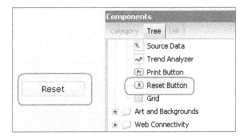

How it works...

When you first load the dashboard, the state of the first load is remembered. So when you click on the **Reset** button, it will go back to the original state.

 Warning: Using the **Reset** button will reset the whole dashboard and not just certain components.

Making selections from a custom image (the push button and image component)

As shown in the *Adding a Mac OS X-looking dock to your dashboard* recipe, we can use a **Fisheye Picture Menu** to emulate a program-dock-type style when selecting items. However, there may be cases where we may want images in different locations that we can click on to perform different actions.

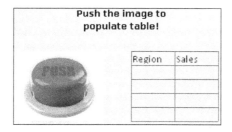

In this recipe, we will go through an example of how to use a push button combined with an Image Component to create a clickable image that can perform actions when clicked.

How to do it...

1. Drag an **Image Component** from the **Arts and Backgrounds** section of the **Components** window onto the canvas.

2. Open up the image properties window and click on the **Import** button. Select the image from your computer that you want to show.

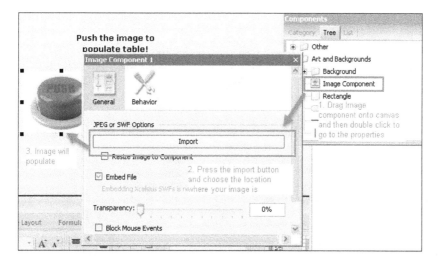

3. Drag a **Push Button** object from the **Selectors** section of the **Components** window and put it on top of the image. Then, resize the **Push Button** so that it is the same size as the image. To make the button the same size as the image, use the sizing icons on the toolbar circled in red, as shown in the following screenshot. Make sure you click on the image first and then on the push button in order for the push button to match the sizing properties of the image, and not the other way round.

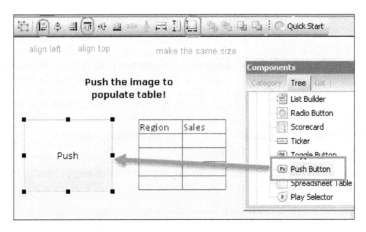

4. In the **Push Button** properties, first bind the **Source Data** and **Destination** to the appropriate cells. In our example, we want to transfer the table data from the yellow section to the destination section highlighted with a black border. Also, in the **Label** section, don't forget to delete all text.

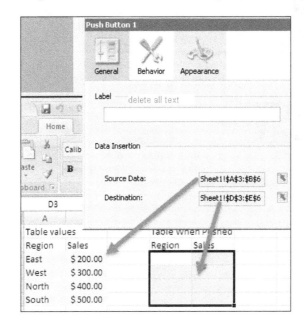

5. Go to the **Appearance** tab of the push button and set the **Transparency** to **100%**. Then, uncheck the **Show Button Background** checkbox.

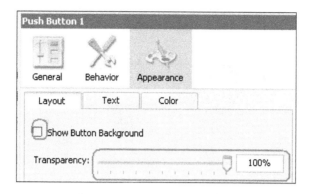

6. Drag a **Spreadsheet Table** component onto the canvas and bind it to the destination cells **D2:E6** of the push button.

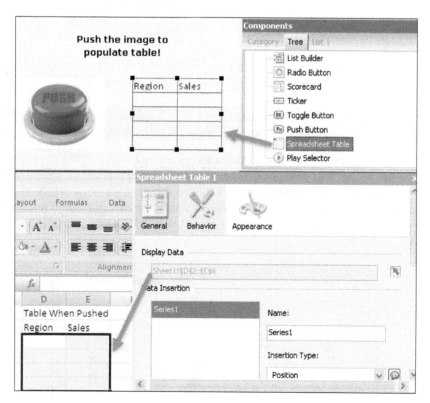

7. Preview and make sure that when you click on the image, the details of the image show up on the table.

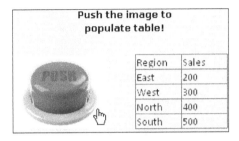

How it works...

In this recipe, we overlay a **Push Button** on top of an **Image Component**. By default, an image component can't perform any actions. However, with an invisible push button on top, it will seem as though we can click on the image to perform an action.

See also

For more information on formatting objects in terms of sizing and alignment and setting the appearance of objects, please read *Chapter 7, Dashboard Look and Feel*.

Inputting data values

The ability to input values into the dashboard is a very useful feature. In the following example, we have a sales forecast that changes according to an inputted number value. If we were to use a slider component for the input value, it would be more difficult for the user to select their desired input value. Another good example could be a search box to find a value on a selector which has over 100 items. This way you don't need to hunt for your value. Instead, you can just type it in.

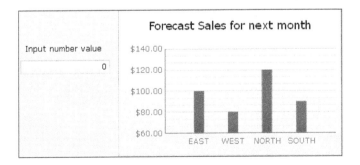

In this recipe, we will create an input textbox to control a what-if scenario.

Getting ready

Create a chart with its values bound to cells that will be controlled by the input textbox value. The following is an example of a sales forecast chart and its cells that are controlled by the what-if scenario:

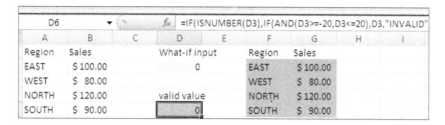

 You may refer to the source file `Inputting data values.xlf` from the code bundle to retrieve the pre-populated data from the preceding image if you don't want to manually type everything in yourself.

How to do it...

1. Drag an **Input Text** object from the **Text** section of the **Components** window onto the canvas.

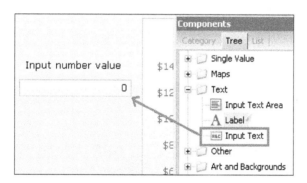

2. In the properties window of the **Input Text** component, bind the **Link to Cell** as well as **Destination** to cell **D3** from the *Getting ready* section.

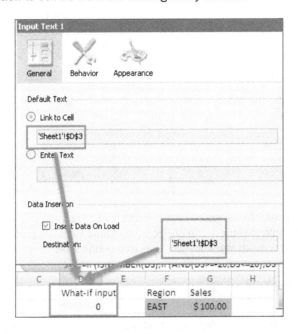

3. Go to the **Behavior** icon of the input text properties and make sure **Treat All Input As Text** is unchecked.

4. The blue cell **D6** from the *Getting ready* section that's labeled as **valid value** will check to make sure the input text entered by the user is valid. To do this, we use the following formula:

```
=IF(ISNUMBER(D3),IF(AND(D3>=-20,D3<=20),D3,"INVALID"),"INVAL
ID")
```

The formula checks to make sure that the cell contains a number that is between -20 and 20.

Now every cell in the chart binding destination will depend on **D6**. The binding destination cells will not add the **D6** value if **D6** is "**INVALID**". In addition, a pop up will appear saying "**Input is invalid**" if **D6** is "**INVALID**".

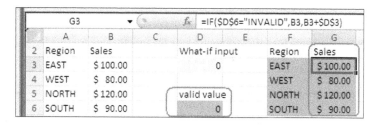

5. Create the pop up by dragging a **Label** text component onto the canvas with **Input is invalid** as its text. Next, go to the behavior tab and for dynamic visibility, bind it to **D6** and set the **Key** as **INVALID**.

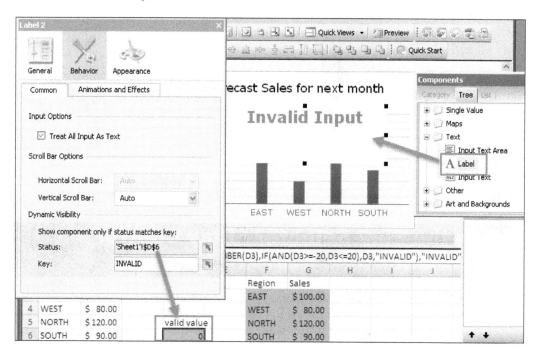

How it works...

In this example, we use an input value textbox to control the forecast bars on the chart. If we type 20, it will add 20 to each value in the forecast. If we type -20, it will subtract 20 from each value in the forecast.

We also add a check in step 4 that determines whether the value entered is valid or not; hence the use of Excel formulas. If a value is invalid, we want to output an error to the user so that they are aware that they entered an invalid value.

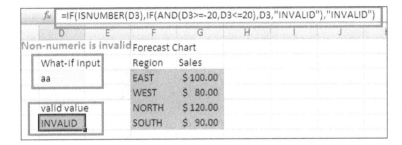

See also

For more information on dynamic visibility, please read *Chapter 4, Dynamic Visibility*.

Using the Play Selector / Play Control component

The Play Selector component can be used when you want to change chart values or components on a dashboard without having the user do anything. Some common uses where we need an automatic change of components are listed as follows:

▸ A company dashboard presented on a large LCD monitor in a company common room; this dashboard will refresh or switch views every 20-30 seconds

▶ A dashboard at a technical support office that shows information on calls coming in and how they are being handled; this dashboard will change views every 20-30 seconds

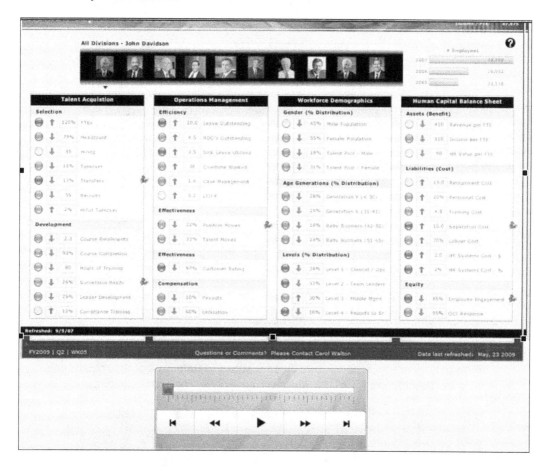

In this recipe, we will create a Play Selector component that changes the image every 20 seconds. We can pretend that the images are different dashboards.

Getting ready

Have a set of three images ready on the canvas, and overlay them on top of each other.

There are three dashboard images that you may use for this example. They are hr1.png, hr2.png, and hr3.png, and can be found in the images folder.

How to do it...

1. Drag a **Play Selector** component from the **Selector** section of the **Components** window onto the canvas.

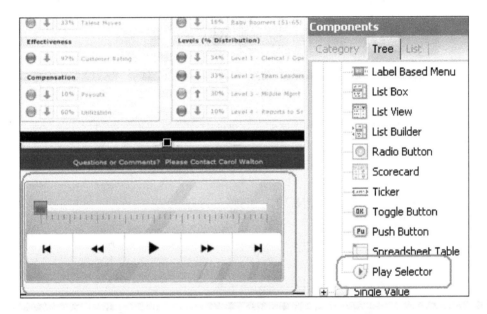

2. In the **Play Selector** properties, select **Row** as the **Insertion Type** and bind the **Source Data** to the dynamic visibility rows that are set up in **Column A** of the spreadsheet. Bind the **Destination** to cell **C2**, which will control the image to be shown.

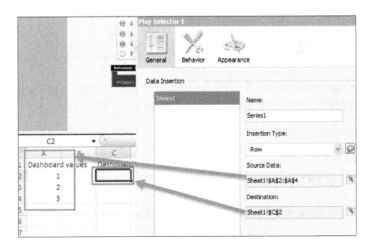

3. Go to the **Behavior** icon of the **Play Selector** properties and check the **Auto Play** checkbox. Change the **Play Time** value to 20 seconds.

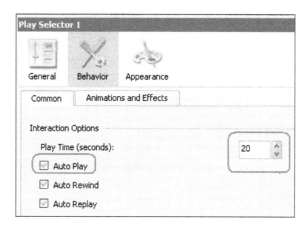

4. Go to the **Appearance** icon of the **Play Selector** properties and set the **Transparency** to **100%**. Also uncheck all the checkboxes.

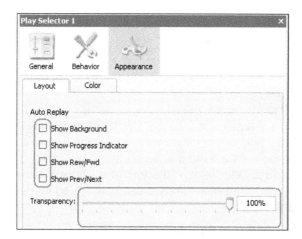

5. On each of the image components, set the **Dynamic Visibility** status binding on the **Behavior** icon to the yellow colored destination cell **C2** from step 2. The key values will be **1**, **2**, or **3** depending on which order you want your images to play in. In the following screenshot, we've shown the dynamic visibility example for the first dashboard:

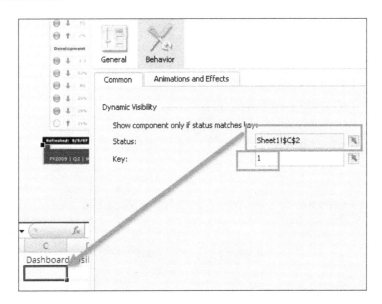

How it works...

In this example, we use a play selector to control which image is being shown. In each 20-second iteration of the play selector, the next row from the **Source Data** range will be moved into the destination cell **C2**. In step 4, we set the transparency of the play selector to **100%** because we wanted to hide the play selector but still have it active. Finally, in step 5, we configured the dynamic visibilities of the images appropriately so the correct one shows up as the play selector runs.

See also

To learn how to use dynamic visibility, please read *Chapter 4, Dynamic Visibility*.

Opening up a Web Intelligence report using dashboard parameters

It is important to distinguish between a dashboard and a report. A dashboard should be a one-page visualization of the most important data a user needs to see. A report contains details that are usually of the lowest granularity, and thus should remain at the SAP BusinessObjects Web Intelligence (Webi) report level. It is a common dashboard requirement to drill down from a chart or scorecard to view individual details. Instead of showing the detailed items on the dashboard, we can pop up a Webi report using parameters passed from the dashboard. In this example, we will pop up a Webi report using one input parameter from the dashboard.

Getting ready

A Webi report with a prompt must be set up first. In our example, the Webi report will ask for a Region parameter.

 You can use the source file `Opening up a Web Intelligence report using dashboard parameters.xlf` from the code bundle as a reference to help guide you through the OpenDocument URL construction part of the recipe.

How to do it...

1. Drag a **Combo Box** selector onto the canvas and bind the label values to the list of Regions on the Excel spreadsheet as shown in the following screenshot. Set **Label** as the **Insertion Type** and bind the **Destination** to the cell highlighted in yellow, which will be the input parameter passed to the OpenDoc call.

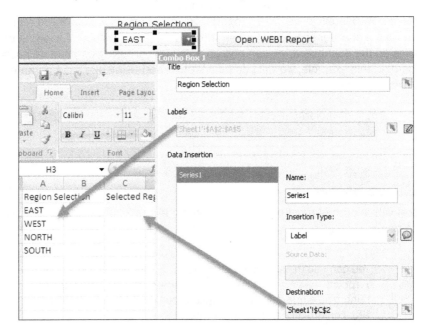

2. Log in to **BI Launchpad** (formerly **Infoview**) and go to the location where the Web Intelligence report is placed. Right-click and select **Document Link**.

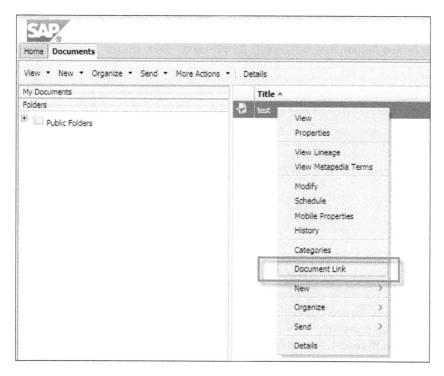

3. Copy the static portion of the **Opendoc URL** as well as the reference **CUID**. Every object in the SAP BusinessObjects repository has a unique CUID reference identifier.

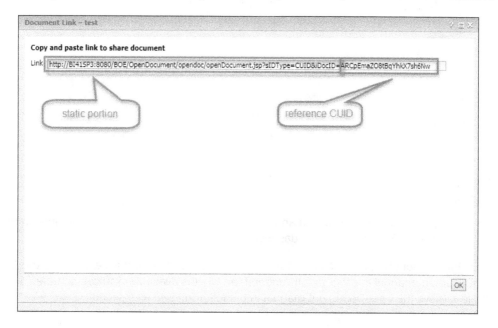

4. An OpenDocument URL is constructed in cell **B14** as shown in the following screenshot. Paste the **CUID** from step 3 onto cell **B23**. Cell **C23** equals the **Selected Region** destination cell, **C2** (**Sheet 1**), from step 1.

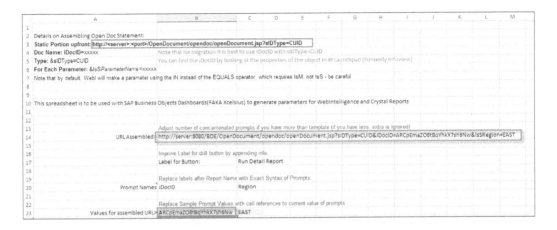

5. Drag a **URL Button** component onto the canvas from the **Web Connectivity** section of the **Components** window. In the **URL Button** properties, change the **Label** text to **Open WEBI report**, and bind the URL to the OpenDoc URL cell **B14** from step 2.

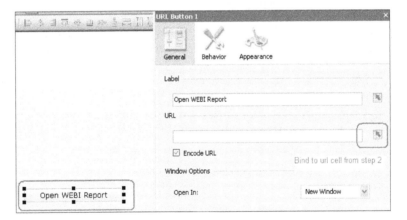

How it works...

In this example, we use what is called an OpenDocument call to open up a Webi report with our desired input parameter from the dashboard.

The OpenDocument URL is quite powerful and has many options, so it is best to read the OpenDocument manual in order to fully understand what is available. You can find the URLs to retrieve the OpenDocument manual in the following *See also* section.

The **URL Button** component is used to open up an external link from the dashboard. An example of a fully constructed URL is as follows:

```
http://server:8080/businessobjects/BOE/OpenDocument/opendoc/
openDocument.jsp?sIDType=CUID&iDocID=ARCpEmaZO9tBqYhkX7sh6Nw&lsSRegio
n=EAST
```

There's more...

The syntax for OpenDocument in SAP BusinessObjects 4.1 is different from previous versions; however, the concept is the same. In this recipe, the OpenDocument URL was generated for SAP BusinessObjects BI 4.1+.

See also

You can find the OpenDocument guide for SAP BusinessObjects BI4.1 at `http://help.sap.com/businessobject/product_guides/sbo41/en/sbo41_opendocument_en.pdf`.

You can find the OpenDocument guide for SAP BusinessObjects XI 3.1 at `http://help.sap.com/businessobject/product_guides/boexir31/en/xi3-1_url_reporting_opendocument_en.pdf`.

Selecting calendar dates

A calendar is a common component found in dashboards if a user is interested in seeing values on a particular day. This is great for going back in history to see past performance.

In this example, we will work with one month of data for September 2010, and the chart will change according to what the user selects on the calendar.

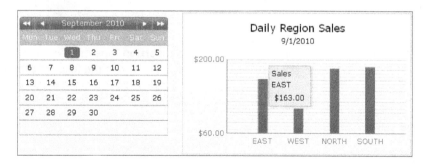

Getting ready

The portion of the spreadsheet containing the chart data will need to be set up in the following fashion. Each row of chart data will belong to a selectable day in the calendar. In this example, each row contains region sales data for a particular date.

	A	B	C	D	E
2	Date	EAST	WEST	NORTH	SOUTH
3	1-Sep	$163.00	$107.00	$183.00	$186.00
4	2-Sep	$182.00	$294.00	$147.00	$268.00
5	3-Sep	$260.00	$134.00	$112.00	$242.00
6	4-Sep	$109.00	$250.00	$161.00	$129.00
7	5-Sep	$298.00	$247.00	$239.00	$292.00

How to do it...

1. Drag a **Calendar** component from the **Other** section of the **Components** window onto the canvas.

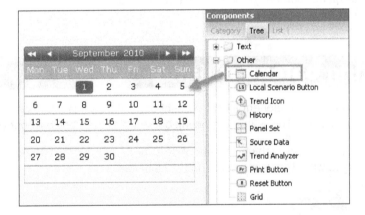

2. In the calendar properties, select **Date** as the **Insertion Type** and bind the **Destination** to the cell **G3** of the spreadsheet, as shown in the following screenshot:

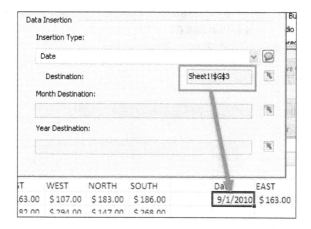

3. Now, we will need to take the value from the destination date cell **G3** in step 2 to find the corresponding row data from the *Getting ready* section. To do this, drag a **Combo Box** selector onto the canvas. In the **Combo Box** properties, select **Row** as the **Insertion Type** and bind **Source Data** to the chart dataset. Then, bind the **Destination** to the cells in the spreadsheet area in yellow (**H3:K3**). Set the **Labels** to the date values of the dataset.

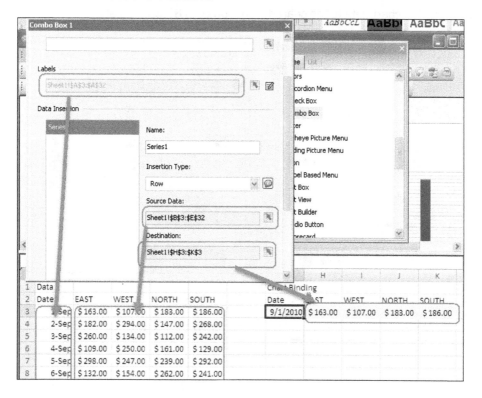

4. On the **Behavior** icon of the **Combo Box** selector, bind the **Item** from the **Selected Item** area to the **Destination** cell **G3** of the calendar set from step 2. Then, drag the **Combo Box** selector to the same position as the chart, and order the **Combo Box** selector to the back of other components so that the user does not see the **Combo Box** selector during runtime.

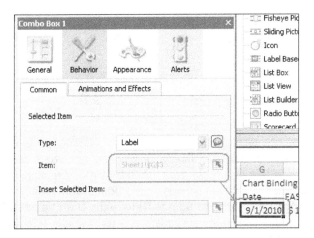

5. Bind the chart data to the chart destination cells **H3:K3** from step 3.

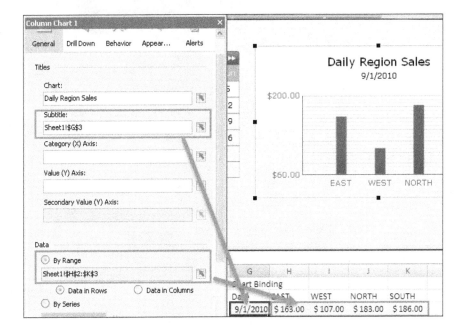

How it works...

In this example, we used a combination of a **Calendar** date component, a **Combo Box** selector, and a **Column Chart** component. The **Calendar** date component controls the date selected in step 1. Then, the **Combo Box** selector connects the date to the appropriate data row from the chart dataset in steps 3 and 4. Finally, in step 5, the chart is bound to the correct data row that was selected in steps 3 and 4.

 Watch out for date format issues when using dates. The date in the dataset may not match up properly with the date value that comes back from the **Calendar** component.

See also

You can read recipes on using chart objects to display data and how to use the **Combo Box** selector in *Chapter 2, Data Visualization*.

Using sliders to create a what-if scenario

What-if scenarios are very important as they allow users to project what future values will look like depending on one or more variables.

In our recipe, we will reuse the simple what-if scenario from a previous recipe, *Inputting data values*. The only difference here is that we will use a horizontal slider instead of inputting the values with text.

Getting ready

Set up the sales data as shown circled in red in the following screenshot, and have a column chart ready on the canvas. You can also reuse the column chart from the previous recipe.

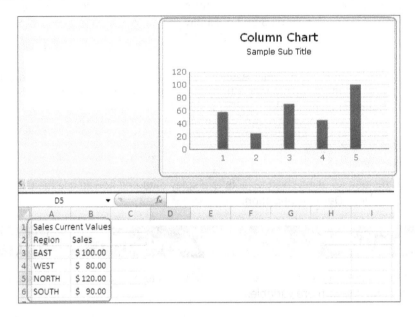

How to do it...

1. Insert a **Horizontal Slider** component from the **Single Value | Horizontal Slider** section of the **Components** window into the canvas.

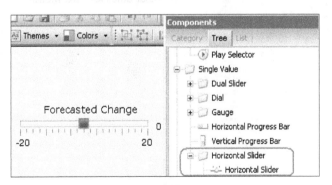

2. Set the **Title** text to `Forecasted Change`. Bind the **Data** to cell **D3** highlighted in yellow. Set the **Minimum Limit** to `-20` and **Maximum Limit** to `20` in the **Scale** section.

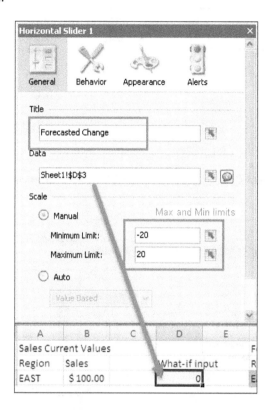

3. Go to the **Appearance** section of the slider properties and make sure that the **Limits** checkbox is checked.

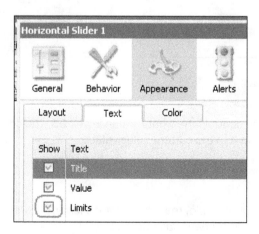

4. Now, in the blue chart data area, each formula will be adding the what-if value **D3** to the chart data values **B3:B6** prepared in the *Getting ready* section.

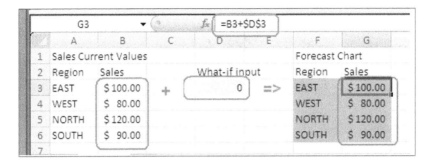

5. Bind the **Forecast Chart** values in cells **F2:G6** to the **Chart Component** and then click on **Preview**.

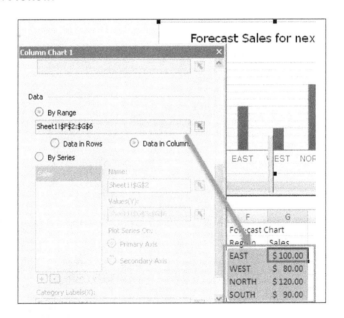

How it works...

In this example, the slider controls the what-if value in cell **D3**. The chart data cells take the user's what-if rate and add it to the current sales values.

See also

For a more complex what-if example, read the *What-if scenario – Mortgage Calculator* recipe in *Appendix A, Real-world Dashboard Case Studies*.

4

Dynamic Visibility

In this chapter, we will cover the following recipes:

- ▶ Switching between different charts
- ▶ Building a pop-up screen
- ▶ Creating a mouseover help text popup
- ▶ Password protecting your dashboard

Introduction

Dynamic visibility makes it possible to control the visibility of components on the dashboard. With this functionality, a component can be made visible or hidden on a running dashboard, based on a status value that is inserted in a certain spreadsheet cell.

Dynamic visibility is useful when your dashboard contains many visual components and you don't want to overload the user with information. Usually, it is used in combination with selectors that let the users choose what they want to see and when.

Switching between different charts

This recipe will show you how to create a dashboard with the option of switching between two charts.

Getting ready

Open a new SAP BusinessObjects Dashboards file and drag two different chart components (for example, a **Line Chart** and a **Pie Chart** component) into the empty canvas. Drag the **Label Based Menu** component found in **Selectors** into the canvas as well.

How to do it...

1. Click on the **Line Chart** component and go to the **Behavior** tab of its properties pane. At the bottom of the pane, you will see a section called **Dynamic Visibility**.

2. Bind the **Status** field to spreadsheet cell **B1**.

3. Put value 1 in the **Key** field:

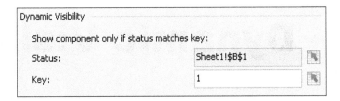

4. Click on the **Pie Chart** component and go to the **Behavior** tab.

5. Here also, bind the **Status** field to cell **B1**.

6. In the **Key** field, fill in the value 2:

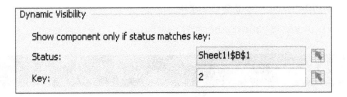

7. Go to the spreadsheet and type Status: in cell **A1** and put value 1 in cell **B1**:

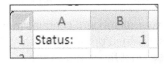

8. Now click on the **Label Based Menu** component and go to the **General** tab of its properties pane.

9. To set the **Labels,** click on the button on the extreme right-hand side, as shown in the following screenshot:

10. Enter two labels: `Trend` and `Division`. Make sure that `Trend` has the first position and `Division` has the second position. You can change the positions by using the little arrows on the bottom left-hand side of the window. In addition, by default there are five entries. To remove the other three entries, just click on the **X** icons to the right.

11. In the **Data Insertion** area, set **Insertion Type** to **Position**.

12. Bind the **Destination** field to spreadsheet cell **B1**:

13. Click on the **Preview** button to run the dashboard. You will only see the label-based component. Click on **Trend** or **Division** and the appropriate chart will appear. Now leave preview mode.

14. To display an initial chart (shown before the first selection), deselect the **Clear Destination When No Selected Item** option in the **General** tab of the properties of the **Label Based Menu** component.

15. Place both charts on top of each other. Use the options in the **Format** menu for precise alignment and sizing:

16. Try your dashboard!

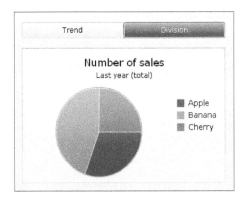

How it works...

In this recipe, we used one of the selector components in combination with the **Dynamic Visibility** functionality to switch between the two charts. Each chart has a unique key assigned: value 1 for the line chart and value 2 for the pie chart. By making a selection in the **Label Based Menu** selector, either the value 1 or value 2 was inserted into spreadsheet cell **B1**. The **Dynamic Visibility** setup in this recipe implies that if cell **B1** has value **1**, **Line Chart** will be shown. If cell **B1** has value **2**, the **Pie Chart** will be shown.

Thus, a component is hidden when any other value than its key is entered in the status cell.

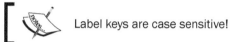

There's more...

This recipe used two chart components with **Dynamic Visibility** settings. But, the **Dynamic Visibility** functionality is embedded in all other components too, except for the **Source Data** component and the **History** component. You can even use **Dynamic Visibility** with grouped components to dynamically show or hide a group of components!

When you set up **Dynamic Visibility** you are not restricted to using only numerical values; you can use any value you want as a **Dynamic Visibility** key for a component. If you do this, make sure you also change the **Insertion Type** of your selector component into **Label**. The labels should always match the key exactly.

Label keys are case sensitive!

Building a pop-up screen

This recipe will show how a pop-up screen can be created within a dashboard. Such a pop-up screen can, for example, be used to provide additional information related to the content of the dashboard. In this recipe, the pop-up screen can be activated and deactivated by clicking on buttons.

Getting ready

No specific preparation is needed for this recipe. You can use any dashboard you already created or just start with an empty one. In this example, we will use the dashboard from the previous recipe.

How to do it...

1. Drag a **Background** component into the canvas from the **Art and Backgrounds** category.

2. Drag the **Label** component from the **Text** category, place it on top of the **Background** component, and enter some text:

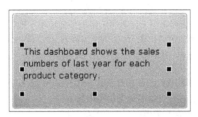

3. Now, drag a **Push Button** component from the **Selectors** category into the canvas and position it in the upper right-hand side corner of the **Background** component. Rename its label as `Close`. We will use this button to close the pop-up screen:

4. Set up the spreadsheet. Enter value 1 in cell **E1** and value 0 in cell **E2**:

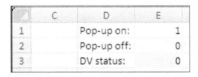

5. Bind the **Source Data** field in the **Push Button** component properties to spreadsheet cell **E2** and bind the **Destination** field to cell **E3**:

6. Group the three components (see the *Grouping the canvas components* recipe in *Chapter 1, Staying in Control*).

7. Add another **Push Button** component to the canvas and rename its label `Info`. This button will be used to activate the pop-up screen.

8. Bind the **Source Data** field of this second **Push Button** component to spreadsheet cell **E1** and bind the **Destination** field to cell **E3**:

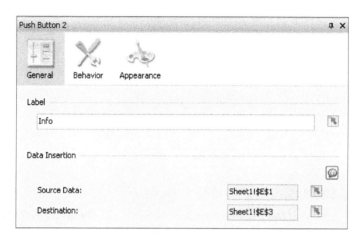

9. Now we are ready to set up the **Dynamic Visibility** functionality. Select the grouped components and go to the properties pane. You will see only one **Common** tab now. Bind the **Status** field to spreadsheet cell **E3**. Also, enter the value 1 in the **Key** field:

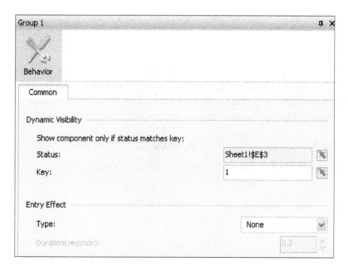

10. **Preview** the dashboard to test the functionality!

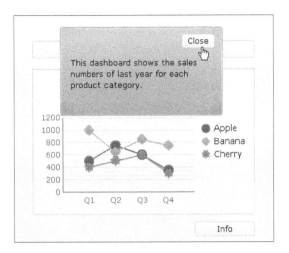

How it works...

In this recipe, we combined the **Push Button** functionality with **Dynamic Visibility**. The three grouped components are only visible when the **Dynamic Visibility** status is **1** (spreadsheet cell **E3**). When clicking on the **Info** push button, the value 1 is put into spreadsheet cell **E3**, following which the grouped components appear. After clicking on the **Close** push button, the value 0 is put into this cell and the grouped components disappear as the status cell does not match value 1 anymore.

There's more...

After clicking on the **Info** push button, the pop-up screen appears. Now this button does not have any useful functionality. Nothing happens if you click it as the pop-up screen is already active. To make this button disappear, you can easily use the **Dynamic Visibility** functionality you already set up by following these steps:

1. Go to the **Behavior** tab of the **Info** push button properties pane.

2. Bind the **Status** field to spreadsheet cell **E3** and enter value 0 into the **Key** field.

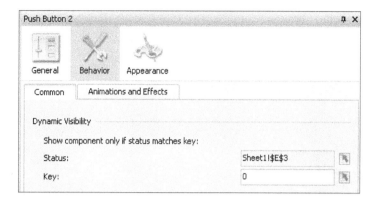

3. Now preview the dashboard to see the effect:

Creating a mouseover help text popup

This recipe shows how you can create a pop-up screen that is activated by making the mouse hover over a certain area of the dashboard. This can be handy if you want to add some minor information on a specific part of a dashboard.

Getting ready

No specific preparation is needed for this recipe. You can use any dashboard you already created or just start with an empty one. In this example, we are reusing the dashboard we created in the previous two recipes.

How to do it...

1. Drag a **Chart** component (for example, a **Pie Chart** component) into the canvas. If you are using an existing dashboard, you can use one of the components of your dashboard instead.

2. Drag a **Label** component found in the **Selectors** category into the canvas and enter the text you want to show.

3. Go to the properties pane of this **Label** component. Select the **Appearance** tab and select the **Show Fill** option.

4. Now, select the **Show Border** option and set **Border Thickness** to **2**:

5. Move the **Label** component over the chart:

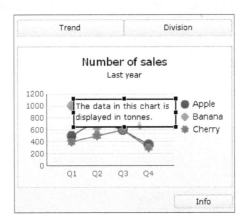

6. Now drag a **Toggle Button** component, found in the **Selectors** category, into the canvas and position it on top of the title of the chart you added to the canvas in step 1. Resize it so that it covers the total area above the chart, as shown in the following screenshot:

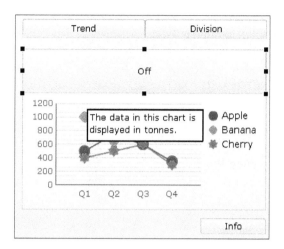

7. In the **Toggle Button** properties pane, go to the **General** tab. Bind **Destination** to spreadsheet cell **H1**:

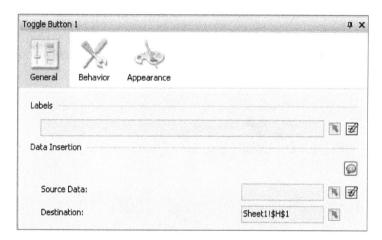

8. Insert value 0 into cell **H1**:

9. Now go to the **Behavior** tab. Under **Interaction Options** in the **Common** menu, change **Mouse Click** to **Mouse Over**:

10. Now go to the **Appearance** tab and set the **Transparency** to **100%** under the **Layout** menu:

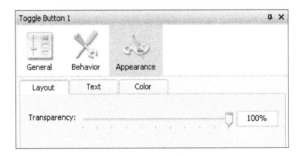

11. Also, under the **Text** menu within the **Appearance** tab, deselect the **Show Labels** option. Now the component won't be visible anymore on the canvas:

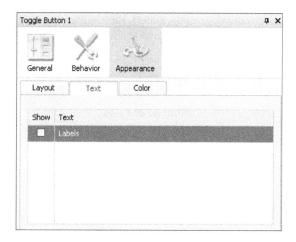

12. To finish this recipe, we have to set up the **Dynamic Visibility** functionality for the **Label** component. First, select the **Label** component. Go to the **Behavior** tab in the properties pane. Within the **Dynamic Visibility** section, bind the **Status** field to spreadsheet cell **H1**. Also put value 1 into the **Key** field:

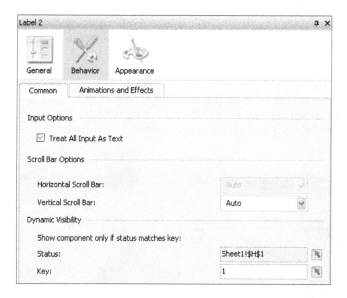

13. Now your dashboard is ready to be tested. Hit the **Preview** button and see what happens!

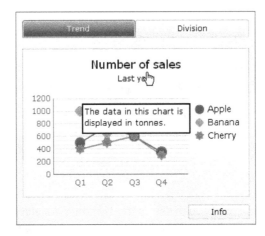

How it works...

For this recipe, we used the **Toggle Button** functionality in combination with **Dynamic Visibility**. Also, instead of clicking on **Toggle Button** to activate it, we switched the insertion trigger from **Mouse Click** to **Mouse Over**. If you run the dashboard and make the mouse hover over the area covered by **Toggle Button**, it will insert value 1 into spreadsheet cell **H1**. This cell triggers **Dynamic Visibility** of the **Label** component that will now appear.

If you go to the properties pane of the **Toggle Button** component, you can set **Source Data**, which is in the **General** tab. Here, you can define which values should be put into the **Destination** cell:

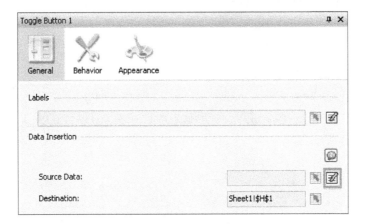

The following screenshot shows the **Source Data** table:

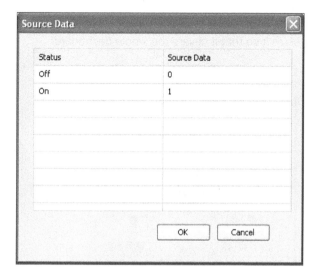

 Keep in mind that if you cover a certain section of your dashboard with a **Toggle Button** component to evoke the **Mouse Over** activation, the interactivity options of the underlying components cannot be activated by the user anymore as **Toggle Button** is blocking it!

Password protecting your dashboard

In this recipe, we will look at a scenario that uses some basic login functionality for a dashboard created with SAP BusinessObjects Dashboards. Before you can use the actual functionality of the dashboard, a password has to be entered.

Getting ready

For this recipe you can use any dashboard you created earlier. We will use the dashboard we created in the previous recipes.

How to do it...

1. Drag a **Rectangle** component found in the **Art and Backgrounds** area into the canvas and resize it so that it covers the whole dashboard:

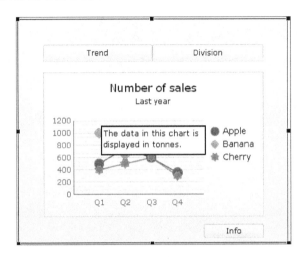

2. Go to the properties pane of the **Rectangle** component and switch the **Fill Type** setting from **None** to **Solid**. You can also change the color and the level of transparency here:

3. The result should look like what is shown in the following screenshot:

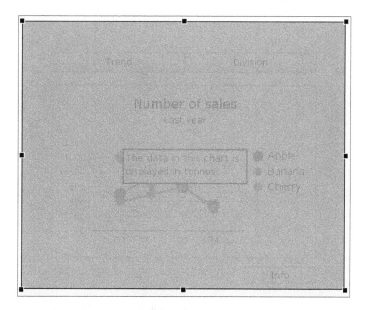

4. Add a **Label** component from the **Selectors** area to the canvas and place it in the middle of the dashboard.

5. Enter `Please enter your password:` in the **Layout** menu of the **Appearance** tab. You can check the **Show Fill** option to show a background color for this component:

The canvas should look like what is shown in the following screenshot:

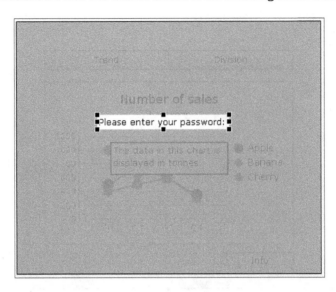

6. Now add an **Input Text** component and place it below the **Label** component. In the **General** tab of the properties pane, bind the **Destination** field to spreadsheet cell **K2**. In the **Behavior** tab, check the option to **Enable Password Protection**. This ensures that only asterisks (*) are displayed when the user enters the password.

7. Select the three components you just added and group them.

8. Go to the properties pane for the grouped components. It is time to set up **Dynamic Visibility**. Bind the **Status** option to spreadsheet cell **K1**. Enter value 1 in the **Key** field:

9. Now we have to set up some Excel logic to make this work. In spreadsheet cell **K1**, enter the =IF(K2="YourPassword",0,1) formula, where YourPassword should be replaced with a password of your choice.

10. Your spreadsheet should now look like what is shown in the following screenshot:

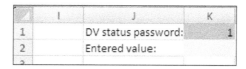

11. Hit the **Preview** button and try to log in to this dashboard by entering your password.

How it works...

In this recipe, the **Dynamic Visibility** functionality is used to make some parts of the dashboard disappear instead of showing them. The **Dynamic Visibility** status is now set by an Excel formula. This *if then* formula checks whether the value in the **Input Text** component matches YourPassword or not. If it does match, the result of the formula will be 0 and the layer we put on top of the dashboard will disappear. Now you can use the dashboard.

This is a method that can be used to protect your dashboard from unauthorized access. However, in an enterprise environment, when the dashboard is published in the SAP BusinessObjects BI Platform, the security is managed by the platform.

5
Using Alerts

In this chapter, we will cover the following recipes:

- ▶ Adding alerts to a column chart
- ▶ Making alert ranges dynamic
- ▶ Displaying alerts on a map
- ▶ Displaying alerts of different thresholds on a map
- ▶ Using bindable colors to control alert coloring from a central location
- ▶ Using alerts in a Scorecard

Introduction

SAP BusinessObjects Dashboards provides a flexible way of alerting a user when something special has occurred. This can be a variety of events, both positive and negative. For example, if certain offices have hit a target threshold for sales, we may want to show these to highlight the positives. If offices fall below a certain threshold for sales, we may also want to highlight these so that we can compare the offices and figure out how to improve the lagging offices.

Adding alerts to a column chart

When looking at a column chart, we might want to see which items are below or above a particular threshold. In this recipe, you will learn how to add alerts to a column chart. Our example will consist of a column chart with a list of regions and their sales. Each region column will be colored appropriately, depending on its sales value versus threshold.

Getting ready

Make sure you set up the sales data and threshold values as shown in the following screenshot. You'll also need to insert a **Column Chart** component into the canvas.

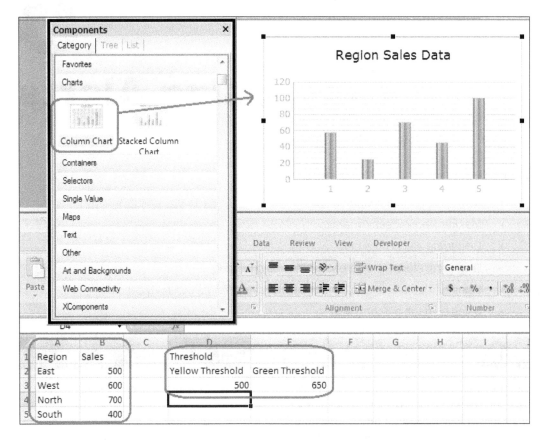

How to do it...

1. First, bind the sales data to the chart as shown in the following screenshot:

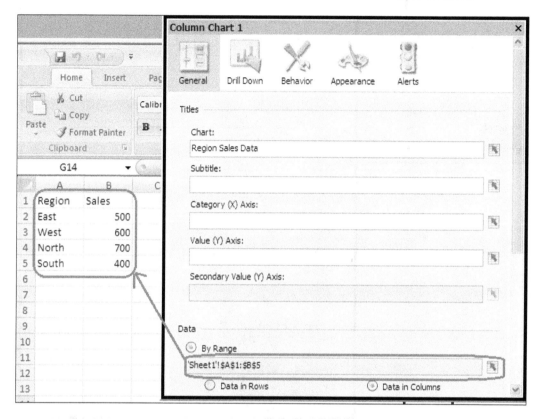

2. Go to the **Alerts** section of the chart properties and ensure that **Enable Alerts** is checked.

3. Select alerts **By Value** as we will be comparing our sales data to the threshold values.

4. In the **Alert Thresholds** section, click on the **Use a Range** checkbox. Bind the data to the threshold data that was set up in the *Getting ready* section.

5. In the **Color Order** section, select the radio button **High values are good**.

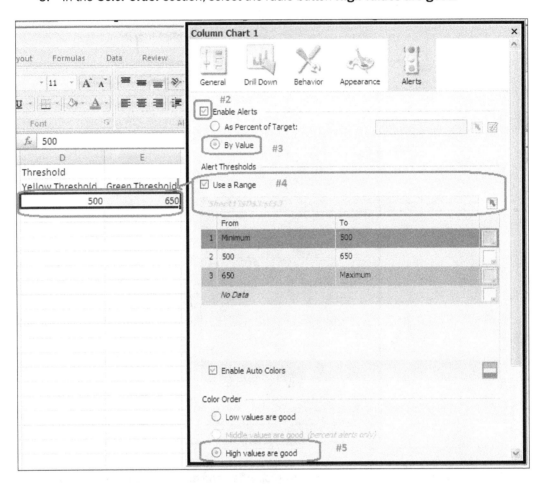

6. In the following screenshot, you will then see that the bars on the chart are now colored according to the sales thresholds:

How it works...

In this recipe, binding the initial data is straightforward, but the part you'll want to take note of is setting up the alerts.

> Note that there will always be *N-1* (*N* minus one) number of threshold values if you are binding the range to your data. For example, if I had two colors (red and green), I would only have one threshold value. If I had four colors, I would have three threshold values set up on my spreadsheet.

In step 4, we bind the threshold range to cells **D3** and **E3** prepared in the *Getting ready* section. Anything that is equal to or greater than the yellow threshold value but less than the green threshold value will be colored as yellow. Anything that is equal to or greater than the green threshold value will be green.

There's more...

Let's say you wanted to display a critical alert that would stand out even if one region was below a threshold. You can accomplish this by following the *Using bindable colors to control alert coloring from a central location* recipe.

Making alert ranges dynamic

It is common that different dimensions contain different thresholds for alert metrics. For example, sales threshold targets may be different for each region of a company, as shown in the following screenshot:

	A	B	C	D	E	F	G	H
1	Region	Yellow Threshold	Green Threshold		Selected Threshold			
2	East	20	50			Yellow Threshold	Green Threshold	
3	West	30	60					
4	North	25	55					
5	South	28	66					
6								

Thresholds / Chart Data / Selection

In our example, we have four regions and different thresholds for each region. So anything below the yellow threshold value will be red, anything that is equal to or greater than the yellow threshold but less than the green threshold will be yellow, and anything equal to or greater than the green threshold value will be green.

This recipe contains a column chart that contains monthly values for a selected region. As the user changes their region selection, the alert threshold will also change. The appropriate alert coloring for each bar will be displayed on the chart.

Getting ready

We will have one worksheet that contains the threshold values as well as a spot that will house the thresholds for the selected region. Please refer to the first screenshot from the introductory section of this recipe. This is how the threshold data layout will look. There will be another worksheet called **Chart Data** that will contain the chart data.

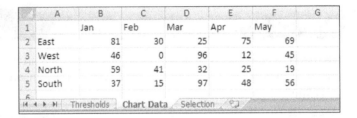

	A	Jan	Feb	Mar	Apr	May	G
1		Jan	Feb	Mar	Apr	May	
2	East	81	30	25	75	69	
3	West	46	0	96	12	45	
4	North	59	41	32	25	19	
5	South	37	15	97	48	56	

Thresholds   **Chart Data**   Selection

How to do it...

1. Insert a **Column Chart** and a **Combo Box** selector into the canvas.

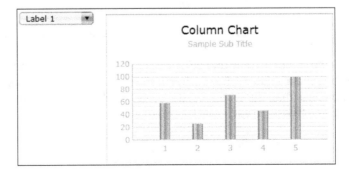

2. Open the **Combo Box** selector properties and bind **Title** and **Labels** to the cells shown in the following screenshot:

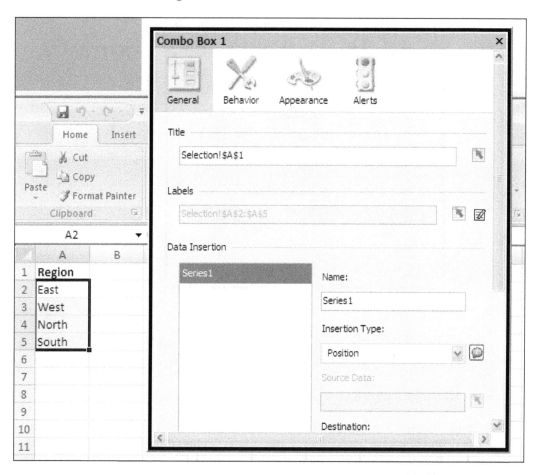

3. Set up the threshold value by linking to the appropriate label. In the **Data Insertion** section of the **Combo Box** properties, rename the text to Threshold. Then, set **Insertion Type** as **Row**. Bind **Source Data** to cells **A2:C5** in the **Thresholds** sheet. Bind **Destination** to the section highlighted in yellow (**E3:G3**).

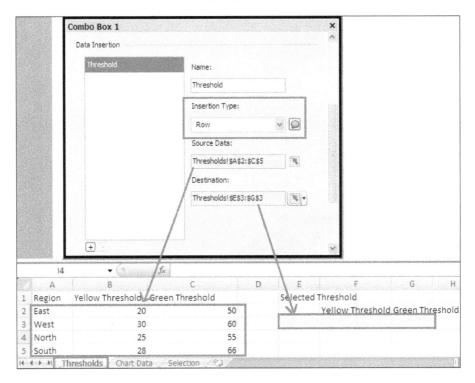

4. Next, press the **+** button in the **Data Insertion** section to add another row selection. Name the next insertion type as Chart Data. Set **Insertion Type** to **Row**. Go to the **Chart Data** worksheet, bind **Source Data** to cells **A2:F5**, and then bind **Destination** to cells **H3:M3**.

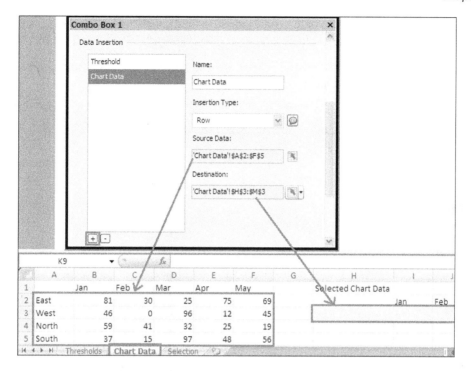

5. Bind the chart data to the **Chart Data** worksheet cells that we populated from step 4. Set the **Subtitle** of the chart to cell **H3**, which contains the selected region name.

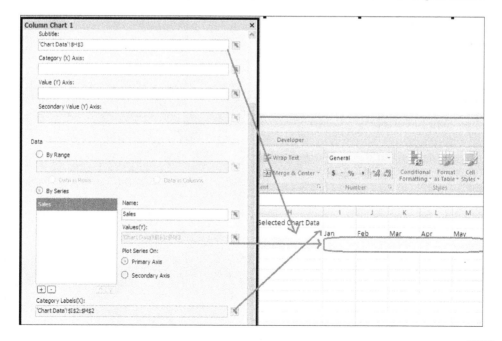

6. Go to the **Alerts** section of the chart properties and check the **Enable Alerts** checkbox.

7. Select the radio button that says **By Value**.

8. In the **Alert Thresholds** section, check the **Use a Range** checkbox and bind to cells **F3:G3** in the **Thresholds** worksheet.

9. In the **Color Order** section, select the radio button that says **High values are good**.

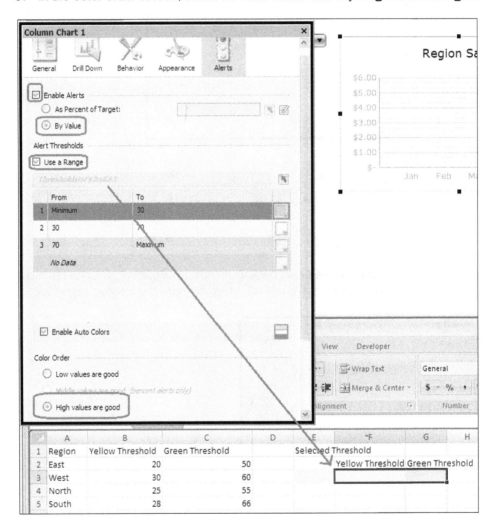

How it works...

In our example, we bind the alert thresholds in steps 6 through 9 to the cells that dynamically change according to the user-selected dropdown. The first threshold, which is red, is anything that is less than the yellow threshold value in cell **F3**. The yellow threshold is anything greater or equal to the yellow threshold value in cell **F3** but less than the green threshold value in cell **G3**. The green threshold is anything that is greater than or equal to the green threshold value in cell **G3**. Using the range bound in the **Alert Thresholds** section, we can dynamically change our threshold settings.

There's more...

In this example, we hardcoded all the threshold and chart data values. But in reality, we can populate the values in the yellow destination cells of steps 3 and 4 using any of the available SAP BusinessObjects Dashboards data connectivity options.

See also

To use different data connectivity options, please read the recipes in _Chapter 8, Dashboard Data Connectivity_.

Displaying alerts on a map

A **map** on a dashboard allows us to visually identify how different regions are doing using a picture instead of a table or chart. With alerts on the map, we can provide even more value. For example, look at the following screenshot. We can see that different regions of the map can be colored differently depending on their value. This allows users to identify at a glance whether a region is doing well or poorly.

Provincial Sales

Getting ready

Insert a Canadian map object into the canvas and bind data to the map. We will use the same example from the *Using maps to select data of an area or country* recipe in *Chapter 3, From a Static to an Interactive Dashboard*.

 [You may also refer to the data prepared in the source file, `Displaying alerts on a map.xlf`.]

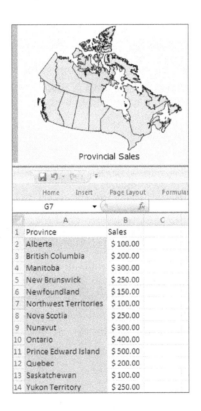

How to do it...

1. In a separate area of the spreadsheet (highlighted in yellow), set up the threshold values. Assume that all provinces have the same threshold.

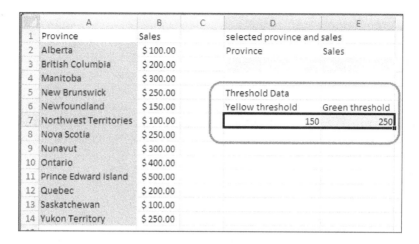

2. Go to the **Alerts** section of the map properties and check **Enable Alerts**.

3. Select the radio button **By Value**.

4. In the **Alert Thresholds** section, check **Use a Range**. Then, bind the range to the **Threshold** dataset in step 1.

5. In the **Color Order** section, select the radio button **High values are good**.

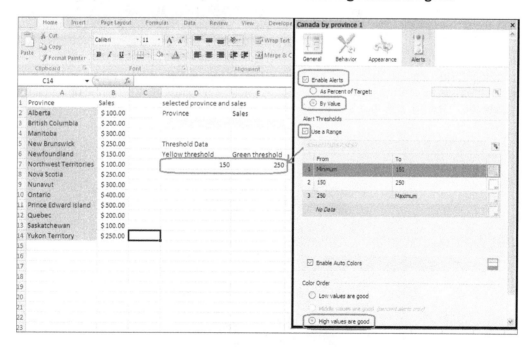

How it works...

In this recipe, we show how to set up alerting for a map component. The way we set it up is pretty standard from steps 2 through 5. Once the alerting mechanism is set up, each province in the map will have its value associated with the alert threshold that we set up in step 1. The province will be colored red if the sales value is less than the yellow threshold. The province will be colored yellow if the sales value is greater than or equal to the yellow threshold but less than the green threshold. The province will be colored green if the sales value is greater than or equal to the green threshold.

There's more...

In our example, we assumed that all the provinces have the same threshold. There is also a way to set up alerts so that each province can have its own threshold. The next recipe, *Displaying alerts of different thresholds on a map*, will explain how to accomplish this. We can also use the CMaps plugin found in the *Integrating Google Maps with the CMaps plugin* recipe in *Chapter 10, Top Third-party Add-ons,* to accomplish the same task, but in a more flexible fashion.

Displaying alerts of different thresholds on a map

The previous recipe was a very useful demonstration of how to set up alerts on a **Map** component. However, the threshold values of all provinces were the same. In reality, this may not be the case for metrics such as sales. For example, a province such as Nunavut is much smaller than Ontario, and thus should not have the same sales threshold as Ontario.

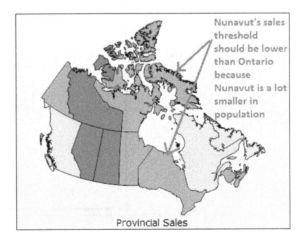

Provincial Sales

Getting ready

Insert a **Canada by province** component into the canvas and bind data to the map. We will use the data setup from the *Displaying alerts on a map* recipe to select the data of an area or country.

 Please refer to the first screenshot in the introductory section of the recipe *Making alert ranges dynamic* to understand how the data should look.

You may also refer to the data setup in the source file, `Displaying alerts of different thresholds.xlf`.

How to do it...

1. To the right-hand side of the **Sales** column (column **B**), add the target thresholds for each province. The larger provinces will have a target threshold of 250, whereas the smaller provinces will have a target threshold of 150. It is important that you use the key-value relationship for the thresholds, as shown in the following screenshot, for the **Map** component:

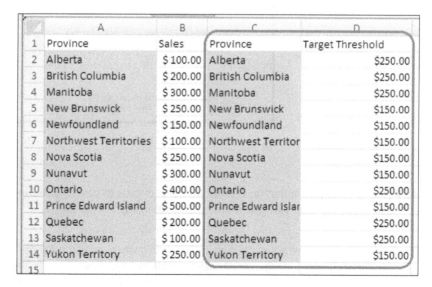

	A	B	C	D
1	Province	Sales	Province	Target Threshold
2	Alberta	$ 100.00	Alberta	$250.00
3	British Columbia	$ 200.00	British Columbia	$250.00
4	Manitoba	$ 300.00	Manitoba	$250.00
5	New Brunswick	$ 250.00	New Brunswick	$150.00
6	Newfoundland	$ 150.00	Newfoundland	$150.00
7	Northwest Territories	$ 100.00	Northwest Territor	$150.00
8	Nova Scotia	$ 250.00	Nova Scotia	$150.00
9	Nunavut	$ 300.00	Nunavut	$150.00
10	Ontario	$ 400.00	Ontario	$250.00
11	Prince Edward Island	$ 500.00	Prince Edward Islar	$150.00
12	Quebec	$ 200.00	Quebec	$250.00
13	Saskatchewan	$ 100.00	Saskatchewan	$250.00
14	Yukon Territory	$ 250.00	Yukon Territory	$150.00
15				

2. Go to the **Alerts** section of the map properties and check **Enable Alerts**.

3. Select the radio button **As Percent of Target** and bind it to the key-value pair cells **C2:D14**.

4. For the target percentage, color anything on the target or above as green. Color anything between 70% of target and the target as yellow. And color anything less than 70% of the target as red.

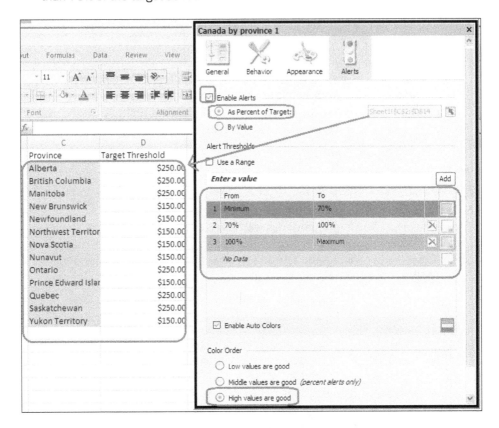

How it works...

Using the **As Percent of Target** option on **Enable Alerts** allows us to have a different threshold for each province, which gives a more realistic alerting mechanism.

 It is important to use a key-value pair relationship when using the **As Percent of Target** alerting mechanism on a **Maps** component. For alerting on the **Charts** components, you don't have to worry about the key-value pair relationship.

In this recipe, we reused the data setup from the *Using maps to select data of an area or country* recipe of *Chapter 3, From a Static to an Interactive Dashboard*.

Using bindable colors to control alert coloring from a central location

With the advent of the option to dynamically bind colors to different parts of a component, we can push alerting to another level. For example, we may have a sales chart for a set of regions and may want to signal whether something is critically wrong. Instead of having a bunch of green and red bars that may look like a Christmas tree, we can set the chart background color to red if one of the values has reached a critical point. In this scenario, a user will be drawn to the chart right away, as it will be ringing alarm bells.

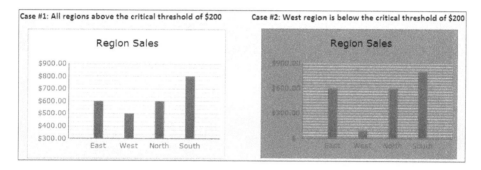

Getting ready

Be sure to have your chart data ready, shown as follows. In this recipe, we will have a set of sales data for each region. You may use the setup from the previous recipe, *Adding alerts to a column chart*, to help save you time.

	A	B
1	Region	Sales
2	East	$ 600.00
3	West	$ 500.00
4	North	$ 600.00
5	South	$ 800.00

How to do it...

1. Drag a **Column Chart** from the **Charts** section of the **Components** window onto the canvas.

2. Bind the chart data to the data set up in the *Getting ready* section.

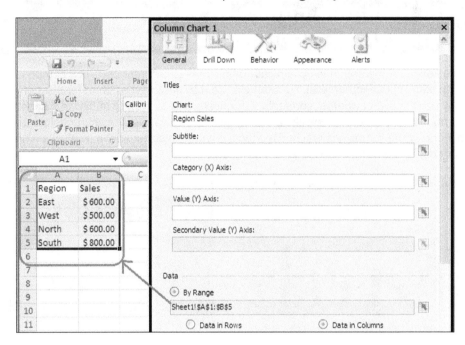

3. Create a section in the worksheet that will contain the critical threshold value. If any region sales go below that value, we want a major alert to show up.

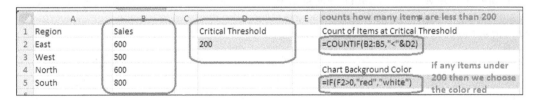

4. Bind cell **F5**, which determines the background color, to the **Background Color** property of the chart.

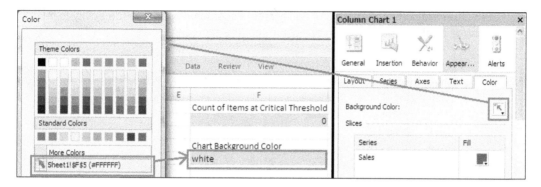

How it works...

Using bindable colors, we can dynamically set color properties for almost any component. In our example, we use a simple COUNTIF statement to determine whether any of the region sales are below the critical threshold. From there, we have another IF statement that determines the coloring of the chart background. The first case (the left-hand side graph in the following screenshot) shows that all our sales are above $200; thus, the chart background is white. The second case (the right-hand side graph in the following screenshot) shows that the sales in the West region are below $200; thus, a major alert is shown and the chart background becomes red.

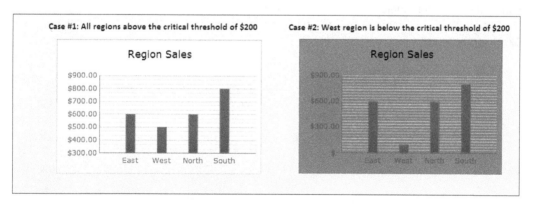

See also

There are many ways to customize alerting for different components. Our example only shows one way to do so. The easiest way can be found in the *Adding alerts to a column chart* recipe. To learn more about customizing charts to your desired look and feel, read the recipes in *Chapter 7, Dashboard Look and Feel*.

Using alerts in a Scorecard

With the **Scorecard** component, we can easily create scorecard KPIs with the ability to insert a user-desired alert / trending icon in any column of the scorecard.

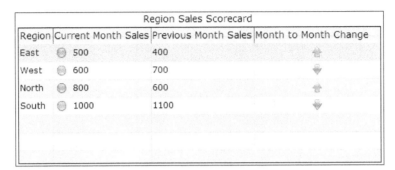

In this recipe, we will go through an example of using the **Scorecard** component to show a table of values, a threshold indicator that will determine whether the current month's sales meet the threshold or not, and a trend indicator that shows whether the current month's sales have risen/fallen compared to the previous month's sales.

Getting ready

Set up your data as follows. We have a list of regions, current month sales, previous month sales, and sales threshold. Note that the **Month to Month Change** column is highlighted because it can either come from the external data source or it could be calculated in the Excel spreadsheet.

	A	B	C	D	E
1	Region	Current Month Sales	Previous Month Sales	Month to Month Change	Sales Threshold
2	East	500	400	100	550
3	West	600	700	-100	550
4	North	800	600	200	850
5	South	1000	1100	-100	800

How to do it...

1. Select the **Scorecard** selector from the **Selectors** category of the **Components** window and drag it onto the canvas.

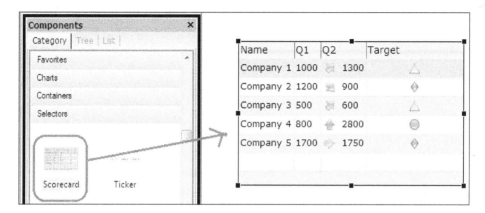

2. Bind the **Scorecard** component to the spreadsheet data prepared in the _Getting ready_ section.

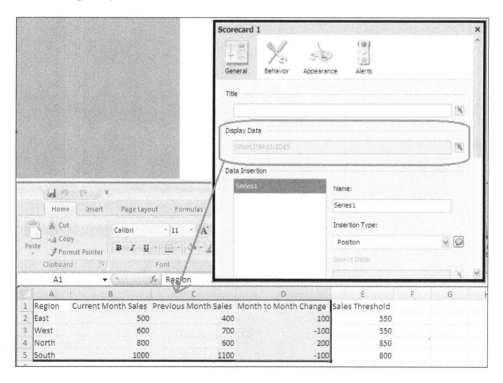

3. Now set up the alert components. First, set up a calculation in column **F** of the spreadsheet, which will determine whether the threshold indicator for the current month will be green or red. Use the incremental formula, `=IF(B2 >= E2, 1, -1)`, in each row in column **F**.

4. Go to the **Alerts** section of the scorecard properties and check the **Current Month Sales** checkbox.

5. Bind **Alert Values** to cells **F2:F5**.

6. Select **By Value**, right below the **Alert Values** section.

7. In the **Alert Thresholds** section, delete the yellow color by clicking on the **X** button in the second last column.

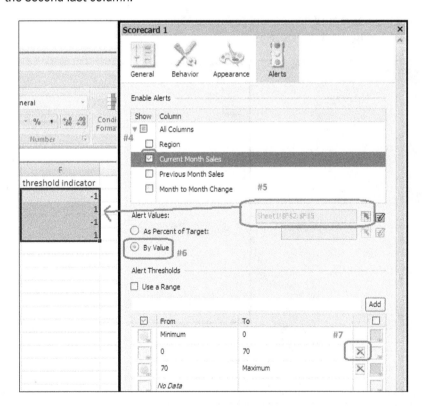

8. In the **Alert Thresholds** section, go to the **To** value of the first row and change it to 0.

9. In the **Color Order** section, select the **High values are good** radio button.

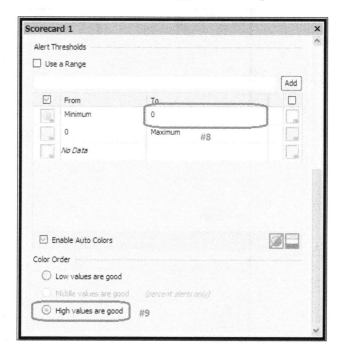

10. In the **Alerts** section of the scorecard properties, check the **Month to Month Change** checkbox.

11. Bind **Alert Values** to cells **D2:D5**.

12. Select **By Value**, right below the **Alert Values** section.

13. Set **Alert Threshold** values to what is shown in the following screenshot. The numbers will be explained in the *How it works...* section.

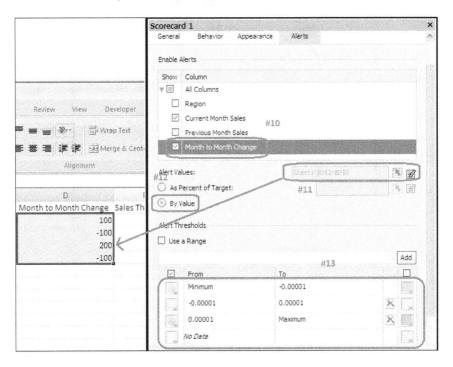

14. Click on the highlighted icon in the **Enable Auto Colors** section and select the arrow icons circled in red.

15. In the **Color Order** section, select the **High values are good** radio button.

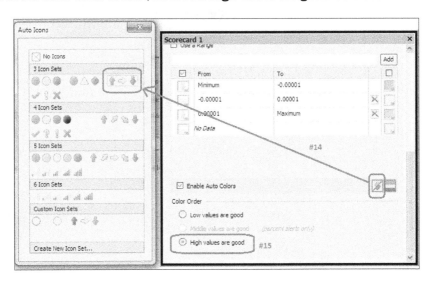

16. Go to the **Appearance** section of the **Scorecard** component. Select the **Text** tab. Uncheck the **Month to Month Change** checkbox because we only want to see the trending icon here and not the text.

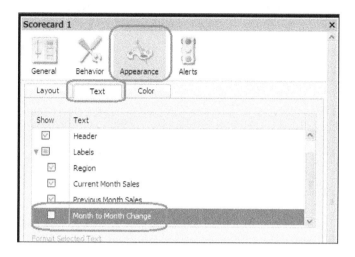

How it works...

In the **Scorecard** component, we can combine different types of alerts together with our table data, as shown in the following screenshot. Now, let's discuss some important points from the steps in the *How to do it...* section.

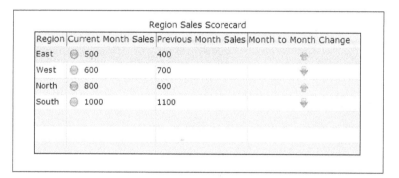

In step 2, you will notice that we do not bind to the **Sales Threshold** column because that column is used to calculate whether the **Current Month Sales** are above or below the **Sales Threshold**. As you can see in step 3, we have column **F** that houses the calculation. The calculated values in column **F** are then bound as the alert values in step 5. From there, we are able to determine whether the threshold indicator on the **Current Month Sales** column should be green or red.

The trend icons shown in the **Month to Month Change** column are determined from the values in the **Month to Month Change** column. In step 13, you will notice the funny **0.00001** values. This is to take into account **Month to Month Change** values that are 0. Unfortunately, we cannot set (if value = 0, then show no change arrow), so **0.00001** is the next closest alternative. In the **Month to Month Change** column, we want to show the arrows, so in step 16, we hide the text values.

See also

You can customize the scorecard look by modifying the appearance settings. Read the recipes in *Chapter 7*, *Dashboard Look and Feel,* to learn how to change the appearance settings of a component.

6

Advanced Components

In this chapter, we will cover the following recipes:

- ▸ Printing your dashboard
- ▸ Grouping and organizing components with the Canvas Container
- ▸ Using dashboard scenarios
- ▸ Using the Grid component
- ▸ Creating a slideshow
- ▸ Using the Panel Set component
- ▸ Using the History component
- ▸ Inserting data with the Source Data component
- ▸ Analyzing trends

Introduction

In the previous chapters, we discussed the functionality and applicability of a lot of SAP BusinessObjects Dashboard components. In this chapter, we will be looking at a number of components that have a somewhat unique, non-standard functionality, but that may deliver great added value to your dashboards.

Printing your dashboard

The **Print** button has a single and pretty straightforward functionality: it will print your dashboard.

Getting ready

You can use any dashboard you created earlier or just open a new blank dashboard file.

How to do it...

1. Drag a **Print** button component into the canvas:

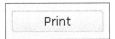

2. Go to the **Behavior** tab and select **Scale to**.
3. Set the scale to **70%**:

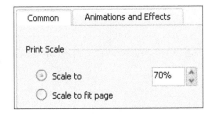

4. Try the **Print** button by previewing the dashboard.

How it works...

After clicking on the **Print** button, you will see a standard Windows Print window, where you can select and configure a printer, and set the number of copies to be printed.

As we can see, the only specific settings for this component were the **Print Scale** option. The default **Scale to fit page** option makes sure that the dashboard fits on a single page. If you select the other option and scale the dashboard to a certain percentage, it might be using more than one page to be printed on.

 Although the **Print** button will appear in the dashboard, it will not appear on the printed result!

There's more...

Read the *Advanced printing with Xcelsius Dashboard Printer* recipe in *Chapter 10, Top Third-party Add-ons* to learn about a third-party printing solution for SAP BusinessObjects Dashboards that offers more features than the **Print** button component.

Grouping and organizing components with the Canvas Container

In the *Grouping the canvas components* recipe in *Chapter 1, Staying in Control*, we discussed how grouping multiple components works. This solution is a good option when a limited number of components are involved. But if you are building a dashboard with a lot of overlapping layers in combination with the **Dynamic Visibility** functionality, you are recommended to use the **Canvas Container** component.

Getting ready

No preparation is required. Just open a new SAP BusinessObjects Dashboard file.

How to do it...

1. Drag a **Canvas Container** component found in the **Containers** category into the canvas.

2. Resize the **Canvas Container** component to almost half the same size of the canvas.

3. Drag a **Line Chart** component directly into the **Canvas Container**:

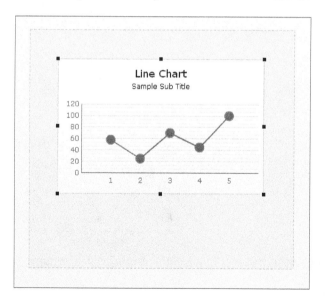

4. Take a look at the **Object Browser**. You will notice that the **Line Chart** component is placed one level below the **Canvas Container** component. This indicates that the **Line Chart** component is now part of **Canvas Container**:

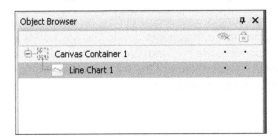

5. Select **Canvas Container** and drag it to the far right of the canvas. As you will see, the **Line Chart** component also moves along with **Canvas Container**.

6. Now drag a **Pie Chart** component directly into **Canvas Container**.

7. Resize the **Canvas Container** so that only one chart remains fully visible. A scroll bar will show up on the right side of the **Canvas Container** component:

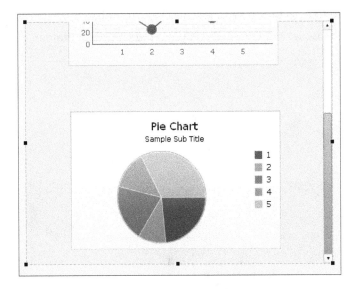

8. Preview the dashboard and check out how this looks in runtime.

How it works...

The **Canvas Container** component looks a lot like the grouping of multiple components as we saw earlier in the recipe in *Chapter 1, Staying in Control* called *Grouping the canvas components*. But with this component, we also have the option to include horizontal or vertical scroll bars. In the properties pane, you can determine whether the **Canvas Container** will show these scroll bars or not. By default, the **Auto** option is selected, which means that scroll bars are only shown if a component that is part of the **Canvas Container** component lies (partly) outside **Canvas Container**. This was explained in step 7 of this recipe.

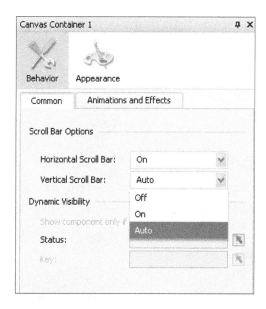

The gray background of **Canvas Container** is only shown in design mode. If you run the dashboard, only the possible scroll bars are visible. In addition, one of the biggest benefits of using **Canvas Container** is that you do not have to ungroup the components when you want to resize or move the grouped components around.

Using dashboard scenarios

If your dashboard has a typical what-if scenario setup with a number of variables, it would be a nice option for the dashboard user to save a scenario with some particular settings to be reviewed or compared later. The **Local Scenario Button** component delivers this functionality.

Getting ready

Create a new dashboard file.

How to do it...

1. Drag a **Vertical Slider** component into the canvas.

2. Drag a **Local Scenario Button** component from the **Other** category into the canvas.

3. Hit the **Preview** button.

4. Set the slider value to **50**.

5. Now click on the **Scenario** button. A menu with four new buttons will appear. Click on the **Save** button and name it Scenario 1 as shown in the following screenshot:

6. Set the slider to value **75** and click on the **Scenario** button again.

7. Click on the **Load** button and select the scenario you just saved. The value of the slider will now be set to **50**.

How it works...

The **Local Scenario Button** component enables the user of a dashboard to save the exact state a dashboard is in at that moment, including all the variables the user has set. These scenarios are saved locally on the user's computer. This means that if you open the dashboard on another computer these saved scenarios cannot be loaded!

With the **Delete** button, the user can delete previously saved scenarios and with the **Set Default** button, a default scenario can be chosen, which will be loaded when the dashboard is opened.

There's more...

If the dashboard user wants to return to the initial state of the dashboard, they can close the dashboard and reopen it. Using the **Reset** button component for this task is a better option. The **Reset** button does exactly what its name says; it resets the entire dashboard to its initial state when clicked upon:

Using the Grid component

The **Grid** component can display a table with data in your dashboard. Therefore, it looks a bit like the **List View** and **Spreadsheet Table** components. There are a number of differences between these two sets of components, stated as follows:

- The **List View** and **Spreadsheet Table** components allow us to make data selections; the **Grid** component does not

- The **Grid** component not only displays data, but its values can also be changed by the dashboard user

- The **Grid** component doesn't have a header row

Getting ready

Open a new SAP BusinessObjects Dashboards file and enter the values in the spreadsheet as shown in the following screenshot:

	A	B	C
1			
2			
3			
4			
5	50	40	35
6	25	25	25
7	90	80	70

How to do it...

1. Drag a **Grid** component into the canvas.
2. Bind the **Data** field to spreadsheet cells **A5** until **C7**.
3. Go the **Behavior** tab and set **Increment** to 5.
4. Click on the **Appearance** tab. Set the **Vertical Margin** as well as the **Horizontal Margin** to 5.
5. Resize the **Canvas Container** component to almost half the size of the canvas.

6. Preview the dashboard to see how this works. Move your mouse over one of the cells and click on it as soon as the cursor changes into an up down arrow as shown in the following screenshot. Now drag your cursor up or down to change the value of the cell.

 This only works when the data bound to the **Grid** component is static. When it is formula-based this will not work.

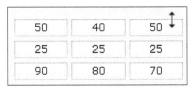

How it works...

As you can see, the way the **Grid** component works is quite straightforward. It displays a simple table with the values in the spreadsheet cells we bound to the component. The value of each cell can then be adjusted when we run the dashboard. As with all the insertion-like components, the actual value in the spreadsheet cell will change as well and can be used in Excel functions or other components that refer to this cell.

There's more...

In the **General** tab, we can set the **Minimum Limit** and **Maximum Limit** fields that we can change a value to. This means that if the initial value of a cell lies outside this range and you want to change the value, you can only change it to a value within the range.

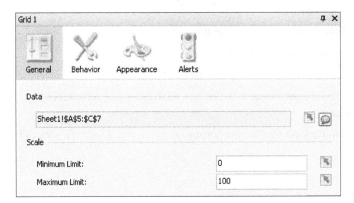

Under the **Common** sub-tab of the **Behavior** tab, these limits can be set to **Fixed** or **Open**. If you choose the **Open** option, the **Scale** fields on the **General** tab are grayed out.

Furthermore, you can set the **Mouse Sensitivity** level. This will set the speed in which the values will increase or decrease when changing them. If you set **Scroll Behavior** to **Auto**, the values keep changing if you click the cell and drag the cursor a bit above or below the cell. If you use the **Manual** option instead, you have to keep moving your cursor up or down to change the value.

Creating a slideshow

As we already discussed in the *Making selections from a custom image (the push button and image component)* recipe in *Chapter 3, From a Static to an Interactive Dashboard*, you can use the image component to show pictures or Flash (.swf) files in your dashboard. This recipe will show how you can create slideshows of multiple images and/or SWF files with the **Slide Show** component.

Getting ready

For this recipe, we need some images and/or SWF files. Make sure that these are files of the following types: .jpg, .png, .gif, .bmp, or .swf. The files can reside on your local computer or on the Web.

How to do it...

1. Enter the URLs of the images or SWF files you want to show in the spreadsheet:

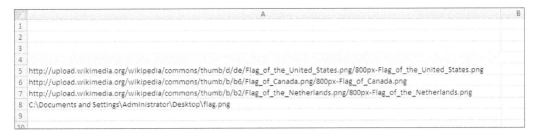

	A	B
1		
2		
3		
4		
5	http://upload.wikimedia.org/wikipedia/commons/thumb/d/de/Flag_of_the_United_States.png/800px-Flag_of_the_United_States.png	
6	http://upload.wikimedia.org/wikipedia/commons/thumb/b/b6/Flag_of_Canada.png/800px-Flag_of_Canada.png	
7	http://upload.wikimedia.org/wikipedia/commons/thumb/b/b2/Flag_of_the_Netherlands.png/800px-Flag_of_the_Netherlands.png	
8	C:\Documents and Settings\Administrator\Desktop\flag.png	
9		
10		

2. Drag a **Play Selector** component into the canvas. Set the component to insert rows to **Destination** cell **A4**. The **Source** field will be bound to the URL cells **A5** to **A8**. For more information on this component, see the *Using the Play Selector / Play Control component* recipe in *Chapter 3, From a Static to an Interactive Dashboard*.

3. Now drag a **Slide Show** component into the canvas.

4. Bind the **URL** field to cell **A4**.

5. Switch to the **Behavior** tab and set **Transition Type** to **Wedge**.

6. Preview the dashboard to see how the **Slide Show** looks.

How it works...

The **Play Selector** component does most of the work here actually. We need it to change the image that should be displayed by using data insertion. The slide show component only displays the images and provides a nice transition between two images.

There's more...

In the **Appearance** tab, there are some options that are specific to this component. First is **Sizing Method**, where you can set how the image or the SWF file should be displayed: in its original size, in scale, or stretched to the size of the component. Next, there are settings for **Horizontal Alignment** and **Vertical Alignment**. Besides these options the standard **Transparency** option is also available:

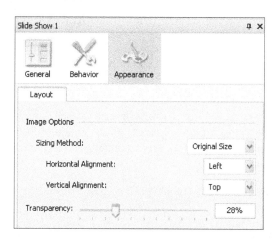

Using the Panel Set component

The **Panel Set** component is one of the few features of SAP BusinessObjects Dashboards that looks really cool at first, but is something you most likely won't use. The purpose of this component is to create a showcase of images and/or Flash (.swf) files in one window. The user is able to zoom in on each panel. Unfortunately, the SWF files that are created with SAP BusinessObjects Dashboards are not supported and cannot be displayed, which instantly decreases the value of the component.

Getting ready

For this recipe, we need some images and/or SWF files. Make sure these files are of the following types: .jpg, .png, .gif, .bmp, or .swf.

How to do it...

1. Drag a **Panel Set** component into the canvas.

2. In the **General** tab of the properties pane, select **Layout2**:

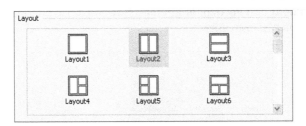

3. Click on the **Import** button in the **Content** area and click on the **Click to Add Images** button in the upcoming window. Browse to your image or SWF file and click on **Open**. The file is now added to **Panel 1**. Repeat this step to add another file and close this window by clicking on **OK**:

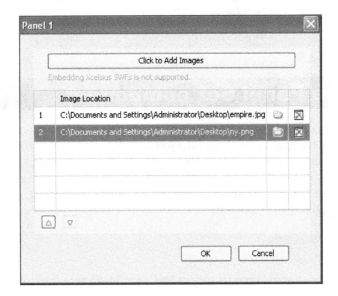

4. Click on the button on the far right-hand side of the **Drop-Down Menu Labels** field. Enter a label for each file you just added:

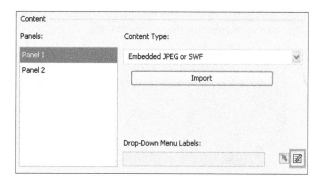

5. Select **Panel 2** and repeat steps 3 and 4 to add some images and/or SWF files to this second panel.

6. Now switch to the **Behavior** tab. In the **Selected Item** area, select **Panel 1** and set the **Item** field to **Image 1**. Do the same for **Panel 2**:

7. Preview the dashboard.

8. Click on the maximize buttons:

9. Now click on the little arrow next to the maximize button to show the menu labels. Select a label to switch to another image or SWF file:

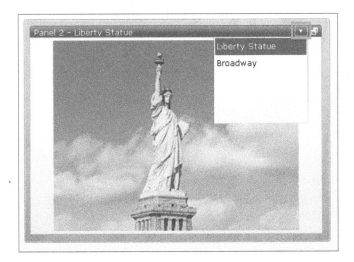

How it works...

As we saw in this recipe, the **Panel Set** component lets us display a set of panels to show multiple images and/or SWF files. There are even 27 different layouts to choose from with up to 10 panels each.

The lack of support for SAP BusinessObjects Dashboard SWF files has already been mentioned, but there are more problems with this component. First, it does not have any selector capabilities, so even if you want to use this component to build a dashboard, it only functions as a sort of product catalog. It is very difficult to make it interactive and let it pass data through to other components.

Another problem is performance-related. The more (high-resolution) images you embed in the component, the bigger your final dashboard SWF file will become. Big SWF files take longer to load and therefore decrease your dashboard's performance. So if you are using this component, make sure you test your final dashboard on different computer setups to check whether the dashboard's performance is acceptable for users.

There's more...

In the following sections, there are some additional features that are available with the **Panel Set** component.

Linking to files instead of embedding

In the recipe, we embedded the images/SWFs in the **Panel Set** component. Another way to show these files is by using the **By URL** option for **Content Type** and linking to them using **URLs**. You can enter these URLs by putting them in the spreadsheet and binding to these cells. Or, you can add them as labels by clicking on the button on the far right-hand side. The **Drop-Down Menu Labels** field can be entered in the same way:

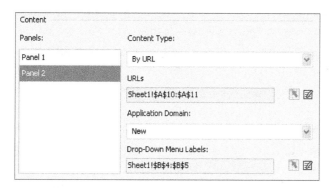

Panel behavior

A nice option for this component is the **Zoom Speed** setting. Play around a bit with this slider to make the panel transition as smooth as you want it to be. Also, here you can enable/disable the maximize button:

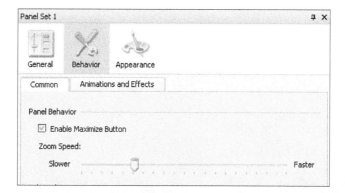

Using the History component

The **History** component makes it possible to plot a value in a chart that changes in real time, while preserving its historical data. If that sounds confusing, think about the stock market charts that track the fluctuation of a stock price. At the start of the day, the line in such a chart is short, while at the end of the day the complete trend of the stock price for that day is shown. This recipe will show you how to set up this kind of functionality in your dashboard.

Getting ready

Just open a new SAP BusinessObjects Dashboards file.

How to do it...

1. Drag a **Line Chart** component, **History** component from the **Other** category, and a **Horizontal Slider** component into the canvas.

2. Select the **Horizontal Slider** component and bind the **Data** field to the spreadsheet cell **B1**.

3. Now select the **History** component and bind its **Data** field to the spreadsheet cell **B1**.

4. Bind the **Data Destination** field to the spreadsheet range **B3:J3**.

5. Go to the **Line Chart** component. Bind the **Data | By Range** field to the spreadsheet range **B3:J3**.

6. Your setup should now look like what is shown in the following screenshot:

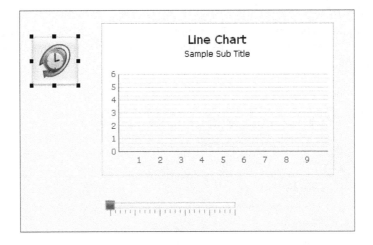

7. Hit the **Preview** button and test the dashboard. Each time you move the slider, a new value should be plotted in the chart:

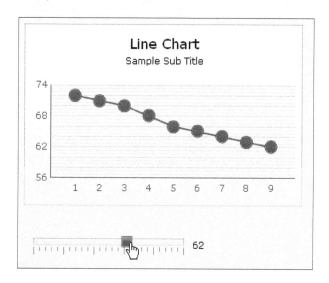

How it works...

The **History** component picks up a value from a certain source cell (cell **B1** in this recipe) and pastes it in a horizontal or vertical range of cells, which in fact store the history of the value. These cells are bound to a chart and so a real-time changing graph is created.

The **History** component has, besides binding to the source and destination cells, only one other setting. You can determine when a value should be pasted to the destination cells. This can be either when the data changes or on an interval of a certain number of seconds. This component works in the background and will therefore not be shown during runtime.

There's more...

If you need more series of real-time changing values in your chart, just use more **History** components to accomplish this.

Another important feature is that in some cases, we can use the **History** component to remember values from a query so that we can avoid re-running queries when we need to look at past data from past queries.

Inserting data with the Source Data component

The **Source Data** component enables us to insert data into spreadsheet cells by changing the selected index value of the component. This is a different approach to inserting data than the one we saw in *Chapter 3, From a Static to an Interactive Dashboard*, when we were discussing selectors and drilldowns.

Getting ready

Open a new SAP BusinessObjects Dashboard file and enter the following data into the spreadsheet:

	A	B	C	D	E
1	Value:				
2					
3	Inserted data:				
4					
5			Product A	Product B	Product C
6		2007	15%	60%	25%
7		2008	30%	40%	30%
8		2009	25%	25%	50%
9		2010	20%	30%	50%
10					

How to do it...

1. Drag a **Pie Chart** component into the canvas.
2. Bind the **Chart** field to cell **B3** and leave the **Subtitle** field empty.
3. Bind the **Data | Values** field to the spreadsheet range from **C3** to **E3**. Select the **Data in Rows** option.
4. Bind the **Labels** field to cells **C5** to **E5**.
5. Drag a **Horizontal Slider** component to the canvas.
6. Bind the **Data** field to cell **B1**.
7. Set **Minimum Limit** to 0 and **Maximum Limit** to 3.

8. Now drag the **Source Data** component into the canvas:

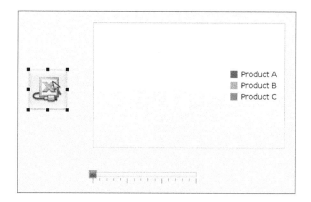

9. Set **Insertion Type** as **Row**.

10. Bind the **Source Data** field to cell range **B6:E9**.

11. Bind the **Destination** field to cells **B3:E3**:

12. Go to the **Behavior** tab. Bind the **Selected Item Index** field to cell **B1**:

13. Preview the dashboard:

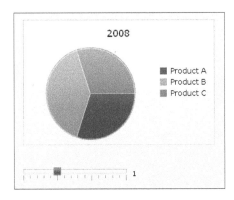

How it works...

As mentioned in the introduction of this recipe, the **Source Data** component has the same data insertion functionality as selector components and drilldowns from charts. But, the data insertion of the **Source Data** component is triggered by a changing value in a spreadsheet cell and not directly by a user interacting with a component.

In this recipe, we used the **Horizontal Slider** component to change a cell value (cell **B1**) to trigger the data insertion. But you can, of course, also use this component in combination with Excel formulas, **Dynamic Visibility**, or the data inserted by other components.

Analyzing trends

Using the **Trend Analyzer** component, you can calculate trends in a series of data. You can then display these trends in a chart so that you can view them next to the actual data and make your analysis. This component can also forecast future trends based on actual data.

Getting ready

For this recipe, we need some data, so open a new SAP BusinessObjects Dashboards file and enter the values in the spreadsheet as shown in the following screenshot:

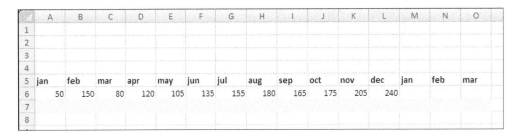

How to do it...

1. Drag a **Combination Chart** component into the canvas.

2. Bind the data **By Range** to the spreadsheet cells **A5:O7**.

3. Drag a **Trend Analyzer** component from the **Other** category into the canvas.

4. Bind the **Data** field to cells **A6:L6**.

5. Set **Trend/Regression Type** as **Linear**.

6. Bind the **Analyzed Data Destination** field to cells **A7:O7**.

7. Set **Number of Forecast Periods** to 3:

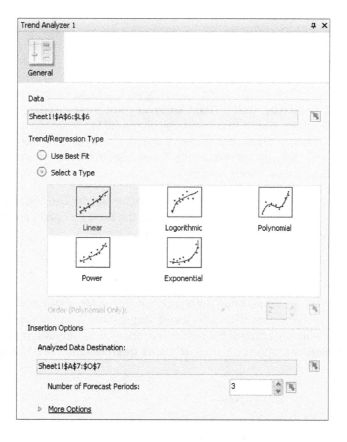

8. Now preview the dashboard:

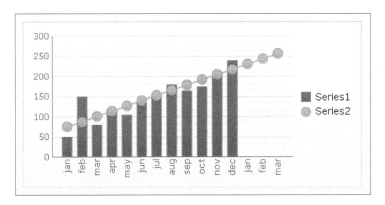

How it works...

In the previous example, we created a chart that shows a data series over a 12-month period. We selected **Linear trend type**, so the **Trend Analyzer** component calculates a linear trend based on all the 12 values. Also, a forecast is calculated for the three months we didn't have data for. The combination chart visualizes both the actual and the calculated trend data series, where the latter is a straight line. As the **Trend Analyzer** component is a background component, it won't be shown during runtime.

Besides the **Linear** option for **Trend/Regression Type**, we can choose **Logarithmic**, **Polynomial**, **Power**, or **Exponential**. Also, we can use the **Best Fit** option and trust SAP BusinessObjects Dashboards to choose the correct one for us.

There's more...

The properties pane of the **Trend Analyzer** component has a **More Options** section. Here you can bind information about the chosen **Trend/Regression Type** to the spreadsheet cells and display them in your dashboard. The fields you can show are **Equation Type Destination**, **Equation Destination** (that's the equation), **R^2 Value Destination**, and **F Value Destination**:

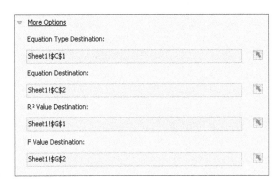

7
Dashboard Look and Feel

In this chapter, we will cover the following recipes:

- ▶ Changing the look of a chart
- ▶ Adding a background to your dashboard
- ▶ Using color schemes
- ▶ Sharing a color scheme
- ▶ Working with themes
- ▶ Making component colors dynamic
- ▶ Dynamic XY positioning and sizing of components
- ▶ Using the Panel Container
- ▶ Using the Tab Set container
- ▶ Making tables look pretty
- ▶ Using quadrants smartly
- ▶ Creating/using a dashboard template

Introduction

SAP BusinessObjects Dashboards provides a powerful way to capture the audience by allowing developers to build dashboards with the important *wow* factor. When a dashboard is visually striking, the user will be more engaged and will thus make better use of it. Poor dashboard design can frustrate users, causing them to quickly give up on getting what they need out of the dashboard, even if it has all the information and functionality that they desire.

Changing the look of a chart

This recipe will explain how to change the look of a chart. Particularly, it will go through each tab in the appearance icon of the chart properties. We will then make modifications and see the resulting changes.

Getting ready

Insert a chart object into the canvas. Prepare some data and bind it to the chart.

How to do it...

1. Click on the chart object on the canvas/object properties window to go to chart properties.

2. In the **Layout** tab, uncheck **Show Chart Background**.

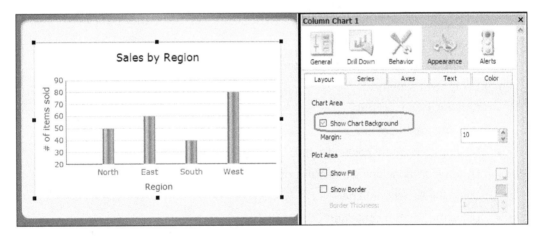

3. In the **Series** tab, click on the colored box under Fill to change the color of the bar to your desired color.

4. Then change the width of each bar; click on the **Marker Size** area and change it to **35**.

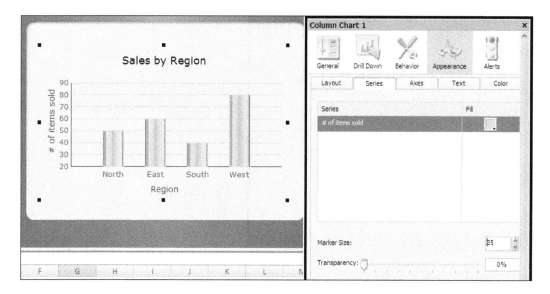

5. Click on the colored boxes circled in red in the **Axes** tab and choose dark blue as the **Line Color** for the horizontal and vertical axes separately.

6. Uncheck **Show Minor Gridlines** to remove all the horizontal lines in between each of the major gridlines.

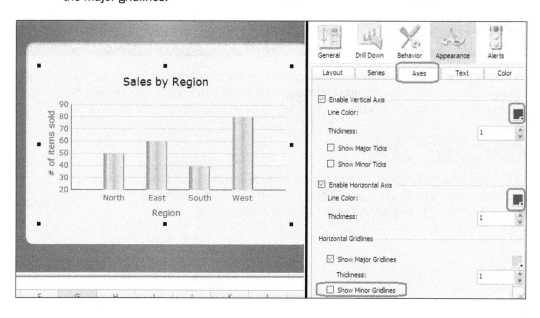

7. Next, go to the **Text** and **Color** tabs, where you can make changes to all the different text areas of the chart, as shown in the following screenshot:

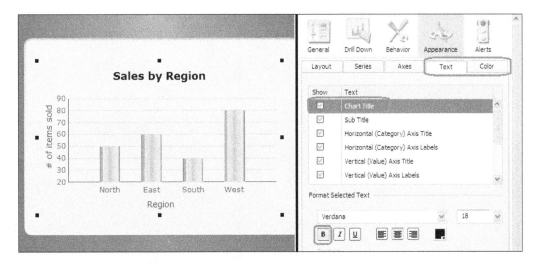

How it works...

As you can see, the default chart looks plain and the bars are skinny so it's harder to visualize things. It is a good idea to remove the chart background if there is one so that the chart blends in better. In addition, the changes to the chart colors and text provide additional aesthetics that help improve the look of the chart.

Adding a background to your dashboard

This recipe shows the usefulness of backgrounds in the dashboard. It will show how backgrounds can help provide additional depth to objects and help to group certain areas together for better visualization.

Getting ready

Make sure you have all your objects such as charts and selectors ready on the canvas. The following is an example of the two charts before the makeover. Bind some data to the charts if you want to change the coloring of the series.

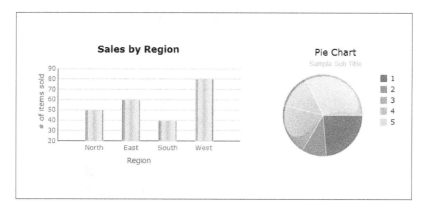

How to do it...

1. Choose **Background4** from the **Art and Backgrounds** tab of the **Components** window.

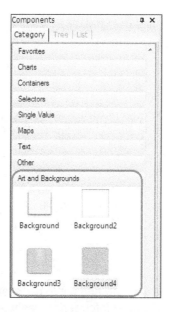

2. Stretch the background so that it fills the size of the canvas.

3. Make sure that the ordering of the backgrounds is behind the charts. To change the ordering of the background, go to the object browser, select the background object, and then press the - key until the background object is behind the chart.

4. Select **Background** from the **Art and Backgrounds** tab and put two of them under the charts, as shown in the following screenshot:

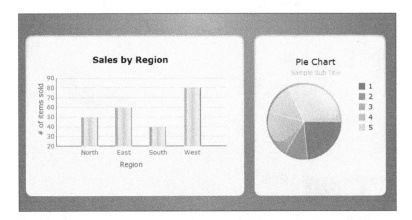

5. When the backgrounds are in place, open the properties window for the backgrounds and set the background color to your desired color. In this example, we chose dark grey and light grey for each background.

How it works...

As you can see with the before and after pictures, having backgrounds can make a huge difference in terms of aesthetics. The objects are much more pleasant to look at now and there is certainly a lot of depth in the charts.

The best way to choose the right backgrounds that fit your dashboard is to play around with the different background objects and their colors. If you are not very artistic, you can come up with a bunch of examples and demonstrate them to the business users to see which one they prefer the most.

There's more...

It is important to use backgrounds carefully and not to use them in the wrong places. A good reference that we recommend is the book *Information Dashboard Design*: Displaying data for at-a-glance monitoring, *Stephen Few, Analytics Press*. This is a great book that will guide you on the best dashboard design practices and on when to use backgrounds.

Using color schemes

SAP BusinessObjects Dashboards conveniently has a set of built-in color themes that developers can use to instantly change the look of their dashboard. Using color themes helps provide consistent coloring among your objects and allows you to change the colors of multiple objects at a time, without having to go into the properties of each object to make any color changes.

Getting ready

Have a set of objects ready on the canvas that you want to make color changes to. In this example, we have the sales by region chart, a pie chart, and a set of backgrounds.

How to do it...

1. Click on the **Colors** icon and make sure that **Current Theme Colors** is selected under the **Built-in** section. The backgrounds will be grey and the charts bluish.

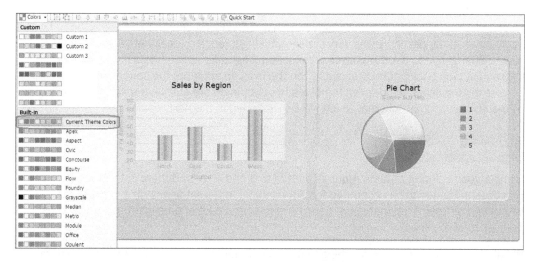

2. Click on the **Colors** icon again and select the **Concourse** color scheme.

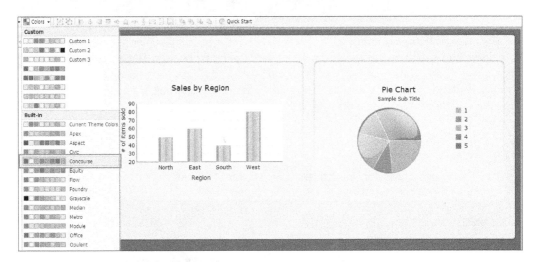

How it works...

As you can see, the default color scheme initially looked kind of bland and the coloring for each series in the pie chart was very similar, making it tough to decipher between each of the series. Changing it to the **Concourse** color scheme lightens up the background considerably with a light blue background that is easy on the eyes. In addition, the series on the pie chart is more distinguishable; however, the blues in our opinion are still too similar. We can fix that by modifying the color scheme, which will be explained in the next recipe.

There's more...

Using a good coloring scheme requires a lot of trial and error and there are many best practices that need to be accounted for. For example, different series on a chart should be colored differently so that users don't have to spend a lot of time figuring out which bar belongs to which series.

We also want colors that are soothing to the eyes. Colors that are too bright or too dark may cause strain on the eyes, thus making it more difficult to find information.

When going through color schemes, it is best to show a demo to the end users who will be using the dashboard and go with a coloring scheme that is most comfortable to their eyes, as it will allow them to find information more easily.

Sharing a color scheme

Developers may want to customize a dashboard's charts and objects to follow a company's coloring guidelines. Most likely, the company's coloring guidelines will not match any of the built-in color schemes, so we'll need a way to create one that we can reuse every time a new dashboard is built for the same company.

Getting ready

You must be able to view hidden files and folders in the `c:\Documents and Settings\ your_user_id` folder. If you are a Windows Vista or Windows 7 user, you must be able to view hidden files and folders in `c:\Users\your_user_id`.

How to do it...

1. Click on the **Colors** icon and select **Create New Color Scheme** at the bottom of the list.

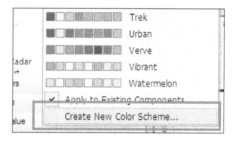

2. Change the background color to whatever color you want from the **Backgrounds** tab in **Advanced Settings** as highlighted in the following screenshot:

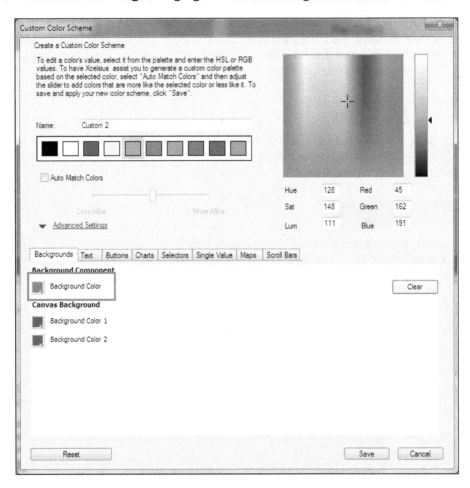

3. Click on the **Charts** tab and change the first **Series** color to something other than the default color. Also change the name of the Color Scheme to a name that you desire.

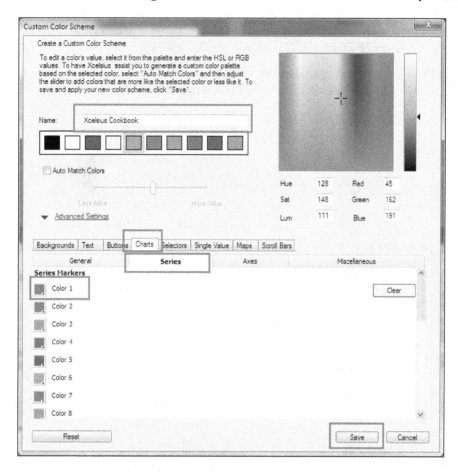

4. Click the **Save** button when you are finished.

5. Your color scheme has now been saved and you can now transfer it to other computers. Copy the XML files of the theme that you want to share from the following two folders to the exact same directory in the destination computer. The XML filenames will be named as you saved them, as follows:

    ❑ c:\Documents and Settings\your_user_id\Application Data\ XcelsiuscustomThemes

    ❑ c:\Documents and Settings\your_user_id\Application Data\ XcelsiuscustomThemesAutoInfo

6. For Windows Vista and Windows 7, the directory path for Xcelsius will be c:\Users\your_user_id\AppData\Roaming\.

How it works...

Every time you save a custom color scheme, it will create two XML files in the aforementioned directories. From there, you can easily share the color scheme with other developers or other machines that have SAP BusinessObjects Dashboards installed.

As you can see in the following screenshot, once you have the XML files of the color scheme in place, you will be able to select it from the **Color Scheme Toolbar**:

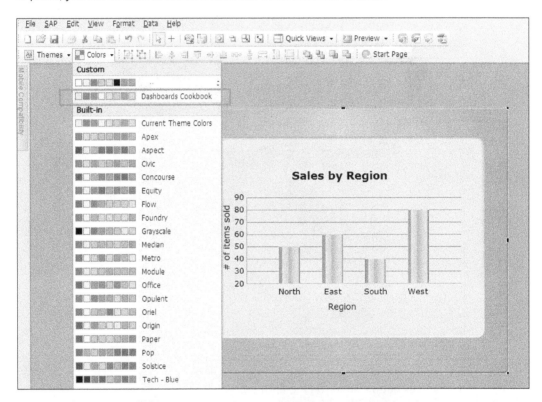

Working with themes

SAP BusinessObjects Dashboards has a library of themes that developers can use to change chart and object styles to a look that suits them most. The ability to select different themes is important because it gives developers more options for customizing the look of their dashboards to what fits best. There are eight themes that developers can choose from. In this recipe, we will be showcasing the default theme along with two other themes.

How to do it...

1. Click on the **Themes** icon and you will see that **Aqua** is selected by default.

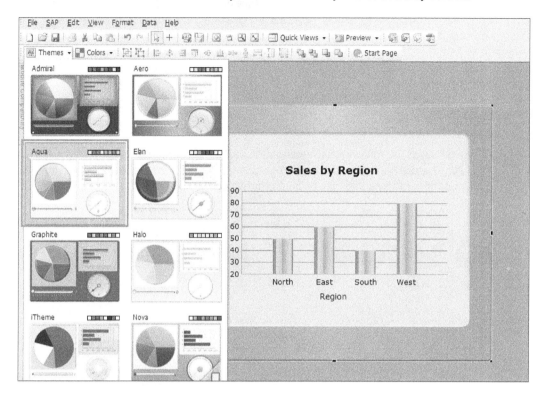

2. Try out other themes such as **Aero**, **Halo**, and so on.

How it works...

As you can see, SAP BusinessObjects Dashboards provides a large library of themes, allowing you to customize the style of your backgrounds, objects, and charts. For example, some themes may have more gradient backgrounds and charts such as the Aero theme, whereas the Halo theme has a flat but bold look.

 Note that some themes have more types of components than others. For example, the Aqua theme has more background components than the Admiral theme.

Making component colors dynamic

SAP BusinessObjects Dashboards allows users to fully control the coloring of their components based on whatever event they desire. For example, if a major alert were to occur we would be able to dynamically change our background to red in order to signal an emergency. This is extremely useful because developers can not only dynamically control the color of bars on a chart but also the rest of the chart components such as the background and text as well.

How to do it...

1. Take a look at the following screenshot. In cell **E2** (highlighted in yellow), we have a COUNTIF statement that will set the bar color to red if any of the regions have sold a number of items less than 40, or blue otherwise.

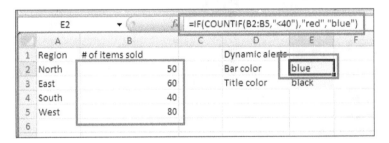

2. In the chart properties, go to the **Color** tab and click on the square colored box in the **Fill** column. At the bottom of the color palette, choose the **Bind to a Color** option and bind to the cell with the color control (**E2**, in our case).

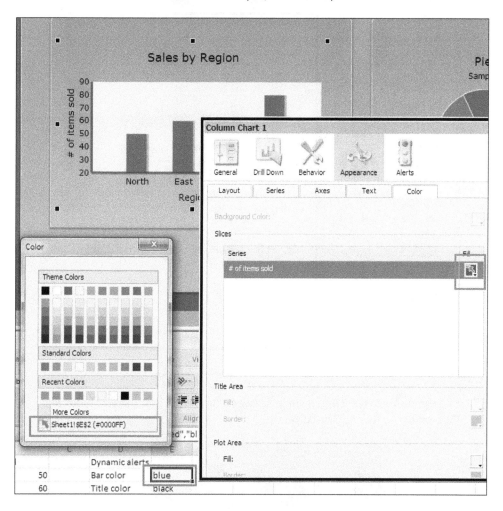

3. Go to the **Text** tab of the chart properties and click on the color square of the **Chart Title**. Bind the color to the cell that controls the title text color (in our case, **E3**).

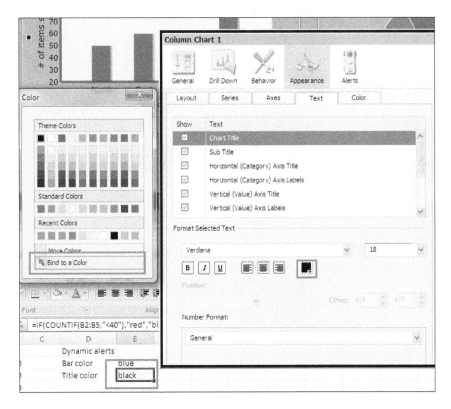

4. Change the cells **B2:B5** to a value below 40 and verify that the **Bar color** and **Title color** are functioning correctly.

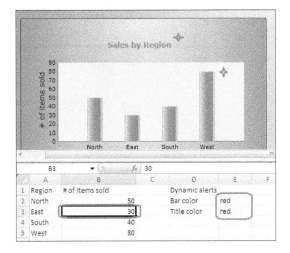

How it works...

As seen in our example, we can easily control the coloring of our chart components with the help of some Excel formulas. Using this method, we are able to alert users if something significant has occurred. For example, if it is critical that all of the regions surpass a sales threshold of 40 units, we can send out an alert signal (red title and bars) if one of the regions fails.

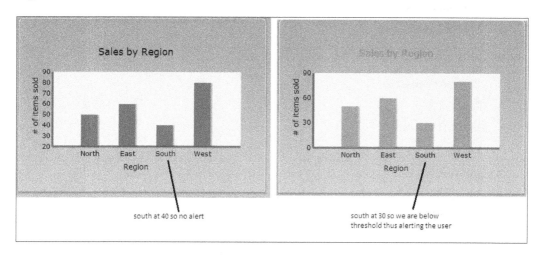

There's more...

Because the dynamic coloring depends on Boolean logic, you'll need the aid of Excel formulas to determine which color is displayed. We recommend that you become familiar with Excel Boolean logic to fully utilize the functionality of dynamic coloring.

Dynamic XY positioning and sizing of components

The ability to move components around dynamically as well as changing their size is a useful feature new to SAP BusinessObjects Dashboards 4.1. For example, there may be a case where the placement of a chart is different depending on user selection. Instead of having to duplicate the chart, you can change its XY positioning.

Although dynamic XY positioning and sizing is a great feature, not all components support this. There is a trick that we will show you so that you can take advantage of dynamic XY positioning. However, it will not work for dynamic sizing.

The following components support both dynamic XY positioning and sizing:

- **Background**
- **Image Component**
- **Rectangle**
- **Ellipse**
- **Horizontal Line**
- **Vertical Line**

The following components support dynamic XY positioning only:

- **Canvas Container**
- **Tab Set**
- **Input Text Area**
- **Label**
- **Input Text**
- **Input Text2**
- **Query Refresh Button**

Getting ready

Our example will consist of a Image Component that supports both dynamic XY positioning and sizing, as well as four sliders that can reposition and resize the component.

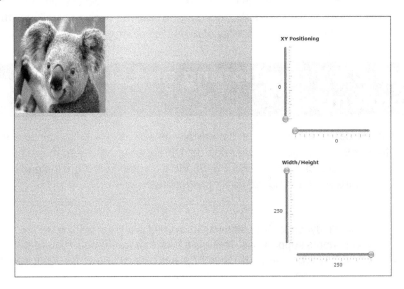

How to do it...

1. For the component that you want to reposition and resize, bind the XY axis as well as the width/height to the appropriate Excel cells.

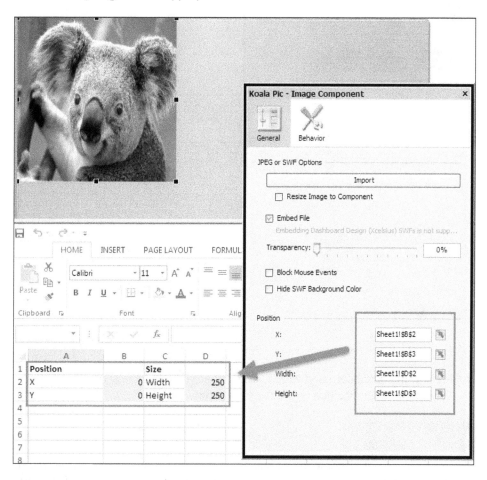

2. Bind the data output from each slider to the appropriate Excel cell.

3. Set the minimum and maximum values of the sliders to whatever values suit your range.

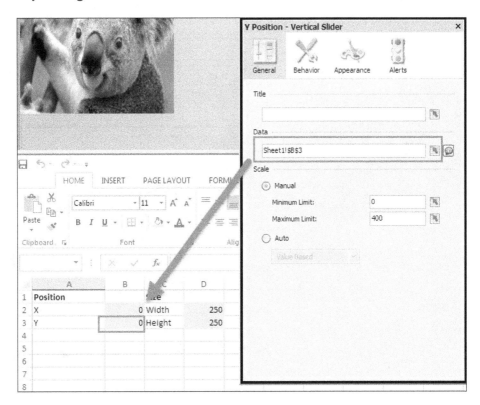

4. Preview the dashboard and you will see that as you move the sliders around, the component will reposition or resize appropriately.

There's more...

As mentioned earlier, not all components support dynamic XY repositioning and sizing. For the components that do not support this feature, we can still enable dynamic XY repositioning.

All you need to do is put the component inside a Canvas Container and then control the XY positioning from the Canvas Container, as shown in the following screenshot:

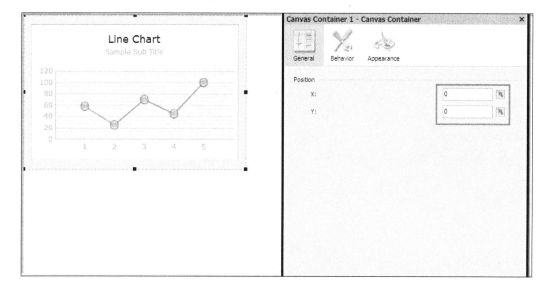

You'll notice that the component(s) will move along with the Canvas Container.

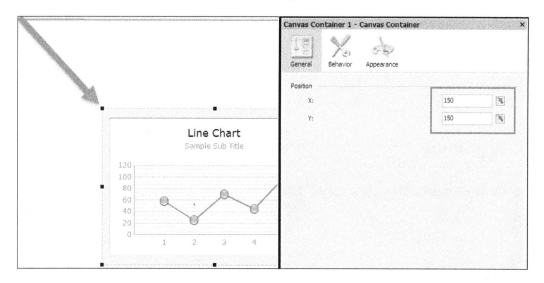

 Note that resizing an image to a larger size may deteriorate the quality of the image.

Using the Panel Container

The Panel Container component is useful if a designer thinks that a set of item(s) is too large for the canvas and wants to be able to scroll the inside of the canvas. A good example would be a scrolling set of charts. Let's say real estate on the dashboard is an issue and we have many charts that need to be shown, but it is not mandatory to show all charts in one view. If we put them in a Panel Container, we can scroll through each chart, similar to a slideshow.

How to do it...

1. Select the **Panel Container** from the **Containers** tab.

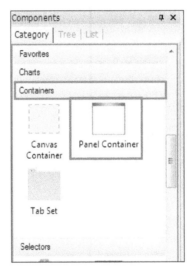

2. Insert a set of charts (these can be any type of charts that you wish to insert) inside the Panel Container.

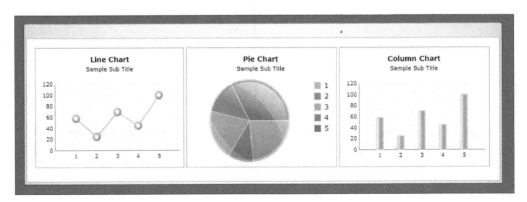

3. Shrink the Panel Container so that it doesn't take up too much real estate on the dashboard. You can do this by taking your mouse to the edge of the panel and resizing from there.

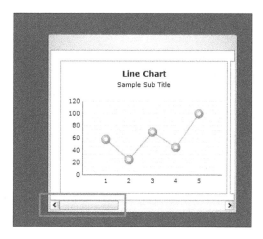

How it works...

In our example, we were able to emulate a slideshow of charts. This is useful if all the charts do not need to be visible in one screen, and will allow designers to save on real estate.

There's more...

If you are inserting multiple objects in a Panel Container you must make sure that the business is okay with the scrolling. In the majority of cases, it is a best practice to show everything on the same screen without having to scroll. In some cases, such large tables with many columns of information, we may have to resort to using the Panel Container in order to facilitate the best use of the real estate.

Using the Tab Set container

The best analogy to a **Tab Set** would be the tabs that you see in Internet Explorer and Mozilla Firefox. Before the advent of tabs, we would have multiple windows of Internet Explorer open, which was very cumbersome. With tabs we can flip through the different pages that we have opened very easily. With the Tab Set container, we can separate different pages within the dashboard. This allows us to flip through pages that are independent of each other but related to the same topic, without having to reload separate dashboards or set dynamic visibility for each page.

How to do it...

1. Select the **Tab Set** container from the **Containers** tab.

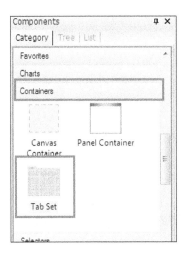

2. In the **Properties** window of the canvas, you can rename the tab. In our example we named the first tab as `Sales`.

3. To add a new tab, press the **+** button on the top left-hand side of the canvas. It will then pop up a window that lets you name your tab. In our example, we named the second tab `Trend Analysis`, as shown in the following screenshot:

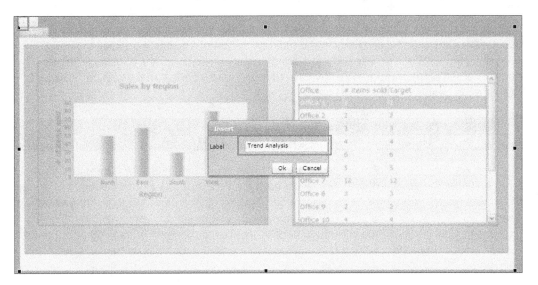

4. Each tab is separated into a different canvas in the **Object Browser** window. All components residing in each canvas will show up as child objects of the canvas.

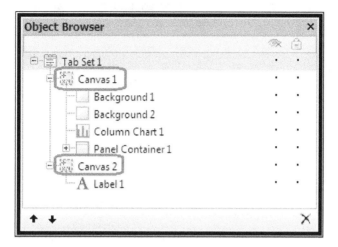

How it works...

The Tab Set container is basically a set of Canvas Containers that hold your objects. The set of Canvas Containers is distinguished by the tab at the top of the main container. Users can switch through tabs at runtime very easily. This functionality emulates the tabs found on popular browsers such as Internet Explorer and Mozilla Firefox.

There's more...

When building Tab Set containers, designers should be wary of having too many tabs or too many levels of tab hierarchies. It is recommended to keep the number of tabs in each level to a maximum of five.

Take the following image for example. With nine tabs, we can see that the dashboard starts to become overwhelming and complex. It is also good to keep the number of hierarchies to a maximum of two. Again, we can see that once we get past two hierarchies, it starts to become messy and users will have too many paths to choose from.

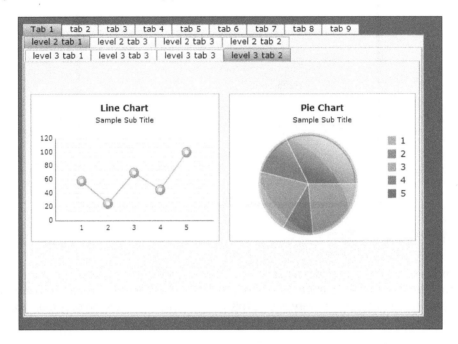

Finally, each additional tab means an additional page. With each additional page comes a set of components and charts, which equate to a larger footprint. Dashboards with a larger footprint will take longer to load due to the size of the SWF file and performance will take a hit due to the number of objects.

 Although the Tab Set container is a useful tool, in terms of performance, it is best to create a tab panel by using the Label Based Menu and then simply use Dynamic Visibility. Instructions can be found in *Chapter 3, From a Static to an Interactive Dashboard* and *Chapter 4, Dynamic Visibility*.

Making tables look pretty

With SAP BusinessObjects Dashboards, we can create tables that look just like a table in an Excel spreadsheet. Unfortunately, our everyday tables look quite bland. If we start off with a default spreadsheet table, it will look kind of like this:

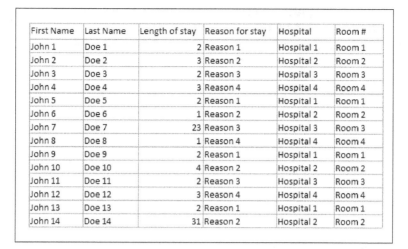

First Name	Last Name	Length of stay	Reason for stay	Hospital	Room #
John 1	Doe 1	2	Reason 1	Hospital 1	Room 1
John 2	Doe 2	3	Reason 2	Hospital 2	Room 2
John 3	Doe 3	2	Reason 3	Hospital 3	Room 3
John 4	Doe 4	3	Reason 4	Hospital 4	Room 4
John 5	Doe 5	2	Reason 1	Hospital 1	Room 1
John 6	Doe 6	1	Reason 2	Hospital 2	Room 2
John 7	Doe 7	23	Reason 3	Hospital 3	Room 3
John 8	Doe 8	1	Reason 4	Hospital 4	Room 4
John 9	Doe 9	2	Reason 1	Hospital 1	Room 1
John 10	Doe 10	4	Reason 2	Hospital 2	Room 2
John 11	Doe 11	2	Reason 3	Hospital 3	Room 3
John 12	Doe 12	3	Reason 4	Hospital 4	Room 4
John 13	Doe 13	2	Reason 1	Hospital 1	Room 1
John 14	Doe 14	31	Reason 2	Hospital 2	Room 2

It looks okay, but with the help of some additional objects, we can spice it up to look a bit more attractive.

Getting ready

Prepare the data on your Excel spreadsheet and set up a Spreadsheet Table component as shown in the previous screenshot.

How to do it...

1. Add color to the row header, and make the header text bold.

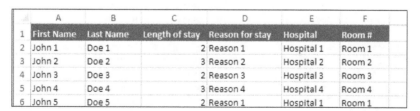

	A	B	C	D	E	F
1	**First Name**	**Last Name**	**Length of stay**	**Reason for stay**	**Hospital**	**Room #**
2	John 1	Doe 1	2	Reason 1	Hospital 1	Room 1
3	John 2	Doe 2	3	Reason 2	Hospital 2	Room 2
4	John 3	Doe 3	2	Reason 3	Hospital 3	Room 3
5	John 4	Doe 4	3	Reason 4	Hospital 4	Room 4
6	John 5	Doe 5	2	Reason 1	Hospital 1	Room 1

2. In the Spreadsheet Table component properties, rebind **Display Data** to the corresponding cells (**A1:F15**) so that the updated header text format will show up. Go to the **Appearance** category and uncheck **Show Gridlines**.

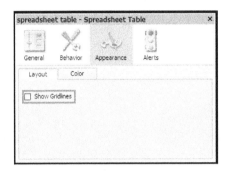

3. Change the theme to **Aero**.

4. Select the first Background object from the **Art and Backgrounds** tab from the **Category** window. Place the background so that it is under the table.

5. Select **Label** from the **Text** tab of the **Category** window. Center it on the title background to give the table a title.

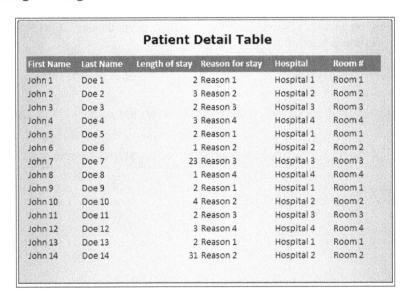

First Name	Last Name	Length of stay	Reason for stay	Hospital	Room #
John 1	Doe 1	2 Reason 1		Hospital 1	Room 1
John 2	Doe 2	3 Reason 2		Hospital 2	Room 2
John 3	Doe 3	2 Reason 3		Hospital 3	Room 3
John 4	Doe 4	3 Reason 4		Hospital 4	Room 4
John 5	Doe 5	2 Reason 1		Hospital 1	Room 1
John 6	Doe 6	1 Reason 2		Hospital 2	Room 2
John 7	Doe 7	23 Reason 3		Hospital 3	Room 3
John 8	Doe 8	1 Reason 4		Hospital 4	Room 4
John 9	Doe 9	2 Reason 1		Hospital 1	Room 1
John 10	Doe 10	4 Reason 2		Hospital 2	Room 2
John 11	Doe 11	2 Reason 3		Hospital 3	Room 3
John 12	Doe 12	3 Reason 4		Hospital 4	Room 4
John 13	Doe 13	2 Reason 1		Hospital 1	Room 1
John 14	Doe 14	31 Reason 2		Hospital 2	Room 2

Patient Detail Table

How it works...

As you can see, with the help of a couple of components, such as backgrounds and labels, we are able to spice up the look of a table.

▸   The *Adding a background to your dashboard* recipe

Using quadrants smartly

It is very important when designing a dashboard to make it as easy to read as possible. In addition, we want to make a dashboard conform to how humans analyze a picture. A common concept is to move from the top left-hand side to the top right-hand side and then to the bottom. This is a flow that the majority of users are comfortable with.

Now we bring in the concept of quadrants. Quadrants allow us to create groupings so that a user is not overwhelmed when looking at a dashboard.

Getting ready

Gather the desired charts and selectors on your dashboard.

How to do it...

1.   Set up your charts so that the dashboard is divided into four quadrants.

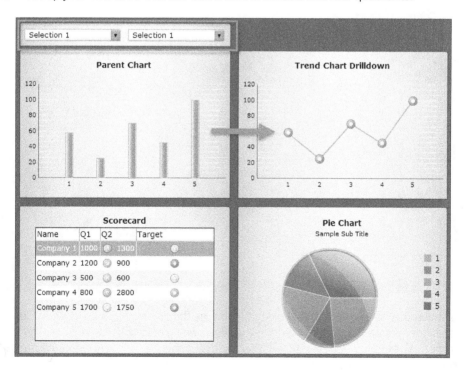

2. Selectors should be on the top left-hand side if they control the whole chart.

3. Use backgrounds to separate your quadrants.

4. Parent charts should be on the left-hand side or on top of the drilldown chart.

5. Charts that we want users to look at first should be at the top.

6. If possible, size all the quadrants equally.

7. Align the components neatly so that it is easier on the eyes when looking for different items.

How it works...

As you can see, when we group things into four quadrants, it is very easy to read the dashboard. In addition, we are comfortable with navigation as we start at the top left-hand side. The drilldown is easy to understand and navigate through as we have the parent chart on the left-hand side of the drilldown chart. Secondary information should be at the bottom of the chart and not at the top, as users are interested in the highest-level data first when viewing the dashboard. Finally, it is important to align everything neatly and size everything as equally as possible. This makes the dashboard much easier to read.

Now let's take an example of a dashboard that is not set in quadrants but is aligned neatly, as shown in the following screenshot:

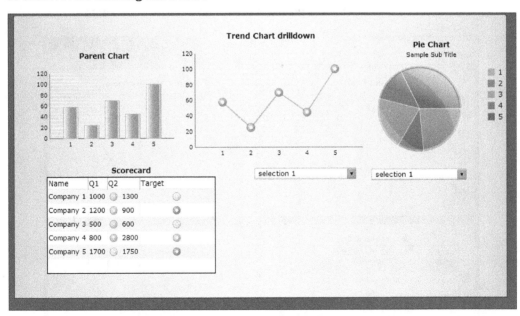

This dashboard is harder to read and navigate now, as things are not in quadrants. The drop-down selectors are on the bottom right-hand side, so we have to shift our focus to the main parent chart diagonally whenever we want to make a change, which is not very user friendly.

▸ The *Adding a background to your dashboard* recipe

▸ In addition, for a good dashboard layout designs you can read *Information Dashboard Design*, *Stephen Few*

Creating/using a dashboard template

To ensure consistency among dashboards within an organization, it is good to create a dashboard template. This also saves time on having to redevelop recurring objects.

Getting ready

Set up a dashboard that contains components and colors that would be common among dashboards in the organization. In our example, we have a common background and color scheme, as shown in the following screenshot:

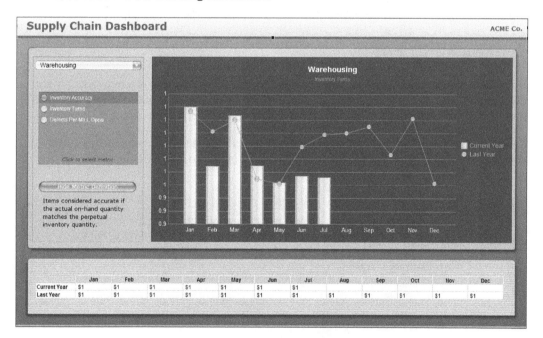

How to do it...

1. Go to **File | Save as...**.

2. Browse to `<Installation Path>\Xcelsius 4.0\assets\template`.

3. Create a folder with a name or category of your choice.

4. Save the file with a filename of your choice.

5. Exit and reopen SAP BusinessObjects Dashboards.

6. Go to **File | Templates**... or press *Ctrl + T*.

7. Select the folder that you created from the category selection.

8. Select the dashboard that you saved earlier.

How it works...

As you can see, dashboard templates are stored in `<Installation Path>\Xcelsius 4.0\assets\template`. Once you create a dashboard template, you can easily access it without having to remember the exact directory you have stored the template in.

There's more...

Unfortunately, this method works only on local machines unless there is a network shortcut at `<Installation Path>\Xcelsius 4.0\assets\template` directory. Because of this, it is quite cumbersome to set up; however, once set up, it works great.

An alternative is to create a dashboard template directory in a shared network area, then create a shortcut to that directory on your desktop. From there, you can then open the dashboard template and work on it.

It is important to note that if you use the method of storing the dashboard templates in a shared network directory, you'll need to make sure that the dashboard templates are read only; otherwise, you'll risk having the templates accidentally modified.

8

Dashboard Data Connectivity

In this chapter, we will cover the following recipes:

- ▶ Creating a news ticker with Excel XML Maps
- ▶ Using Query as a Web Service (QaaWS)
- ▶ Using Live Office Connection
- ▶ Using BI Web Services to consume a Webi report
- ▶ Using the SAP NetWeaver BW Connection
- ▶ Using the Query Browser
- ▶ Passing values from dashboard to dashboard with Flash Variables

Introduction

Dashboards get really powerful when they are able to display recent or even real-time data. Of course, you can manually enter the updated data in the SAP BusinessObjects Dashboards spreadsheet and publish a new dashboard every time the data changes. If your dashboard uses a lot of data that changes regularly, you will quickly find out that this is a very time-consuming task.

A good solution is to set up one or more data connections between the dashboard and an external data source. If the data in the source changes, the dashboard will show this updated information.

Creating a news ticker with Excel XML Maps

In this recipe, we will show you how to integrate a real-time news ticker into your dashboard. The user will then be able to click on a news article and the website will automatically pop up. To set up this connection to an online news website, we will use the Excel XML Maps connection.

Getting ready

Make sure the spreadsheet has a **DEVELOPER** tab, and that you are connected to the Internet.

If you do not see the **DEVELOPER** tab, please follow these instructions:

1. Click on **FILE**.
2. Click on **Options**.
3. Click on **Customize Ribbon**.
4. Check the **DEVELOPER** box.

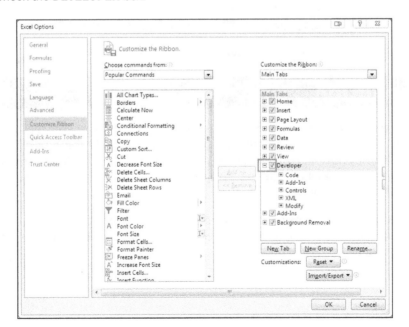

How to do it...

1. Go to `http://www.cnn.com/`. At the bottom of this page, you will see an RSS link. You can also directly go to `http://www.cnn.com/services/rss/`.

2. Copy the URL of the **Top Stories** RSS feed: `http://rss.cnn.com/rss/edition.rss`.

 RSS is an XML-based method by which web content can be easily and quickly distributed when it is changed or newly entered into a website.

3. Open a new SAP BusinessObjects Dashboards file, go to the **DEVELOPER** tab, and click on **Source**. The **XML Source** pane will appear.

 If you are using MS Excel 2003, you can find the **XML Source** pane at **Data | XML | XML Source**.

4. Click on the **XML Maps...** button.

5. In the upcoming **XML Maps** window, click on the **Add...** button.

6. Paste the RSS URL into the **File name** field and click on **Open**. A message might appear stating that this XML source does not refer to a schema and Excel will create one itself. Click on **OK**.

7. Click on **OK** once more in the **XML Maps** window to close it. The **XML Source** window will now show all the fields that are available in this RSS stream.

8. To create a news ticker we only need two of these fields: the title of the article and the URL to the article on the CNN website. Both fields are located in the item folder: **title** and **link**. Click and drag the **title** field to cell **A6** and drag the **link** field to cell **B6**.

9. Hit the **Refresh Data** button in the **DEVELOPER** tab. The cells below **A6** and **B6** will now be filled with data from the RSS feed.

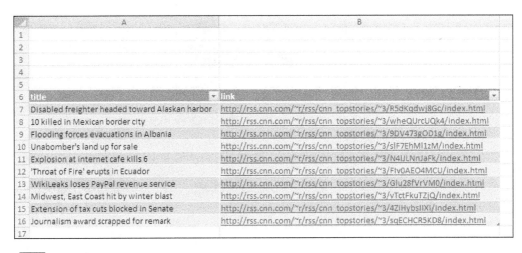

10. Open the **Data Manager** as shown in the following screenshot:

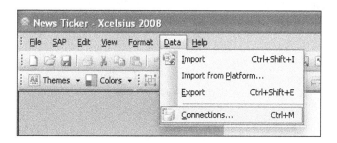

11. Click the **Add** button and select **Excel XML Maps**. You can find this connection type in the **Existing Connections** area.

12. As you can see, the **Data Manager** has already picked up the RSS feed we added to the spreadsheet.

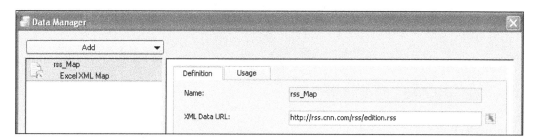

13. Go to the **Usage** tab. Select **Refresh Before Components Are Loaded**. Also, set **Refresh Every** to **1 Minutes**. Close the **Data Manager**.

14. Add a **Ticker** component from the **Selectors** category to the canvas.

15. Bind its **Labels** to cells **A7:A16**.

16. Select **Insertion Type** as **Row**. Bind the **Source Data** field to cells **B7:B16**. Bind the **Destination** field to cell **B4**.

17. The next steps explain how to trigger the website popup. Add a **URL Button** component to the canvas.

18. Bind the **URL** field to cell **B4**.

19. Empty the **Label** field.

20. Go to the **Behavior** tab, bind the **Trigger Cell** field to cell **B4**, and ensure that the **When Value Changes** option is checked.

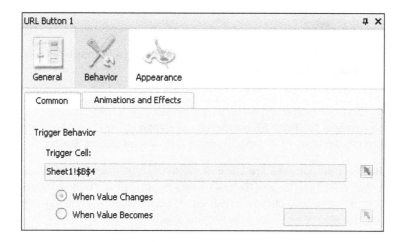

21. Finally, go to the **Appearance** tab and deselect the **Show Button Background** option. The **URL Button** component should now be invisible.

22. Try your dashboard!

> Large spike in radiation detected at Japan nuke plant   -   Radiation from plant d

How it works...

Let's recap what we just did. First, we added an RSS feed from `http://www.cnn.com/` to our spreadsheet. We used the standard Excel XML Maps functionality to do this. A big advantage of this method is that we can preview the data directly in the spreadsheet, which eases the setup of components and data bindings.

Next, we created a data connection in the **Data Manager**. This step is necessary to let SAP BusinessObjects Dashboards know where to get the data from and under what conditions (refresh rate). If we do not do this, the dashboard will not get fresh data from the RSS feed and will only use the data that is already stored in the spreadsheet cells.

We bound a **Ticker** component to the cells containing the titles of the news stories. If the user clicks one of the titles, a web page should open with the right story. We set up row insertion to fetch the right URL for the **URL Button**. Finally, we configured the **URL Button** component so it would be triggered without clicking it.

There's more...

In this section, we will take a look at the **Usage** tab under **Data Manager | Connections**, as well as the **Connection Refresh Button** component.

Usage tab

Most connection types in the **Data Manager** have a **Usage** tab like we saw in step 13 of the recipe. There are two sections in this tab: **Refresh Options** and **Load Status**.

With **Refresh Before Components Are Loaded** the data connection will be used to get data as soon as the dashboard starts. The **Refresh Every** option sets the refresh rate in seconds, minutes, or hours. You can also choose to refresh the data when a value in a particular spreadsheet cell changes or a certain value is matched.

During the loading of fresh data it is possible to inform the dashboard user what is happening at the moment (loading data or idle). You can insert these messages in a spreadsheet cell and display them, for example, with a **Label** component. Also, a nice idea is to display a loading-image instead of text. You can use **Dynamic Visibility** to set this up (see *Chapter 4, Dynamic Visibility*).

If you select the **Enable Load Cursor** option, the cursor will change from the standard arrow into an hourglass. The **Disable Mouse Input on Load** option will disable user interactions (mouse clicks and mouseovers) as long as data is being loaded.

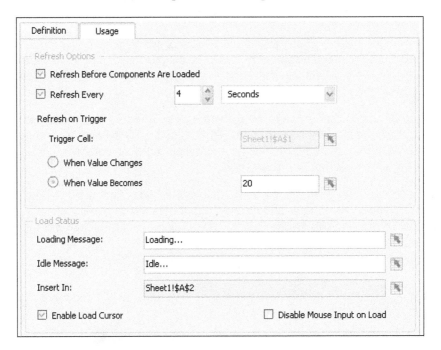

Connection Refresh Button

To manually refresh data when using the dashboard, we can use the **Connection Refresh Button** component, which can be found under **Web Connectivity**. This component can refresh one or more connections that are defined in the **Data Manager**.

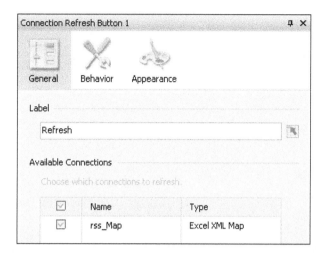

Using Query as a Web Service (QaaWS)

Query as a Web Service is a small but powerful tool in the SAP BusinessObjects BI portfolio. It allows us to create a query on top of a SAP BusinessObjects Universe and publish its results as a Web Service. This recipe shows you how to create a QaaWS and how to consume the data in SAP BusinessObjects Dashboards.

Getting ready

First, you will need SAP BusinessObjects BI Platform to be installed on your machine (along with server and client components). You will also need a Universe that is connected to an underlying database.

How to do it...

1. Open Query as a Web Service and log in to your SAP BusinessObjects BI server. You can find this application in the SAP BusinessObjects BI 4 platform Client Tools folder.

2. Click the **New Query** button on the upper left. Here you can enter a name for this Web Service and a description (not mandatory). Enter a name for your Web Service and click the **Next** button.

3. Select a Universe and click **Next**.

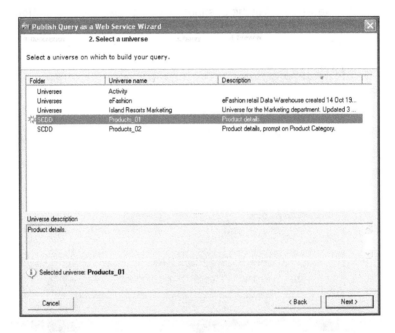

4. The following screen allows us to build our query. The left column contains the available dimensions, measures, and filters from the selected Universe. Drag the ones you want to use into the **Result Objects** window and click **Next**.

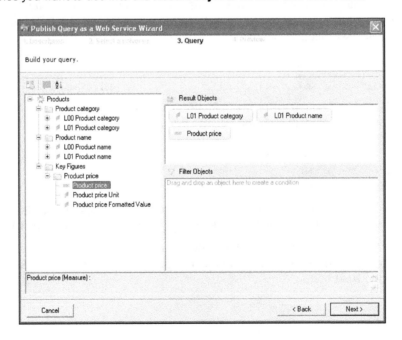

5. If the **Answer prompts** screen pops up, just click the **OK** button. The *There's more...* section of this recipe will discuss the use of prompts.

6. The **Preview** screen provides us with an overview of the QaaWS setup we just created. The most important part of the **Preview** screen is that it shows how the data and its layout will look in SAP BusinessObjects Dashboards after setting up the data connection and binding the columns to the spreadsheet. When you are satisfied with the preview, you can click on **Publish**.

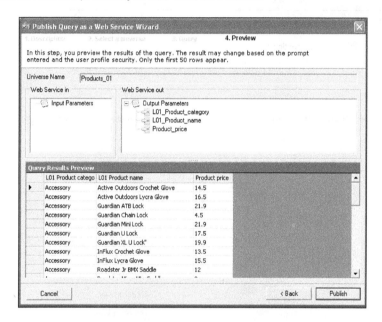

7. Now click the **To Clipboard** button to copy the Web Service URL to your clipboard.

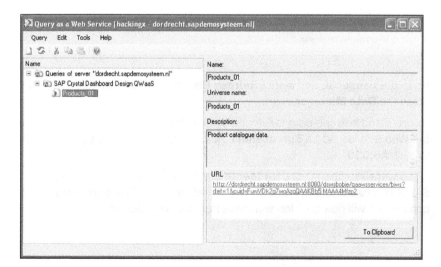

8. In SAP BusinessObjects Dashboards open the **Data Manager** window.

9. Add a **Web service query (Query as a Web Service)** connection.

10. Paste the URL into the **WSDL URL** field and click **Import**.

11. Select the **row** folder in the **Output Values** section. Since we have three columns of data in this Web Service, we have to bind it to a three-column area in the spreadsheet. Bind it to cells **A6:C30**.

12. Go to the **Usage** tab and select **Refresh Before Components Are Loaded**. Close the **Data Manager**.

13. To see if and how the data is fetched by SAP BusinessObjects Dashboards from the Web Service, add a **Spreadsheet Table** component to the canvas and bind it to cells **A6:C30**.

14. Preview the dashboard. A **User Identification** popup will appear. Enter your SAP BusinessObjects BI Platform credentials to log in. The **Spreadsheet Table** component will now be filled with data from the Web Service.

How it works...

In this recipe, we used three stages to get data into our dashboard. First, the SAP BusinessObjects Universe; second, the QaaWS definition on top of the Universe that created a Web Service; and third, the QaaWS-connection setup in the **Data Manager** to connect to the Web Service.

Because we cannot preview the data in the SAP BusinessObjects Dashboards spreadsheet like we did in the *Creating a news ticker with Excel XML Maps* recipe, we used the **Spreadsheet Table** component to check how the cells are populated when running the dashboard.

There's more...

Some other important concepts when using Query as a Web Service include the use of prompts and methods.

Using prompts

QaaWS prompts make it possible to load only the data that the dashboard user needs when using the dashboard.

1. Repeat steps 1 until 4 of the recipe. Before clicking **Next** in the fourth step, add the dimension that you want a filter on into the **Filter Objects** area. Select the **Prompt** option by clicking the little arrow on the right.

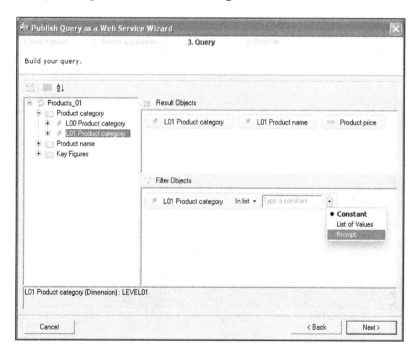

2. The **Answer prompts** window will appear. Here, select one of the available values to enable QaaWS to create a preview of the data in the next screen and click **OK**.

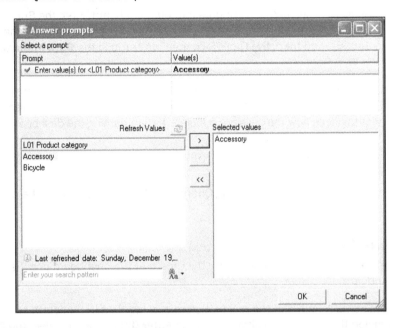

3. As you can see in the **Preview** screen, the prompt filter object we added is now shown as an **Input Parameters**. **Publish** the QaaWS.

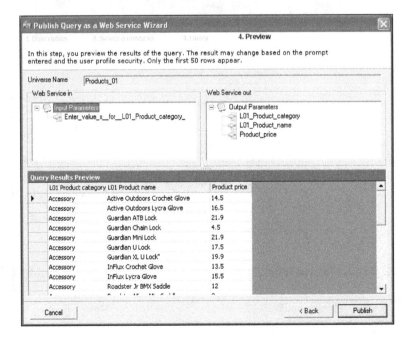

4. Repeat steps 8 until 11 of the recipe.

5. The prompt is now displayed in the **Input Values** area. Bind the prompt to cell **A1**.

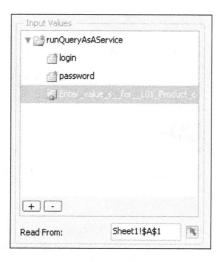

6. Go to the **Usage** tab and bind the **Trigger Cell** field to cell **A1** and ensure that **When Value Changes** is selected. Now the data will only be refreshed when the value in this cell changes. Close the **Data Manager**.

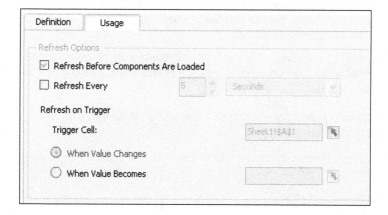

7. Set up a **Spreadsheet Table** component like we did in step 13 of the recipe.

8. Add a **Combo Box** component and add the **Labels** for the prompt. Select **Label** as the **Insertion Type** and bind the **Destination** field to cell **A1**.

9. Preview the dashboard and switch between the different labels to see the different data selections being loaded into the dashboard.

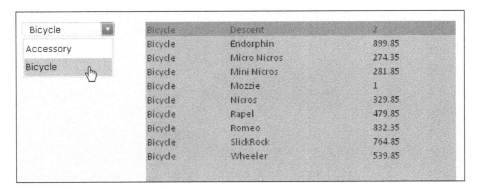

Methods

As you might have noticed while creating a QaaWS connection in SAP BusinessObjects Dashboards, there are several different methods you can use in the **Definition** tab. These methods can be split into two groups: to retrieve data and to list available parameter values:

▶ runQueryAsAService: This is the default selected option that we also used for the examples in this recipe. It enables us to send out parameter values and retrieve data.

▶ runQueryAsAServiceEx: This method gives the same output results as runQueryAsAService, but instead of providing an exact input parameter value, we can now also provide its index.

▶ valuesOf_parameter: This method will return a list of values for its input parameter, which can be used to create a selector like we did in the *Using prompts* section.

Remember that each QaaWS connection can only use a single method, so you might have to set up more than one connection.

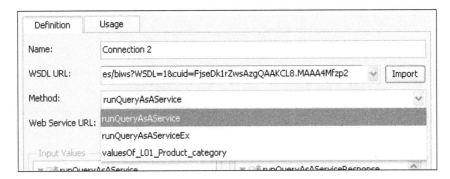

Using Live Office Connection

With SAP BusinessObjects Live Office it is possible to insert data from Crystal Reports documents and Web Intelligence reports into Microsoft Office products (Word, Excel, Outlook, PowerPoint). Since data can also be refreshed with this add-on, the Live Office Connection can be a very useful way to provide our dashboards with fresh data.

Getting ready

For this recipe you will need SAP BusinessObjects BI Platform to be installed on your machine and the Live Office Connection software installed on your client computer. You will also need a Crystal Reports document, a Web Intelligence report, or a Universe to connect to.

How to do it...

1. Open a new SAP BusinessObjects Dashboards file and go to **Preferences...** in the **File** menu. In the **Excel Options** section, check if **Live Office Compatibility** is enabled.

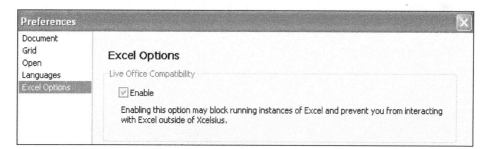

 For better tool stability, only enable this option when you are actually using Live Office in your dashboard.

2. Go to the **Live Office** tab of the spreadsheet. Click the **Crystal Reports** or **Web Intelligence** button to insert a report.

In this recipe we will use a report as a data source. You can also choose **Universe Query** here to connect directly to a Universe.

3. Log in to your SAP BusinessObjects BI Platform and choose a report.

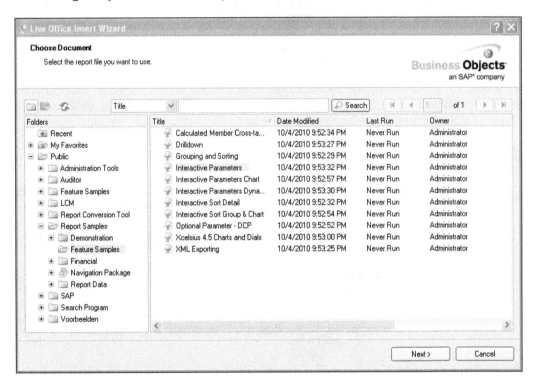

4. If your report contains any parameters, a window will appear in which you can enter the parameter values to filter the dataset that should be retrieved. In the *There's more...* section of this recipe we will discuss how to connect these prompts to the dashboard.

5. In the next window, the actual **Crystal Reports** document or **Web Intelligence** report is shown. With some mouse dragging and selecting you can select the data you want to import.

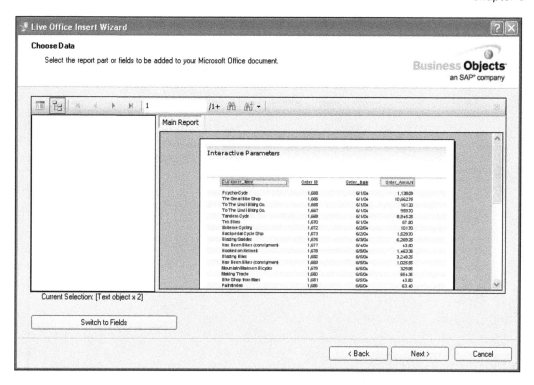

6. Click the **Switch to Fields** button to see an overview of all available fields. Here you can also select which fields you want to use.

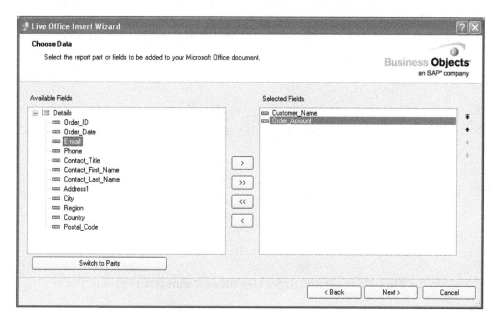

7. If you want to set some more filters on fields, you can use the next window by clicking on **Next**.

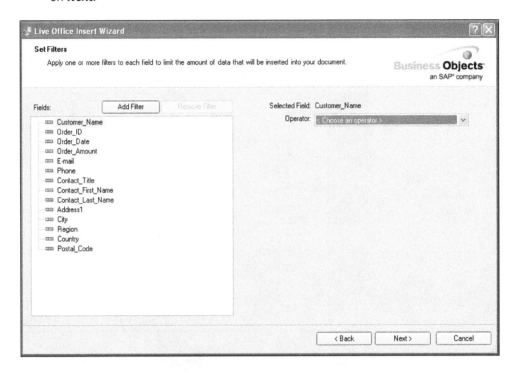

8. In the final window, you can enter a name for the Live Office objects you just set up. Click **Finish**.

9. As you will see, the spreadsheet is now populated with data from the report.

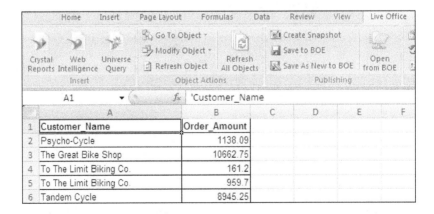

10. Go to the **Data Manager** and add a **Live Office Connections** connection.

11. Change the **Sessions URL** to point to the SAP BusinessObjects BI Platform server. Ranges are already bound to the cells in which the data has been imported. As you can see, Headers and Data Grid are separated. Do not forget to set up the **Usage** tab (see the *Creating a news ticker with Excel XML Maps* recipe).

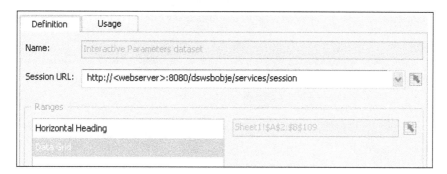

How it works...

With the Live Office Connection we retrieve data from Crystal Reports documents, Web Intelligence reports, or connect directly to a Universe. In this way we can reuse the definitions that are created in these reports as a base for our dashboard data.

There's more...

Just like we have seen in the *Using Query as a Web Service (QaaWS)* recipe, it is possible to use prompts to select the data that we want to retrieve and use it in our dashboard with a Live Office Connection. Use the following steps to set this up:

1. In the **Live Office** tab of the spreadsheet, select the **Modify Object** button and choose **Prompt Setting...**.

2. In the window that appears you will see the available parameters. After selecting the parameter you want to use, select **Choose Excel** data range.

3. Bind the field to a spreadsheet cell.

4. Follow step 6 until 9 of the *There's more...* section on *Using prompts* of the *Using Query as a Web Service (QaaWS)* recipe to use this prompt from within your dashboard.

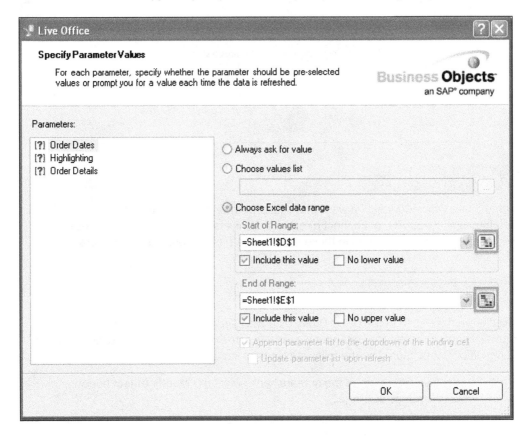

Using BI Web Services to consume a Webi report

BI Web Services is a data connection that works in basically two steps: first, a Web Intelligence (Webi) dataset report is created, similar to that of Live Office. Second, in SAP BusinessObjects Dashboards this dataset is consumed as a Query as a Web Service.

The benefit of using BI Web Services is that it combines the strengths of both Live Office and Query as a Web Service. These benefits include:

▸ The ability to perform complex calculations such as crosstabs, special aggregations, advanced contexts, and so on in the Webi document

▸ The ability to schedule reports so that we don't run into issues with queries that take a long time to execute

▸ We do not have to load the Webi report inside SAP BusinessObjects Dashboards, thus not requiring the extra Live Office bridge connection, which slows down dashboard performance considerably

In addition, BI Web Services has the ability to:

▸ Perform filtering within a dataset. Basically, this is like viewing a scheduled Webi document and filtering further within that dataset. This is extremely important, because one of the limitations with Live Office is its inability to consume datasets greater than 500 rows. Earlier, we would have to consume the entire scheduled dataset from Live Office. However, now we can filter the scheduled dataset beforehand and then consume the filtered set in SAP BusinessObjects Dashboards. We have tested filtering on datasets of 20k+ rows and the performance is great!

▸ Drill up and down hierarchies as shown in the following screenshot:

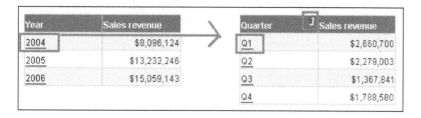

Getting ready

Using the eFashion universe, create the following Webi document that contains **Year**, **State**, and **Sales Revenue**:

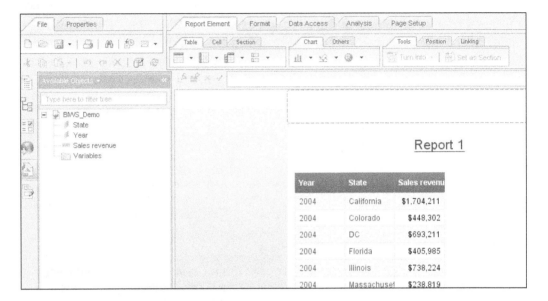

How to do it...

We will first show you how to create a BI Web Service and then how to consume it in SAP BusinessObjects Dashboards.

Creating the BI Web Service

1. Open up the Webi document, right-click on the dataset, and select **Publish as Web Service**.

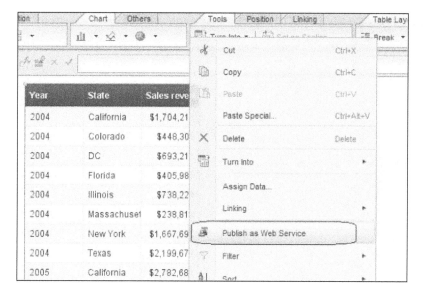

2. You will encounter a series of wizard instructions. Click **Next** until you reach the **Publish Content** menu. Enter a name for your dataset. Then click on the **Set filters...** button to set the appropriate filters on the dataset.

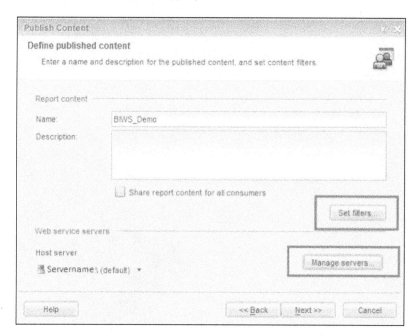

3. Set **Year** as a filter and uncheck the rest. Then click **OK**.

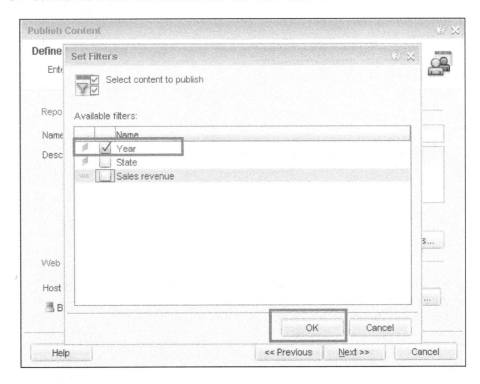

4. Click **Manage servers...** and make sure the correct server setting is in the box.

5. If this is your first BI Web Service, the next window will show an empty tree structure. Click on the folder icon to create the new web service and name it BIWS_Demo.

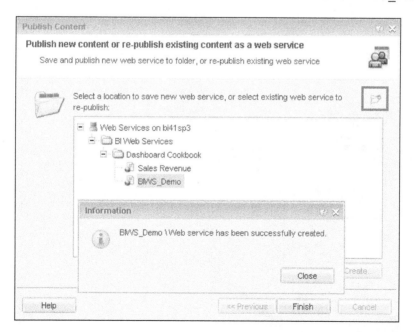

6. Now, if you click on the **Web Service Publisher** icon, on the left you'll be able to see the new BI Web Service that you just created.

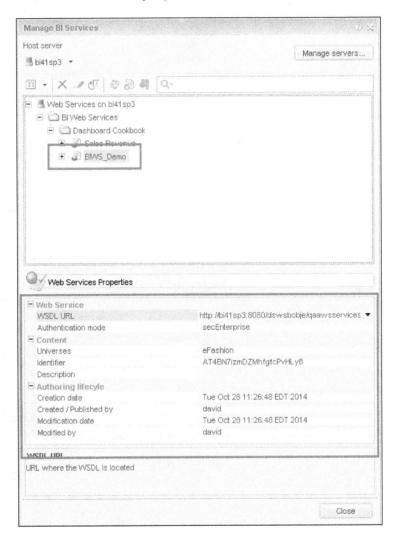

Creating a BI Web Service connection in SAP BusinessObjects Dashboards

1. Click on the **Data Manager** icon and add a **Web service query (Query as a Web Service)*** connection.

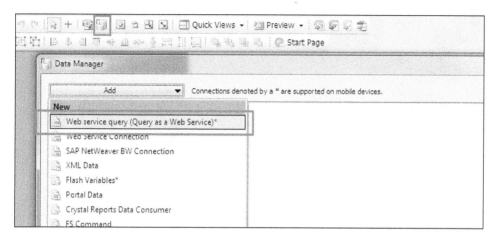

2. Create a **Dropdown** component that allows the user to select a year, which we will use to filter the dataset appropriately.

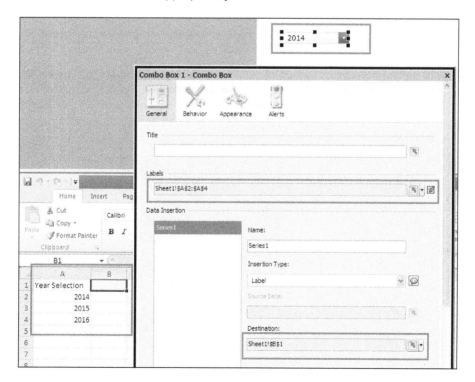

3. Now name the Web service query selection `BIWS_Demo`. On the left-hand input side, bind the value input parameter to the year dropdown output. Set the operator parameter to the value in.

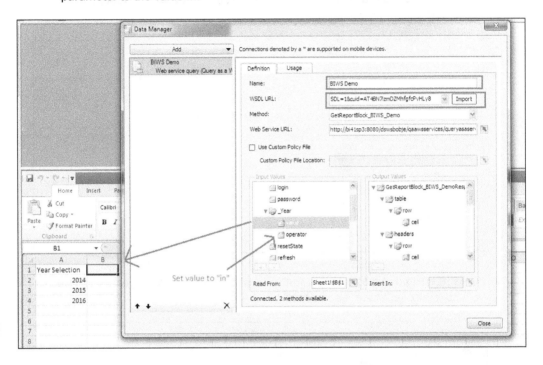

4. Now if you scroll down the input values window, you will see bindings for **refresh** and **getFromLatestDocumentInstance**. Refresh means that the query will execute every time, and **getFromLatestDocumentInstance** means that we will be grabbing the dataset from the latest scheduled instance. In our example, we will just execute the query every time. So set refresh to 1.

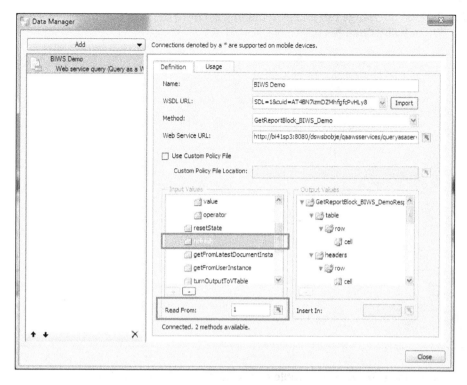

5. In the **Output Values** section on the right, set the output binding for the row. Let's assume that the maximum size we can have for a table is 20 rows. Bind the row output to a 3 x 20 dataset.

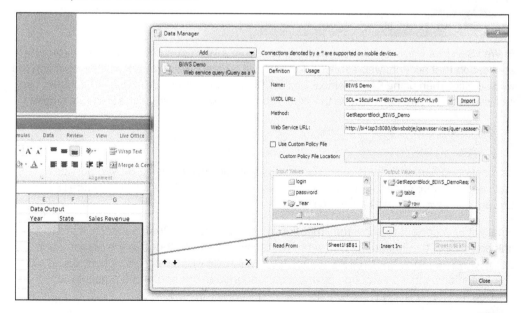

6. Click on the **Usage** tab and bind the trigger cell to the year output cell. Make sure the **When Value Changes** option is selected.

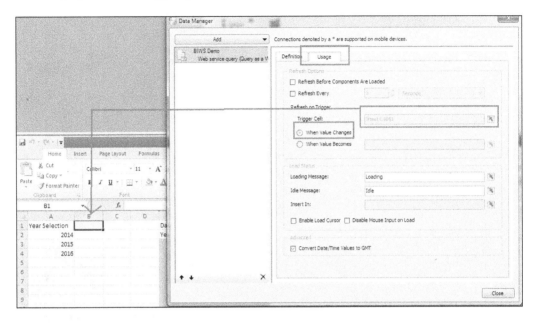

7. Now bind a **Spreadsheet Table** component to the output dataset.

8. Preview the dashboard and you will see that every time the year in the dropdown changes, the data results will also change.

How it works...

BI Web Services works by allowing users to consume a Webi document with any third-party application that accepts web services. In short, we create a Webi report and then publish the web service. Then using SAP BusinessObjects Dashboards or any other application that can call web services, we can retrieve the Webi report data with the appropriate inputs entered.

There's more...

As mentioned earlier, there is drilldown capability in hierarchies using BI Web Services. You can visit `http://blog.davidg.com.au/2011/03/drill-down-in-xcelsius-using-bi.html` to learn how to do so.

Finally, it is important to know the limitations that exist within BI Web Services. A great link on some of the limitations that we have discovered can be found in the presentation at `http://www.scribd.com/doc/94112911/Leveraging-BI-Web-Services`. The limitations and workarounds have been mentioned at the end of the presentation.

Using the SAP NetWeaver BW Connection

With the SAP NetWeaver BW Connection, we can deliver SAP BW data to dashboards that are hosted on the same SAP BW system. With this setup we don't need a separate SAP BusinessObjects BI Platform to host the dashboards, and the connections to source systems.

 The *Using the Query Browser* recipe later in the chapter will demonstrate how to connect to SAP BW data from the SAP BusinessObjects BI Platform, as the workflow is the same as connecting to a Universe.

Getting ready

To set up a connection between SAP BusinessObjects Dashboards and SAP BW, you have to make sure that your SAP installation fulfills the following minimal technical requirements:

- SAP BW 7.01, service pack 05 with ABAP and Java stacks deployed
- SAP BusinessObjects Xcelsius Enterprise 2008 Service Pack 02
- SAP Frontend 7.x installed at client with BI Add-Ons

For this recipe we are using a simple **BEx** Query to connect to.

How to do it...

1. Open a new SAP BusinessObjects Dashboards file. Open the **Data Manager** and add a new **SAP NetWeaver BW Connection**.

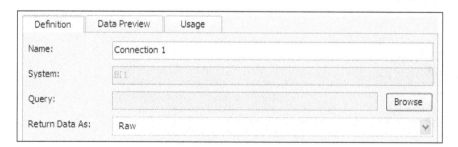

2. Click on the **Browse** button to log in to the SAP BW system. Select the correct SAP BW system, enter your login credentials, and click **OK**.

3. Use the **Find** option to search for your query. Click **Open** to select the query.

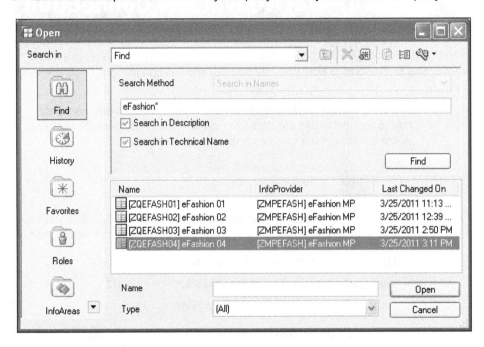

4. Go to the **Data Preview** tab and click the **Refresh Data Preview** button. A preview of the layout of the returned data will now be shown here. In our example, there are seven columns: four characteristics and three key figures.

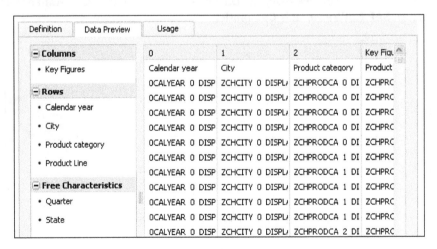

The **Data Preview** tab has the option to rearrange the layout of the output of the BEx Query and add/remove characteristics by using drag and drop.

5. Go back to the **Definition** tab.

6. Select **Cross-Tab Data** from the **Output Values** section and bind it to the spreadsheet. For each column in the **Data Preview** tab (step 4) you need a column in the spreadsheet.

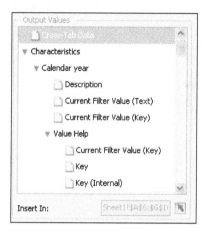

7. Go to the **Usage** tab and select the **Refresh Before Components Are Loaded** option. Close the **Data Manager**.

8. Add a **Spreadsheet Table** component to the canvas and bind it to the same cell range as you did in step 6.

9. If you hit the **Preview** button a message will appear stating that it is not possible to preview this dashboard with BI Query connection data and whether you want to continue. If you hit **Yes**, the dashboard will be previewed without live data from SAP BW.

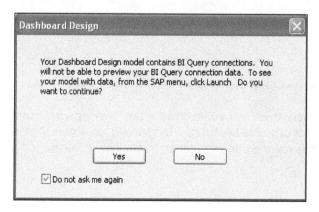

10. For this example, click **No**. The *Publishing to SAP BW* recipe in *Chapter 9, Exporting and Publishing*, covers the Launch function to deploy the dashboard with an active connection to SAP BW.

How it works...

The **SAP NetWeaver BW Connection** enables us to retrieve data from a SAP BW system via a BEx Query. For this example, we used a simple BEx Query we created in the **BEx Query Designer** with four characteristics in the rows and three key figures in the columns. In the properties of the characteristics we defined the **Results Rows** as **Always Suppress** so the output won't include this row.

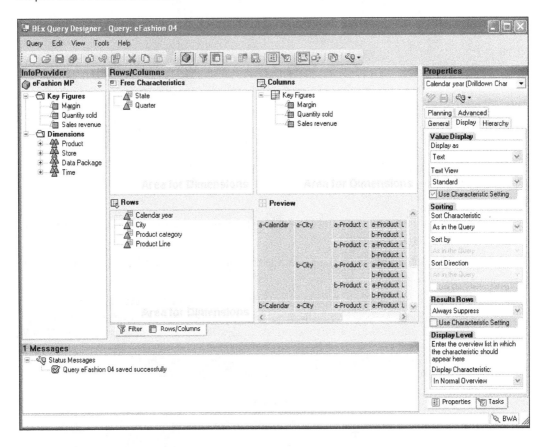

If we run this BEx Query, the result would be as in the following screenshot. The first row shows the headers for the three key figures. The second row shows the headers for the four characteristics. In this row the Unit information for the key figures placed (**EUR**) is also placed when available.

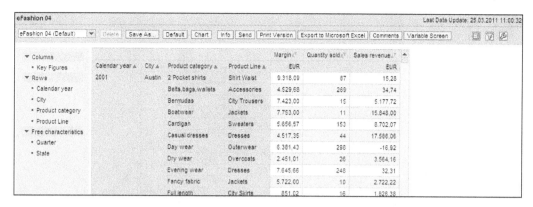

Running the original BEx Query is a great way to get an overview of how the data output will eventually look when setting up the spreadsheet. Moreover, if you are using multiple characteristics and key figures, this will give you a view that is clearer than the **Data Preview** tab in the **Data Manager**.

There's more...

In this section, we will take a detailed look at the options for data input and output in the SAP NetWeaver BW Connection.

Using variables and filters

Just as we have seen how to use prompts in the *Using Query as a Web Service (QaaWS)* recipe, we can use BEx Query variables and filters to fetch a limited set of data by following these steps:

Variables are only available if they are defined in the BEx Query as Input Variables. However, the SAP NetWeaver BW Connection can use any free characteristic from a BEx Query to set filters on. Even the **Key Figures** can be filtered!

1. Go to the **Data Manager**.

2. In the **Output Values** area search for **Variables** and select **Value Help** for the variable you want to use.

3. Bind **Current Filter Value (Key)** to a range of cells. In these cells the values you can choose from will be inserted.

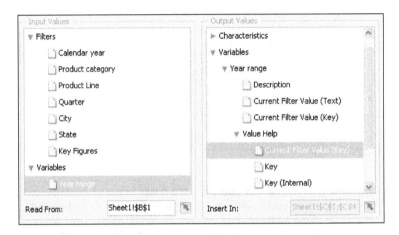

4. In the **Input Values** area select the variable and bind it to a cell. This cell should contain the value that the BEx Query uses as input for the variable.

5. Now add any **Selector** component to the canvas.

6. Bind its **Labels** field to the cell range you bound to in step 3.

7. Set the **Insertion Type** to **Label** and bind the **Destination** field to the same cell as you bound to in step 4.

The procedure for filters is the same as for variables. The only difference is that in the **Output Values** area you need to select the **Characteristics** instead of the **Variables** elements.

If you are using a BEx Query variable that represents a data interval, the value that you use as input for this variable should have the following format: *StartValue - EndValue*, (a space before and after the minus).

For a BEx Query variable that supports the input of multiple values, the input value should have the following format: Value1; Value2; Value3 (a semicolon followed by a space between the values).

You can use the Excel Concatenate function to combine the output of two selectors in a single cell and bind this cell to the variable in the **Input Values** area.

The master data values that we added to the dashboard in steps 2 and 3 of this section contain by default values of posted data. In the **BEx Query Designer**, we can alter this setting in the **Extended** tab of the **Properties** of a characteristic under the **Filter Value Selection at Query Execution** section.

Only Posted Values for Navigation: Only values that are in the result set of the BEx Query are available. This implies that master data values might disappear when a certain filter has been set.

Only Values in InfoProvider: Only the master data values that are in the InfoProvider are used.

Values in Master Data Table: All available master data values of the characteristic will be used, whether they are present in the InfoProvider or not.

Other Output Values

The **Output Values** area includes the following elements:

- ▶ **Cross-Tab Data**: Provides the complete query output
- ▶ **Characteristics**: Provides fields to create a list of values
- ▶ **Variables**: Also provides fields to create a list of values
- ▶ **Static Filter**: Gives information about the filters that have already been created in the BEx Query
- ▶ **Information**: Provides information about the BEx Query itself, like the Query Technical Name or the Last Data Update

▶ **Messages**: Provides BEx Query error messages

Returned data format

The SAP NetWeaver BW connection gives us the option to let the data return as **Raw** or **Formatted**. By default, the **Raw** option is selected, as seen in the following screenshot. If you choose **Formatted**, the BEx format will be used, which means that the data includes information such as the number of decimals and currency.

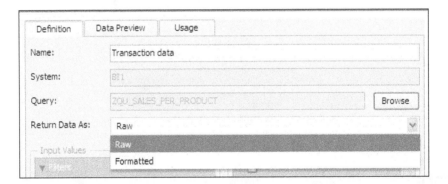

Using the Query Browser

The **Query Browser** feature differs from the other data connection methods in that we can create a query from a Universe or a BEx Query without leaving SAP BusinessObjects Dashboards. Also, with **Query Browser** we can bind the result data not only to the spreadsheet but also directly to the components on the canvas.

Getting ready

Open a new SAP BusinessObjects Dashboards file and activate the **Query Browser** pane from the **View** menu. You will also need a SAP BusinessObjects BI Platform environment with a Universe that you want to connect to.

If you want to connect to a BEx Query, you need an OLAP Connection to a SAP BW system. In the recipe we will follow the workflow for the Universe. In the *There's more...* section of this recipe, we will take a look at connecting to a BEx Query.

> Note that only .unx Universes are supported. You can use the Information Design Tool to convert .unv Universes to .unx.

How to do it...

1. Go to the **Query Browser** pane and click on the **Add Query** button.

2. If you are not already connected to the SAP BusinessObjects BI Platform, a popup will appear asking you to log in. Enter the system and user credentials to log in.

3. You can choose between selecting a **Universe** or a **BEx** query. Choose **Universe**.

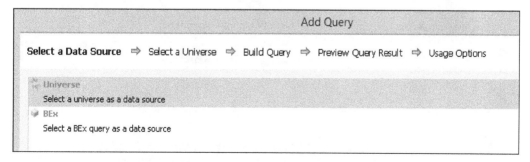

4. A list with available **Universes** appears. Select the Universe you want to use and click **Next**.

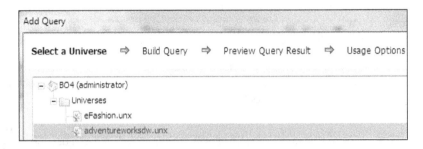

5. In the **Build Query** screen you can define the **Universe** query. Drag a dimension and a measure to the **Result Objects** section.

6. Drag a dimension you want to filter into the **Filter Objects Area**.

7. Set this filter to **Equal to Prompt**. The **Edit Prompt** screen will pop up. **Check Optional** prompt. Click **OK**.

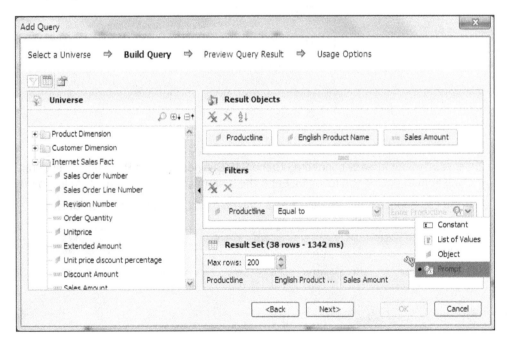

If you are a seasoned Webi developer, you might have noticed that the **Build Query** screen looks a lot like the **Query Panel** in Webi. The Webi version has a lot more advanced features though, such as creating a combined query with union, intersection, or minus nestings.

8. Click the **Next** button to go to the **Preview Query Results** screen.

9. Since we added a prompt, we now need to select a value to fill this prompt to retrieve some preview data. Select a value from the list and click **Run**.

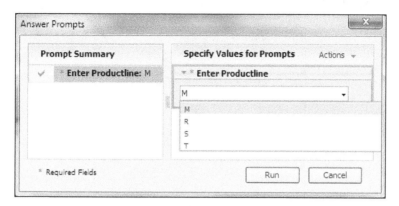

10. The result of the query will be shown now. Click **Next**.

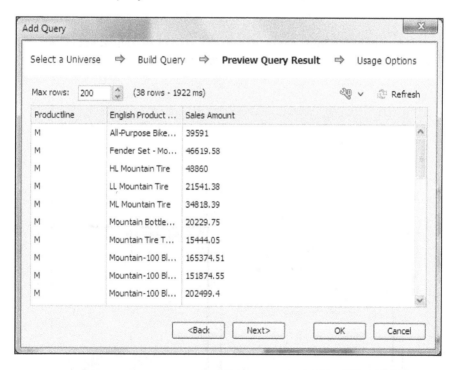

11. The final screen is the **Usage Options** screen, which looks exactly the same as the **Usage** tab in the **Data Manager**. Leave everything with the default values selected and click **OK**.

12. The query will be added to the **Query Browser** pane, including the **Result Objects**, **Filters**, and **Prompts** you selected.

13. Bind each dimension and measure of the **Result Objects** area to a column in the spreadsheet.

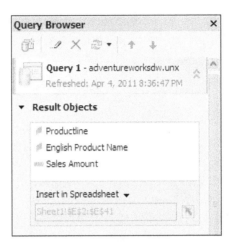

14. Add a **Spreadsheet Table** component to the canvas. Bind its **Display Data** field to the cells you bound the dimensions and measures to in the previous step.

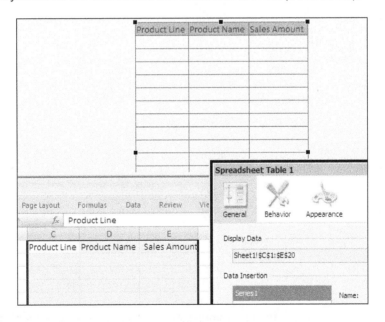

15. Add a **Query Prompt Selector** component from the **Universe Connectivity** category and select the prompt you just created from the **Source Prompt** menu.

You can also select the prompt from the **Query Browser** pane and drag the component into the canvas.

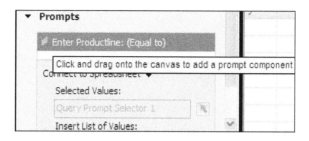

16. At the bottom of the **General** tab you can define whether you want the query to be refreshed after the selection has been made, or after clicking the button. Here you can also change the **Button Label**.

17. Preview the dashboard!

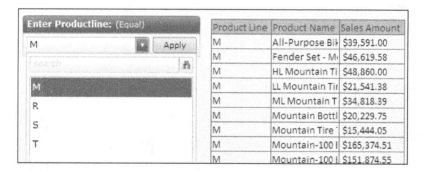

How it works...

The **Query Browser** gives us the opportunity to connect a dashboard to a Universe without leaving SAP BusinessObjects Dashboards to set up QaaWS, Live Office, or a BI Webservice. Also, we don't have to use the spreadsheet in SAP BusinessObjects Dashboards since we can bind the query results directly to the components.

We used the **Query Prompt Selector** component to filter the dataset. The component shows a list of values, and after hitting the **Apply** button the data is refreshed.

From the **Query Browser** we inserted the output of the query into the spreadsheet, from which we used the data to be displayed in a **Spreadsheet Table** component. Of course, you can also add, for example, a chart component and use the **Query Data** option to connect to the result data.

There's more...

In this section, we will look into one more related component and discuss several connectivity options (SAP BW BEx Query, SAP HANA, and SAP ECC).

Query Refresh Button

With the **Query Refresh Button** component, which is also located in the **Universe Connectivity** category, you are able to manually refresh the query. After adding this component to the canvas you need to select the queries that should be refreshed after clicking the button.

SAP BW BEx Query

In step 3 of the primary recipe we chose to connect to a **Universe** instead of a **BEx** query. The workflow with a **BEx** query is almost the same:

1. Instead of choosing **Universe**, choose **BEx** query as a data source.

2. The OLAP Connections that are configured in your SAP BusinessObjects BI Platform are shown now. Select the OLAP Connection to the SAP BW system.

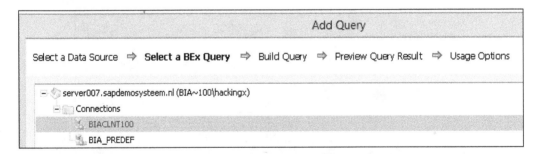

Before a **BEx** query is accessible in the **Query Browser**, the **Allow External Access to this Query** setting has to be enabled in the **BEx Query Designer**. You can find this setting in the **Extended** tab of the **Properties** menu of the BEx query.

3. Now you can select the **BEx** query by either browsing through the **InfoArea** or using the search option. As you can see in the following screenshot, only the first BEx query (**OPT_MP01_Q0003**) is available. The others are grayed out since the **External Access** option isn't switched on yet.

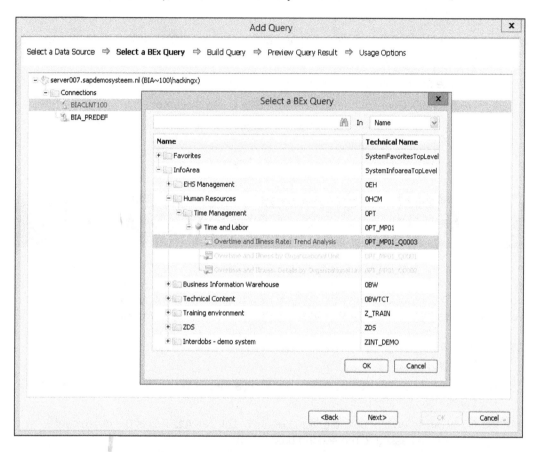

4. You can now continue from step 5 of the primary recipe.

Using SAP HANA as a data source

It is possible to use SAP HANA views (attribute, analytical, or calculation view) as a data source for your dashboard. The only thing you need to do is to create a Universe based on a connection to a SAP HANA system. From there you can reach the Universe in the **Query Browser** in SAP BusinessObjects Dashboards and use it just like any other Universe.

Using SAP ECC tables as a data source

SAP ECC contains its own little SAP BW Client within itself. This provides us with the opportunity to use data directly from SAP ECC tables in SAP BusinessObjects Dashboards. This topic falls a bit outside the scope of this book, so we won't go into detail, but the general steps you have to take are as follows:

1. Activate the SAP BW client within SAP ECC using the RSRTS_ACTIVATE_R3IS program.
2. Create an InfoSet using t-code `SQ02`.
3. Activate the **BI Release** property for the InfoSet using t-code `SQBWPROP`.
4. Create a BEx Query on this InfoSet with **BEx Query Designer**.
5. Create an OLAP Connection in the SAP BusinessObjects Dashboards BI Platform to this BEx Query.
6. Use the **Query Browser** to connect to the BEx Query.

Passing values from dashboard to dashboard with Flash Variables

A common requirement is to be able to have two dashboards interact with each other by passing variables from one dashboard to another. In our example, we have a parent dashboard that encapsulates several children dashboards. In this recipe, we will show you how to pass values from one dashboard to another using **Flash Variables**.

How to do it...

1. Open up a new Dashboard model and drag an **Input Text** component and a **SWF Loader** component into the canvas.
2. Go to the spreadsheet and enter `Company A` in cell **A1**. This is the default value that will be passed to the second dashboard.
3. In cell **A2** type `child.swf?Variable1=` and in cell **A3** type `=CONCATENATE(A2,A1)`.
4. Link the **Input Text** component to cell **A1**. Also make sure you select the **Insert Data On Load** option and bind its **Destination** field to cell **A1**.
5. Bind the **Source URL** field of the **SWF Loader** component to cell **A3**.

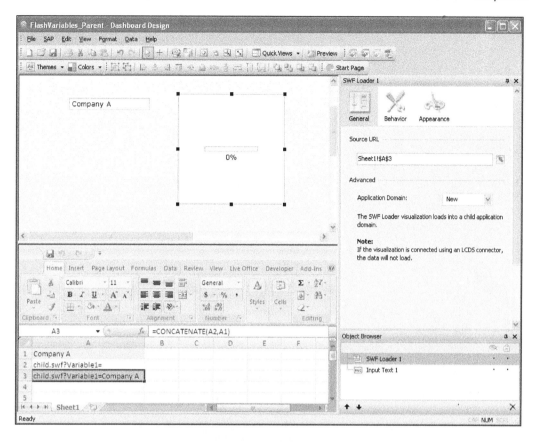

6. Save and export this dashboard to an SWF file. See the *Exporting to SWF, PPT, PDF, and other file types* recipe in *Chapter 9, Exporting and Publishing*, for more information. Name this SWF file `parent.swf`.

7. Open a new SAP BusinessObjects Dashboards file and drag a **Label** component into the canvas.

8. Now bind this **Label** component to cell **A1**.

9. Define this cell as **Named Range Variable1**. See the *Using named ranges* recipe in *Chapter 1, Staying in Control*, for more information on how to do this.

10. Decrease the size of the canvas by clicking the **Fit Canvas to Components** option in the **Standard Toolbar**. You can also find these options in the **View** menu.

11. Your setup should now look like this:

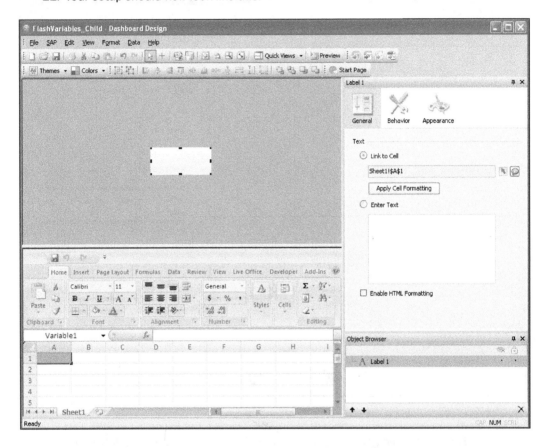

12. Now go to the **Data Manager**. Add a **Flash Variables** connection.

13. Click on the **Import Named Ranges** button. The named range you just created will pop up in the **Ranges** window. You can now close the **Data Manager**.

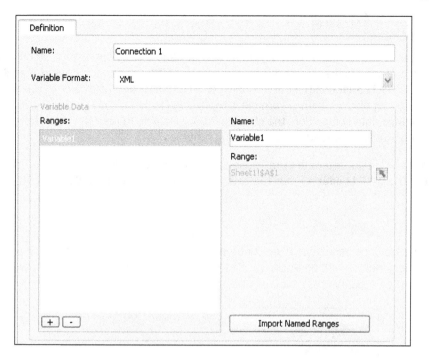

14. Save and export the dashboard to an SWF file. Make sure the name of this file is `child.swf`.

15. Open `parent.swf`. Change Company A into another value, click outside the text input box or hit the *Enter* key, and see what happens.

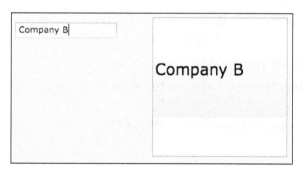

How it works...

We just created two dashboards: a parent dashboard and a child dashboard, where the child dashboard is loaded in the parent dashboard with the **SWF Loader** component. The **Source URL** in this **SWF Loader** component not only points to the location of the child dashboard (`child.swf`) but also contains a variable with a value (`?Variable1=CompanyA`). With a **Flash Variables** data connection, the child dashboard is able to read the value from this variable and put it in a spreadsheet cell during runtime.

We used the Excel Concatenate formula, so each time the variable value changes, a new URL is created. The **SWF Loader** reloads the child dashboard whenever the **Source URL** changes.

There's more...

Using more than one variable is easy. Just repeat the steps of this recipe and make sure you separate the variables with an ampersand (&). For example, a URL with two variables would look like this: `child.swf?Variable1=Value1&Variable=Value2`.

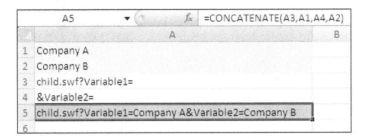

Besides using more than one variable, it is also possible to pass multiple values through a single variable as described in the following steps:

1. Reopen the child dashboard you created earlier.

2. Open the **Data Manager** and select the **Flash Variables** connection you already created.

3. Change the **Variable Format** from **XML** to **CSV**.

4. Bind the **Range** of **Variable1** to cell **A1:A3**. Close the **Data Manager**.

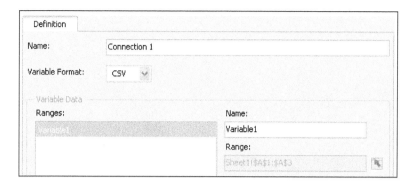

5. Replace the **Label** component with a **Spreadsheet Table** component.
6. Bind this **Spreadsheet Table** component to cells **A1:A3**.
7. Export the dashboard to an SWF file again. Name it `child.swf`.
8. Open the `parent.swf` file.
9. Enter multiple values, separated by a comma (,), and see what happens.

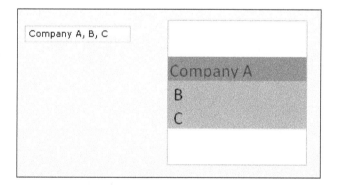

9

Exporting and Publishing

In this chapter, we will cover the following recipes:

- ▶ Exporting to SWF, PPT, PDF, and other file types
- ▶ Publishing to SAP BusinessObjects BI Platform
- ▶ Housing your dashboard in a BI Workspace
- ▶ Publishing to SAP BW
- ▶ Going mobile

Introduction

After creating your dashboard, you will need to publish it into a format that everyone is able to view.

A dashboard model is compiled into a Shockwave Flash (SWF) file format. Compiling to an SWF file format ensures that the dashboard plays smoothly on different screen sizes and across different platforms. It also ensures that users aren't given huge files that are larger than 10 megabytes.

 SWF is an Adobe Flash file format used for multimedia vector graphics and ActionScript. SWF can contain animations or applets of varying degrees of interactivity and function. For more information on SWF, visit `http://en.wikipedia.org/wiki/SWF`.

Developers can publish dashboards to a format of their choice. The available choices include Flash (SWF), HTML, PDF, MS PowerPoint, MS Outlook, MS Word, and the SAP BusinessObjects BI Platform (both desktop and mobile). Once publishing is complete, the dashboard is ready to be shared!

Exporting to SWF, PPT, PDF, and other file types

After developing a visual model in SAP BusinessObjects Dashboards, we will need to somehow share it with users. We want to put it into a format that everyone can see on their machines. The simplest way is to export it to a standard SWF file.

One of the great features SAP BusinessObjects Dashboards has is the ability to embed dashboards into different Microsoft Office file formats. For example, a presenter could have an MS PowerPoint deck, and in the middle of the presentation, have a working dashboard that presents an important set of data values to the audience. Another example could be an executive level user who is viewing an MS Word document created by an analyst. The analyst could create a written document in MS Word and then embed a working dashboard with the most updated data to present important data values to the executive level user.

You can choose to embed a dashboard in the following file types:

- MS PowerPoint (.pptx)
- MS Word (.docx)
- MS Outlook
- PDF (.pdf)
- HTML (.html)

Getting ready

Make sure your dashboard is complete and ready to be shared.

How to do it...

1. In the menu toolbar, go to **File | Export | Flash (SWF)**.

2. Select the directory in which you want the SWF to go to and name your SWF file.

How it works...

SAP BusinessObjects Dashboards compiles the visual model into an SWF file that everyone is able to see. Once the SWF file has been compiled, the dashboard will then be ready for sharing.

 It is mandatory that anyone viewing the dashboard SWF has Adobe Flash installed. If not, they can download and install it from `http://www.adobe.com/products/flashplayer/`.

If we export to MS PowerPoint, we can then edit the PowerPoint file however we desire.

If you have an existing PowerPoint presentation deck and want to append the dashboard to it, the easiest way is to first embed the dashboard SWF to a temporary PowerPoint file and then copy that slide to your existing PowerPoint file.

There's more...

Exporting to an SWF file format makes it very easy for distribution, thus making the presentation of mockups great at a business level. Developers are thus able to work very closely with the business and iteratively come up with a visual model closest to the business goals. It is important though, when distributing SWF files, that everyone viewing the dashboards has the same version, otherwise confusion may occur. Thus, as a best practice, versioning every SWF that is distributed is very important.

Publishing to SAP BusinessObjects BI Platform

Dashboards can be saved to the SAP BusinessObjects BI Platform. The platform hosts the dashboards so that users can easily access them through the BI Launchpad (formerly known as InfoView) or via the SAP BusinessObjects BI Mobile app for mobile dashboards (see the recipe *Going mobile* later in this chapter). Also, administrators can control the dashboard's security on the platform.

Getting ready

Make sure your dashboard is complete and ready for sharing.

How to do it...

1. From the menu toolbar, go to **File** | **Save To Platform** | **Desktop Only**.

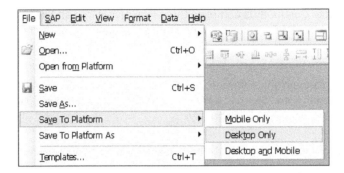

2. Enter your SAP BusinessObjects BI Platform login credentials and then select the location in the SAP BusinessObjects BI Platform system where you want to store the SWF file, as shown in the following screenshot:

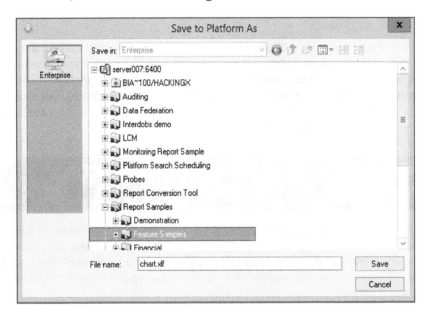

3. Log in to BI Launchpad and verify that you can access and run the dashboard.

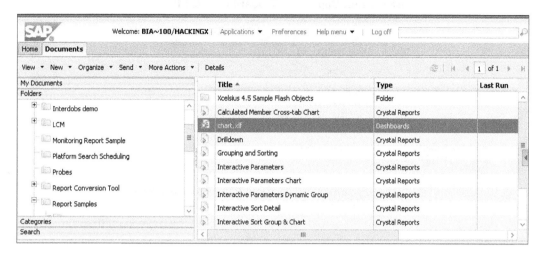

How it works...

When we export a dashboard to the SAP BusinessObjects BI Platform, we store it in the repository. From there, we can control accessibility to the dashboard and make sure that we have one source of of the actual dashboard instead of sending out multiple dashboards through e-mail and possibly getting mixed up with what is the latest version. When we log in to BI Launchpad it also passes the login token to the dashboard, so we don't have to enter our credentials again when connecting to SAP BusinessObjects BI Platform data. This is important because we don't have to manually create and pass any additional tokens once we have logged in.

There's more...

SAP BusinessObjects Dashboards supports saving a dashboard offline at runtime. This means that a user can create an offline snapshot of the dashboard that contains data retrieved at the time of saving and store that copy on their local machine. When doing this, all external data connections are disabled and connectivity-related components, such as the Connection Refresh Button, are also disabled.

Enabling offline dashboards is easy. Go to **File | Document Properties** and select the **Allow This Dashboard to be Used Offline** option.

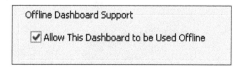

To save the dashboard while running it, right-click anywhere on the background of the dashboard and click **Save Current Copy of Dashboard to Local Disk**.

See also

To give a true website type feel, developers can house their dashboards in a website type format using a **BI Workspace**. This in turn provides a better experience for users, as they don't have to navigate through many folders in order to access the dashboard that they are looking for.

Housing your dashboard in a BI Workspace

Using a BI Workspace (formerly known as Dashboard Builder), which is part of the SAP BusinessObjects BI Platform to organize your dashboards, allows users to customize the look and feel of how dashboards are accessed. In addition, administrators can control access to each navigational layout. When we house dashboards in a BI Workspace, users don't have to navigate through numerous folders in order to reach their desired dashboard, but instead use web page style links to access their dashboard.

In our example, we will set up a BI Workspace, which will contain links to three dashboards.

Getting ready

Make sure you have your dashboards created and saved on the SAP BI Platform. Refer to the previous recipe, *Publishing to SAP BusinessObjects BI Platform*, to learn how to do this. In our example, we use three dashboards, as shown in the following screenshot:

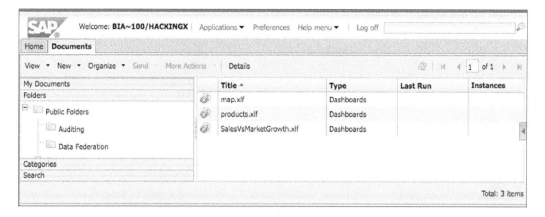

How to do it...

1. Log in to BI Launchpad and choose **BI Workspace** from the **Applications** menu.

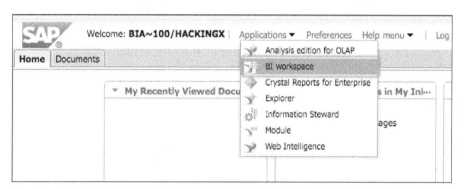

2. Select **Template** from the **Layout** drop-down box. From the **Predefined templates** drop-down box that now appears, select **2 Rows**.

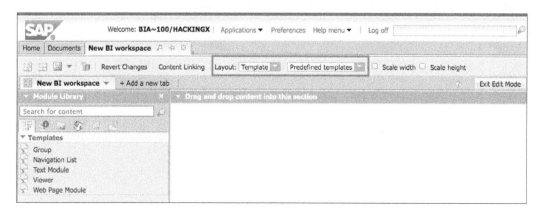

3. In the **Module Library** on the left, click on the **Public Modules** icon (third option). Here you can browse the BI documents on the BI Platform. Drag and drop your dashboards into the two sections.

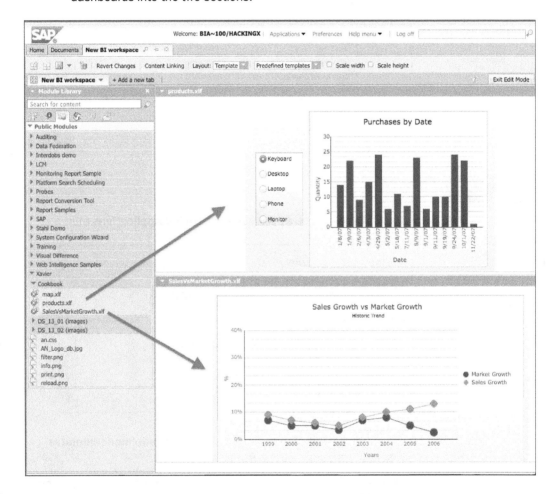

4. Now click the **+ Add a new tab** button and give the new tab a name.

5. Drag the third dashboard into the section.

6. Click on the **Save** button, give your BI Workspace a name, and save it on the BI Platform.

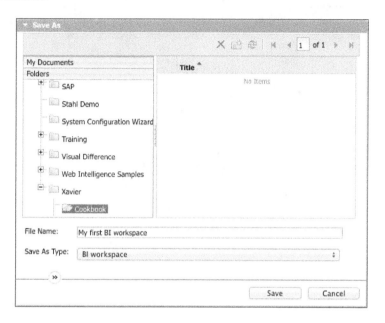

7. Click on the **Exit Edit Mode** button on the upper-right side of the screen. This is how the BI Workspace will look to users:

How it works...

As you can see, when we set up a BI Workspace, it is easier to access the dashboards rather than clicking through a bunch of folders. You can think of a BI Workspace as a container that holds a set of dashboards.

There's more...

There are some more neat things that you can accomplish with BI Workspaces.

Setting a BI Workspace as a home tab for BI Launchpad

In the **General** section of the **Preferences** menu of BI Launchpad, we can define how the **Home tab** for BI Launchpad should look. We can set a BI Workspace as the home tab with the following steps. So, when the user logs in to BI Launchpad, they will instantly see the BI Workspace.

1. Go to the **Preferences** menu of BI Launchpad and select the **General** tab.

2. Deselect **Use Default Settings**.

3. Select the **Home tab** radio option, select **Select Home tab**, and then click on the **Browse Home Tab** button. Now select your BI Workspace and adjust the title text.

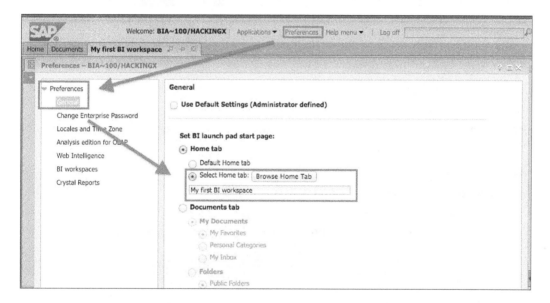

4. Click on **Save & Close** to finish.

5. Log in to BI Launchpad again and you'll see the BI Workspace pop up right away!

Support for other types of BI documents

BI Workspaces not only support dashboards but other BI documents such as Crystal Reports, Web Intelligence Reports, and even websites!

Content linking

A BI Workspace has the option to set up communication between the different documents. This allows the passing of values between documents that are placed on the same tab in a BI Workspace. For example, a selection made in a dashboard can lead to a change of data in a Web Intelligence document.

This feature lies outside the scope of this book, but you can check the BI Workspaces user guide by SAP for more information.

 You can find the *BI Workspaces User Guide* at `http://help.sap.com/businessobject/product_guides/boexir4/en/xi4_bi_workspace_user_en.pdf`.

Publishing to SAP BW

This recipe shows you how to publish a dashboard to a SAP BW system. Once a dashboard is saved to the system, it can be published within a SAP Enterprise Portal iView and made available for users to view.

Getting ready

For this recipe, you will need a completed dashboard. This dashboard does not necessarily have to include a data connection to SAP BW.

How to do it...

1. Select **Publish** in the **SAP** menu. If you want to save the SAP BusinessObjects Dashboards model with a different name, select the **Publish As...** option.

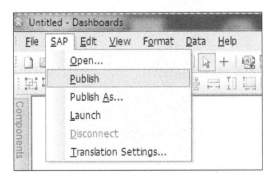

2. If you are not yet connected to the SAP BW system, a pop up will appear. Select the appropriate system and fill in your username and password in the dialog box.

3. If you want to disconnect from the SAP BW system and connect to a different system, select the **Disconnect** option from the **SAP** menu.

4. Enter the **Description** and **Technical Name** of the dashboard. You can choose to save the dashboard as a role or just into your `Favorites` folder. Click on **Save**. The dashboard is now published to the SAP BW system.

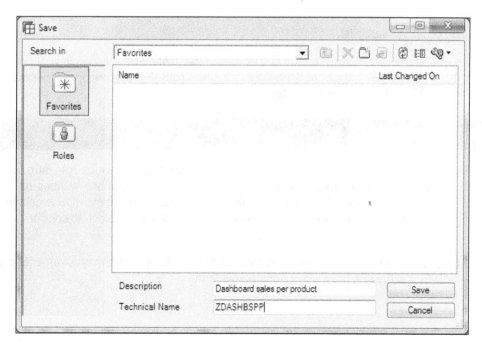

5. To launch the dashboard and view it from the SAP BW environment, select the **Launch** option from the **SAP** menu. You will be asked to log in to the SAP BW system before you can view the dashboard.

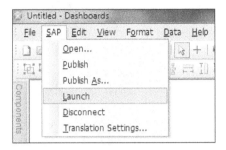

How it works...

As we have seen in this recipe, the publishing of a dashboard to SAP BW is quite straightforward. As the dashboard is part of the SAP BW environment after publishing, the model can be transported between SAP BW systems like all other SAP BW objects.

There's more...

After launching the dashboard in step 5 of this recipe, the dashboard will load in your browser from the SAP BW server. You can add the displayed URL to a SAP Enterprise Portal iView to make the dashboard accessible for portal users.

Going mobile

With SAP BusinessObjects Dashboards 4.0 Service Pack 5, a big new feature was introduced: mobile dashboards. This feature enables the creation of HTML5-compatible dashboards that can be viewed on mobile devices such as the iPad. Instead of using the mouse pointer to interact with the dashboard, the user can now tap, touch, drag, and pinch to control the dashboard.

In this recipe, we will create a mobile dashboard and have a look at all the requirements and the supported and the unsupported options of this feature.

Getting ready

To work with mobile dashboards, we need to meet the following requirements:

- SAP BusinessObjects Dashboards 4.0 Service Pack 5 or higher
- SAP BusinessObjects BI Platform 4.0 Service Pack 5 or higher, with mobile server deployed
- SAP BusinessObjects Mobile app for iOS or Android

 You can download the latest version of the SAP BusinessObjects Mobile app from the Apple App Store (iOS) or the Google Play Store (Android).

In this recipe, we will use a simple dashboard with some charts but without any connections.

How to do it...

1. First, we want to preview the dashboard to see how it would look in a mobile format. In the menu toolbar, go to **File | Preview | Mobile (Fit to Screen)** or use the button in the standard toolbar.

2. We can now check the look and interactions of the mobile dashboard. Click on a bar or a point on any chart to see how the mouseover values are displayed.

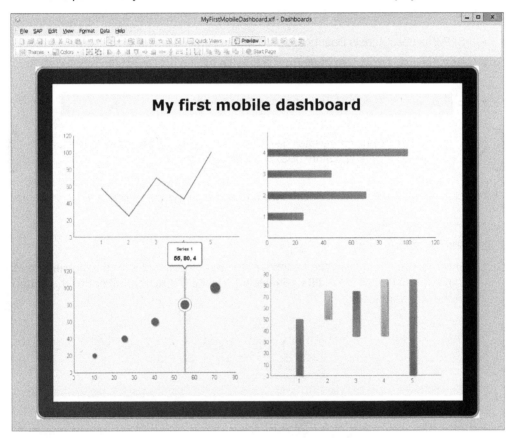

3. Leave the preview mode. Next, we are going to save our dashboard to the SAP BusinessObjects BI Platform. In the menu toolbar, go to **File** | **Save To Platform** | **Mobile Only**. Log in to the platform and select the location where you want to save the dashboard. Click the **Save** button to finish.

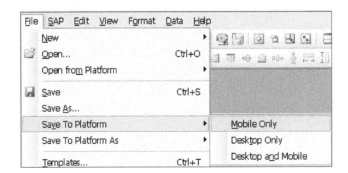

If you want the dashboard to be available both as a mobile dashboard and a traditional desktop that is run through BI Launchpad, select the **Desktop and Mobile** option.

4. Grab your iPad or other mobile device and fire up the SAP BusinessObjects Mobile app. Log in to your SAP BusinessObjects BI Platform. You will see the dashboard that we just saved pop up on top.

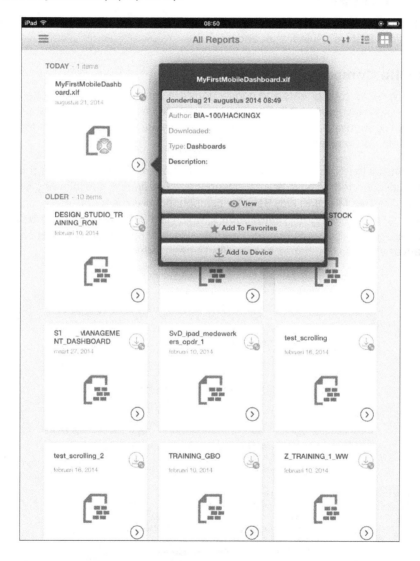

5. Click on the **View** button to start the dashboard.

How it works...

Mobile dashboards are not exported to an SWF file, but to an HTML5-compatible object. We need the SAP BusinessObjects Mobile app to run the dashboard from the SAP BusinessObjects BI Platform.

There's more...

There are some neat features that can be accomplished with mobile dashboards as well as some limitations that we will talk about now.

The Mobile Compatibility panel

Unfortunately, not all components and connections are supported with mobile dashboards. When we use such a component it will simply be excluded from the mobile dashboard and the connection will obviously not work. To check whether we are using an unsupported item, we can use the Mobile Compatibility panel.

This panel lists all the components and connections that are used and notes if they are supported, unsupported, or have several unsupported features. In the following example, we can see that the Tree Map and Play Selector components aren't supported. The Combo Box has a few unsupported features. **Connection 1**, which is a SAP BW connection created with the Data Manager, is also not supported. We can also see that a recommendation is given for the canvas sizing so that it matches the iPad screen format.

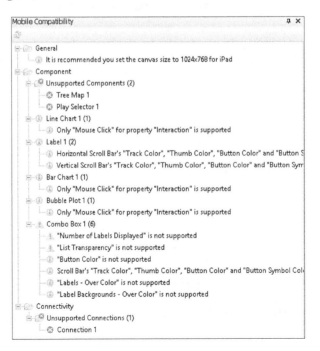

The following connection types are supported in mobile dashboards:

- ▸ All connections created with the Query Browser
- ▸ Web service query (Data Manager)
- ▸ Flash Variables (Data Manager)
- ▸ External Interface Connection

 The supported Data Manager connections are denoted by an asterisk in the Data Manager.

Also, only the Nova theme is supported and you have to make sure that you only use fonts with (iOS5+) appended.

 A detailed overview of all supported components and their specific unsupported properties or features can be found in the **Help | Dashboards Help** menu, under **Mobile support | Supported components in mobile dashboards**.

Sharing and annotating dashboards from the SAP BusinessObjects Mobile app

A nice feature of the SAP BusinessObjects Mobile app is that it not only lets us view the dashboard, but also allows us to make annotations to it and share it through e-mail and SAP StreamWork.

1. In the upper-right corner of the screen, click on the settings button to enable the option bar.

2. Click on **Annotate**. Here you can add lines and text, crop sections, and even add a voice memo to the dashboard.

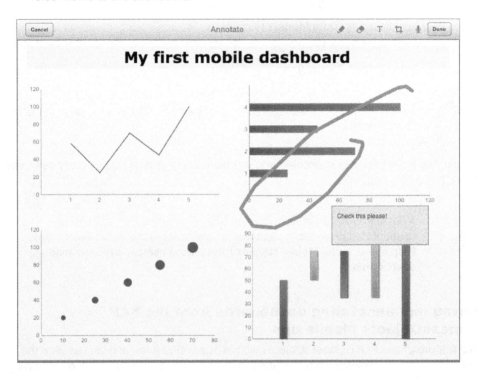

3. Click on **Done**. Now two new buttons will appear: **Email** and **StreamWork**. By clicking on one of these buttons, you can share a print of the dashboard, including the annotations you just made.

10
Top Third-party Add-ons

In this chapter, we will cover the following recipes:

- ▸ Managing add-ons in SAP BusinessObjects Dashboards
- ▸ Connecting to CSV files with the CSV Connector
- ▸ Integrating Google Maps with the CMaps plugin
- ▸ Connecting to Salesforce.com with DashConn
- ▸ Presenting micro charts in a Tree Grid
- ▸ Integrating Web Intelligence with Antivia XWIS Advantage Express
- ▸ Advanced printing with Xcelsius Dashboard Printer
- ▸ SUCCESS with graphomate charts

Introduction

As we have seen throughout this book, SAP BusinessObjects Dashboards gives us an almost overwhelming package of tools to create the most stunning dashboards. Even this may not be enough for your specific dashboard. With SAP BusinessObjects Dashboards, SDK (short for software development kit) developers are able to create add-ons for SAP BusinessObjects Dashboards to provide that extra functionality that does not come with the original software.

This chapter will discuss several of the top third-party SAP BusinessObjects Dashboards add-ons that are available. Some of them can be downloaded for free while others need to be purchased. Without exception, all these add-ons are free to try out before you make the decision to buy one or not. We will not discuss all third-party add-ons that are available at the moment, as there are simply too many of them. We had to limit ourselves to those add-ons that stand out the most and are the most applicable to a large number of users.

The recipes in this chapter will not be as detailed as the other recipes in this book. The goal of this chapter is to give you a quick introduction to the basic functionality of the add-ons and how to set them up. After reading a recipe, you should have a good understanding of the possibilities of the add-on and whether it might be interesting for you to spend more time on it or not. We will also direct you towards useful resources for more information on each add-on.

Managing add-ons in SAP BusinessObjects Dashboards

In this recipe, we will show you where you can find third-party add-ons and how to add and remove them in SAP BusinessObjects Dashboards. Dashboard add-ons will consist of the `.xlx` extension.

Getting ready

To install an add-on, you'll first need to download it. The following recipes in this chapter will guide you to the right places to get these files.

If you are using Windows Vista, you must turn off **User Account Control (UAC)**, otherwise the **Add-On Manager** menu items will be disabled. To do so, go to **Start | Control Panel | User Accounts | Turn User Account Control on or off**.

How to do it...

1. To add or remove add-ons, use the **Add-On Manager**. Go to the **File** menu and select **Manage Add-Ons**.

2. The **Add-On Manager** will pop up and show which add-ons are already installed. If you have already downloaded an add-on, you can click on the **Install Add-On** button. Browse to the add-on's XLX file and open it. The add-on will be installed instantly. You need to restart SAP BusinessObjects Dashboards to use the new add-on(s).

3. If you want to remove an add-on, first select the add-on and click on the **Remove Add-On** button. Confirm the removal and the add-on will be deleted from your SAP BusinessObjects Dashboards installation.

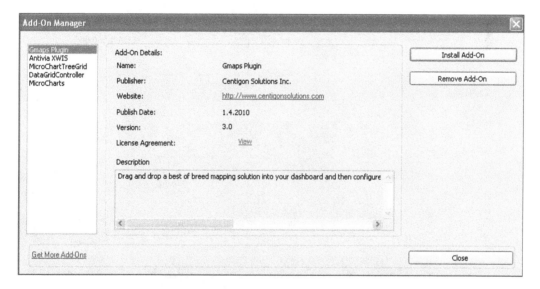

4. A good place to find add-ons is the SAP Store (`http://store.sap.com/`). On this website, you can find certified solutions not only for SAP BusinessObjects Dashboards, but also for other SAP enterprise applications. Since the add-ons don't have their own category, you could search for `Xcelsius` to get the most results.

The reason why it is best to search for Xcelsius is that SAP BusinessObjects Dashboards was recently rebranded and most add-ons were initially developed for Xcelsius. Also, SAP BusinessObjects Dashboards as a search term may lead to generic search results.

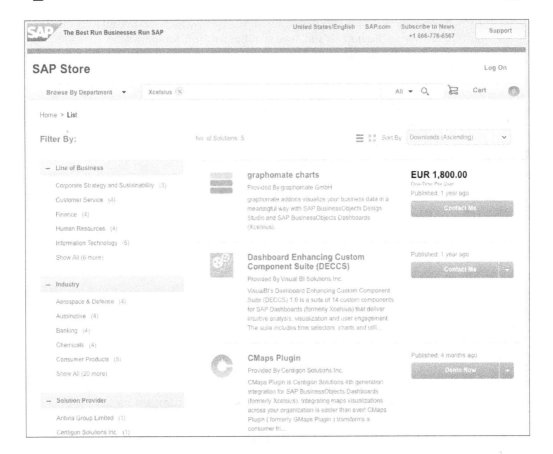

5. Another place to find and download add-ons is on developer websites. In each recipe of this chapter, we will guide you to these sites.

Connecting to CSV files with the CSV Connector

In *Chapter 8, Dashboard Data Connectivity*, we discussed a number of data connectivity options for dashboards in SAP BusinessObjects Dashboards. In addition to these standard data connections, Centigon Solutions has developed an add-on that allows us to use **Comma Separated Value** (**CSV**) files to grab data from. This recipe will give you a quick walkthrough of the features of this add-on.

Getting ready

Go to the Centigon Solutions website (`http://www.centigonsolutions.com/`) and browse for `CSV Connector`. Download the free trial and install it with the **Add-On Manager**. You also need a sample CSV file to use in this recipe.

How to do it...

1. Open a new SAP BusinessObjects Dashboards file and go to the spreadsheet area. Enter the location of the CSV file in cell **C1**.

2. Open the **Data Manager** and click on the **Add** button. Under **Add-On connection**, you will see the **CSV Connector**. Select it.

3. Give this connection a name. Bind the **CSV Data URL** field to cell **C1**.

4. Also, check the **Delimiter** setting. This should match the format of your CSV file.

5. Go to the **Data Preview** tab and click on the **Preview Data** button. The data from the CSV file will now be shown. Note that the number of columns and rows is displayed as well.

If nothing happens, your CSV file location may be wrong or a different delimiter may have been used in the CSV file. The use of a forward slash (/) or backward slash (\) in the URL is also a common cause as \ is used for the local network and / is used for SharePoint.

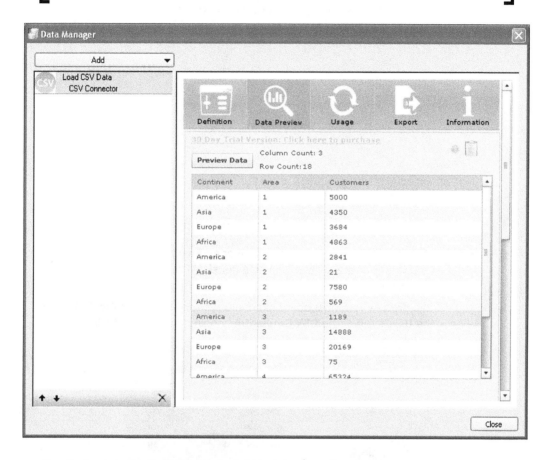

6. Go back to the **Definition** tab and bind the **Data Destination** field to a range of cells that match the format, as shown in the **Data Preview** tab.

7. Now add a filter on the dataset in the CSV file. Bind the **Filter Columns** field to a range of cells with the same number of columns as the data destination range. Close the **Data Manager**.

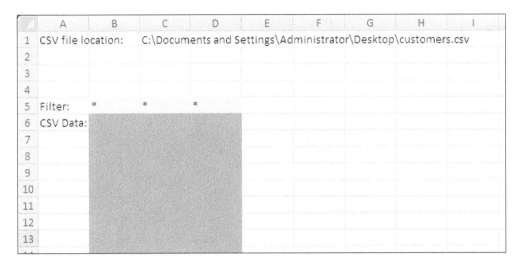

8. You can now set up a **Combo Box** component or another **Selector** component to change the values of these cells. Use an asterisk (*) as a wildcard to show all records in a column.

9. If you want to preview your dashboard, do not forget to select the **Refresh On Load** option in the **Usage** tab of the **CSV Connector** connection in the **Data Manager**.

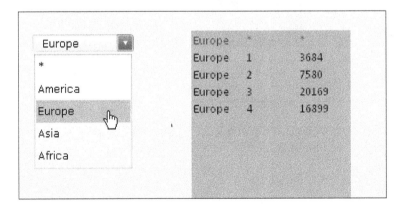

How it works...

The **CSV Connector** add-on from Centigon Solutions is an ideal data connector to handle input from CSV files if you do not have the option to use server data providers such as QaaWS or SAP BW. Especially for smaller enterprises, this is a very good solution to provide dashboards with fresh data. In addition, when comparing a CSV to an XLS data source, CSV files have no row limit, whereas XLS files are restricted to 1 million rows.

A nice feature of this component is the ability to preview the data in the data manager. This will help you to set up the component without having to preview the dashboard every time to check out how the data will be loaded in the spreadsheet.

In this recipe, we showed how to filter the dataset of the CSV file. You can use this option to load only the data you will actually need, which will improve the performance of the dashboard. Furthermore, in the **Data Output Definition** tab of this add-on in the **Data Manager**, you can define which columns and rows should be loaded.

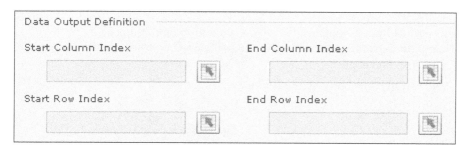

 If you filter a column, that column must be part of the output.

There's more...

Besides displaying the data from a CSV file and filtering the values, the **CSV Connector** add-on can also do some calculations as described in the following steps:

1. Add another row above the **Data Destination** area. There are four calculation values. Enter a calculation value for each column as follows:

   - **Column 1**: Lists the values separated by a comma
   - **Column 2**: Counts the number of rows
   - **Column 3**: Calculates the sum of values
   - **Column 4**: Calculates the average of values

2. Next, enter a single-value index that indicates which column the calculations are applied on.

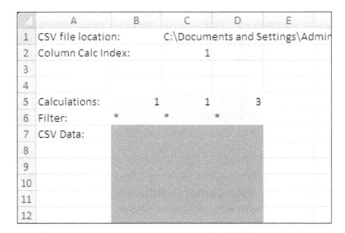

3. Open the **Data Manager** and bind the **Column Calculations** field and the **Column Calculation Index** field to the corresponding cells you just entered in the spreadsheet.

4. Preview the dashboard to try this functionality.

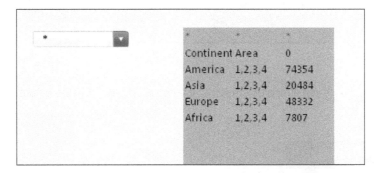

The **CSV Connector** add-on also includes a component that is able to export a data range from a dashboard to a CSV file or to the clipboard. To learn more about this feature, visit the Centigon Solutions website at http://www.centigonsolutions.com/.

Integrating Google Maps with the CMaps plugin

In the *Using maps to select data of an area or country* recipe in *Chapter 3, From a Static to an Interactive Dashboard*, we introduced the standard map options that SAP BusinessObjects Dashboards offers. Then, in the *Displaying alerts on a map* recipe in *Chapter 5, Using Alerts*, we discussed how to use alerts on these maps. Centigon Solutions raised the bar on this topic and introduced the CMaps plugin for SAP BusinessObjects Dashboards.

With this add-on, we can completely integrate Google Maps in a dashboard in SAP BusinessObjects Dashboards. This means that we can use the graphics we know from Google Maps (map, satellite, hybrid, terrain, and so on) and functionalities such as zooming in or out on a map. Furthermore, the CMaps plugin integrates with other SAP BusinessObjects Dashboards components. We can make selections from a map region and display alerts, single points (such as cities or buildings), and heat maps on the map.

This recipe will introduce you to this add-on and show you how to create a map with alerts and selectable regions.

Getting ready

This recipe needs some preparation. First, go to the CMaps plugin website (`http://www.cmapsplugin.com/`) and request the CMaps plugin add-on trial. You'll receive an e-mail with a download link and a trial key. Install the add-on with the **Add-On Manager**.

Next, we need a so-called shapefile. This provides the overlay for a geographical area. There are lots of free SHP files available on the Internet; for example, SHP files can be found at `http://centigonknowledge.com/tutorial/shape-data-explorer-and-download-manager/`.

Download the ZIP archive of any shapefile you want to use and extract it. The extracted folder includes at least the SHP file, a DBF file, and an SHX file.

In this recipe, we will use a shapefile of Europe, but the steps are the same for shapefiles of other regions.

How to do it...

1. Open MS Excel and go to **Open**.
2. Set **Files of type** to **All Files**.

3. Browse for the DBF file and open it.

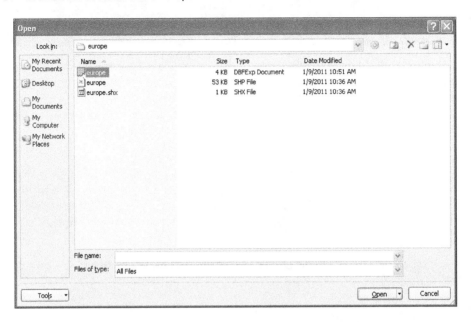

4. A spreadsheet with a list of countries will appear, including some additional, country-specific data.

5. Save the file as an Excel Workbook.

6. Open SAP BusinessObjects Dashboards and import the Excel file you just created by selecting **Import** from the **Data** menu:

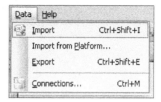

Or by clicking on the **Import** button:

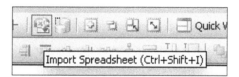

7. A pop up will appear stating that you will lose everything in your existing spreadsheet. As we opened a blank SAP BusinessObjects Dashboards file, we can click on **Yes**.

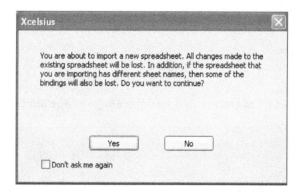

8. Insert five rows above the data from the DFB file. Right-click on row **1** and select **Insert**. Repeat this four times.

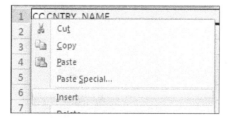

9. Enter your CMaps trial key in spreadsheet cell **C1**.

10. Drag the **CMaps Plugin** component to the canvas. You will find this component at the bottom of the **Maps** section.

11. Bind the **Key** field of the CMaps plugin to cell **C1**. The **CMaps Plugin** component will now change into a real Google Map of the world.

12. Enter the location of the SHP file in cell **C2**.

	A	B	C	D	E	F	G	H	I
1	GMAPS API Key:		ABQIAAAAg1LhVivPWJy5RTpx5QZWVhT7baK43PfWUhem6_3pYhbuy5V60hS7						
2	Shapefile url:		C:\Documents and Settings\Administrator\Desktop\europe\europe.shp						
3									
4									
5									
6	AL	Albania	3416945	Lek	ALL	AL			
7	AD	Andorra	55335	Peseta	ADP	AN			
8	AT	Austria	7755406	Schilling	ATS	AU			
9	BE	Belgium	10032460	Franc	BEF	BE			
10	BA	Bosnia an	2656240			BK			
11	BG	Bulgaria	8943258	Lev	BFL	BU			
12	DK	Denmark	4667750	Danish Kr	DKK	DA			

13. Select the **Shape Data** option and bind the **Single shape file URL** field to cell **C2**.

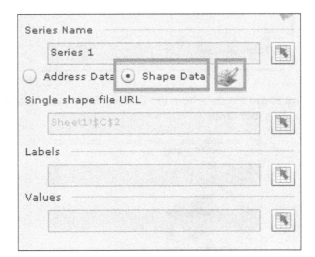

14. Click on the button on the right of **Shape Data** to open the **Shape Data Options** screen. Here, select **Shape File URL** and click on **OK**.

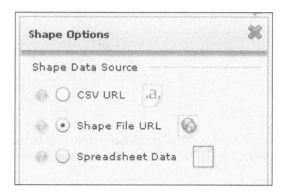

15. If you now hit the **Preview** button, the shapefile for Europe should be visible on top of the Google Map.

 The shapefile will not appear in **Preview** mode if you are using a relative path.

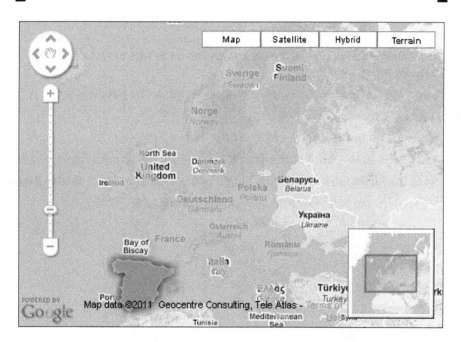

16. Now return to the properties pane of the **CMaps Plugin** component and bind the **Labels** field and the **Values** field to the corresponding cells in the spreadsheet.

17. Set **Insertion Type** to **Row** and bind the **Source Data** field to the cells we just bound to the **Labels** and **Values** fields. Also bind the **Destination** field to cell range **B4:C4**.

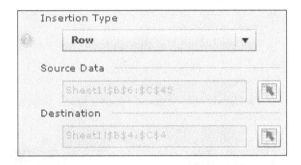

18. Add a **Gauge** component to the canvas and bind the **Title** field to cell **B4** and the **Data By Range** field to cell **C4**.

19. Select the **CMaps Plugin** component again and go to the **Behavior** tab.

20. Deselect **Dynamic Zoom**.

21. Bind the **Pan to Location** field to cell **C3**.

22. Enter 54.52596, 15.25512 in cell **C3**. These are the coordinates for mid-Europe.

23. Go to the **Alerts** tab in the **CMaps Plugin** properties pane. Select **Enable Alerts**.

24. Select **By Value** and set the number of **Alert Levels** to **6**.

25. Now edit the limits by double-clicking on the **Limit** values. If you click on the **Refresh** button, your changes will already be shown in the component.

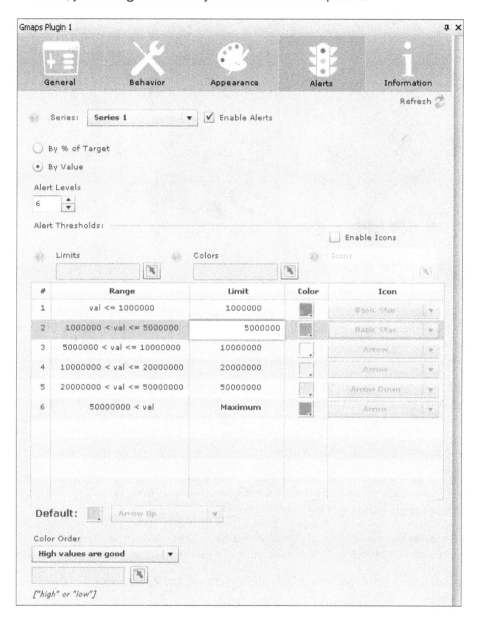

26. Preview and explore the dashboard.

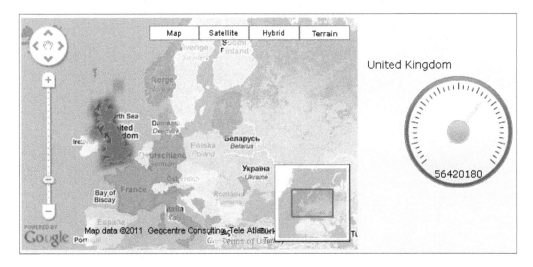

How it works...

This recipe required a lot of preparation before we could perform the actual binding of the data to the **CMaps Plugin** component. In this recipe, we showed you how to use SHP files. These files provide a layer on top of the Google Map. This layer enables us to make regions selectable or fill them with colors to show alerts.

The DBF file provided us with the metadata on the SHP file (that is, the country codes and names). After importing this information into the spreadsheet, the setup of the **CMaps Plugin** component has a lot of similarities with the configuration of standard SAP BusinessObjects Dashboards **Map** components, as we discussed in *Chapter 3, From a Static to an Interactive Dashboard*, and *Chapter 5, Using Alerts*.

The SHX file can be used to combine SHP and DBF files for GIS solutions, where this file is required to maintain the integrity between the files when used in GIS solutions. The CMaps plugin does not utilize this SHX file.

In the **Behavior** tab, we entered the coordinates for Europe, so the map, by default, showed Europe. You can find these coordinates at http://www.map-gps-coordinates.com/.

In addition, if you want to zoom in or out, you can change the **Zoom Level**.

Setting up the alerts in the CMaps plugin works just like configuring the **Alerts** tab in standard SAP BusinessObjects Dashboards components, with the addition that you can also use icons as alerts in the **CMaps Plugin** component.

There's more...

This recipe only covered a few of the possibilities of this add-on. Check out the CMaps plugin website (`http://www.cmapsplugin.com/`) to learn more about the other features. Here you can also find a lot of tutorials, articles, videos, templates, and samples.

Connecting to Salesforce.com with DashConn

What about using live data from your Salesforce.com reports in SAP BusinessObjects Dashboards to create interactive dashboards to show, track, and analyze your sales activities? **DashConn** is an add-on by IdeaCrop for SAP BusinessObjects Dashboards that delivers this integration. Let's have a look at the features of this add-on and how to set it up.

Getting ready

As we are connecting to Salesforce.com, you will obviously need a Salesforce.com Developer account. You can sign up for a free account at `http://developer.salesforce.com/signup`.

To connect to Salesforce.com from a dashboard in SAP BusinessObjects Dashboards, you will require a security token. You can get this security token from the **Personal Setup** menu at Salesforce.com.

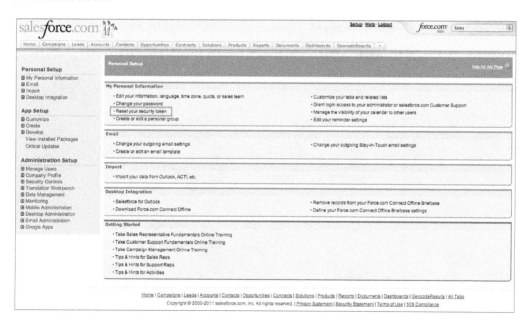

You can download a free trial version of the DashConn add-on from the IdeaCrop website, `http://www.ideacrop.com/`.

How to do it...

1. Open a new SAP BusinessObjects Dashboards file and drag the **Salesforce.com DataViewer** component onto the canvas.

2. Go to the **Reports** tab and enter your Salesforce.com credentials. A list with your Salesforce.com reports will appear.

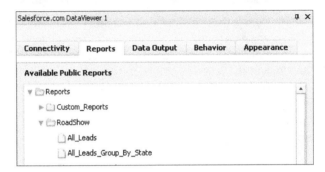

3. Select the report you want to use. A loading message will appear.

4. Now go to the **Data Output** tab and bind the **Main result destination** field to spreadsheet cell range **A6:D20**.

5. Bind the **Selection destination** field to cell range **G6:K20**.

6. Make sure that the **Place column names in the first row** option is selected. We can use these column names later on when we add some chart components and have to bind the series names.

7. Preview the dashboard to see how the data is being returned (and filled in the spreadsheet cells that we bound in step 4). You will be asked to fill in your credentials.

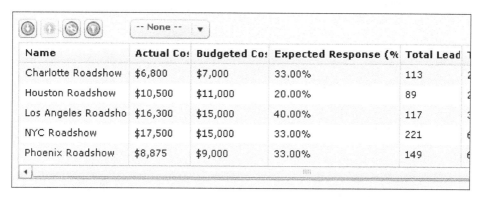

8. Leave the **Preview** mode and drag a **Column Chart** component to the canvas.

9. Bind the **Column Chart** component to the columns you want to show in the chart. Remember that the first row will show the column names. Also, do not forget to select the **Ignore Blank Cells** options in the **Behavior** tab of the chart component. In this recipe example, we are showing two series: **Actual Costs** and **Budgeted Costs**.

10. Now add another chart to the canvas and bind it to one or more columns from the **Selection destination** area (step 5). In this recipe example, we want to show the **Total Leads** in a **Bar Chart**.

11. Preview the dashboard. As you will see, the **Column Chart** will display data right away. If you select a row in the **Salesforce.com DataViewer** component, the **Bar Chart** will also be filled.

You can use *Ctrl* and click or *Shift* and click to select multiple rows.

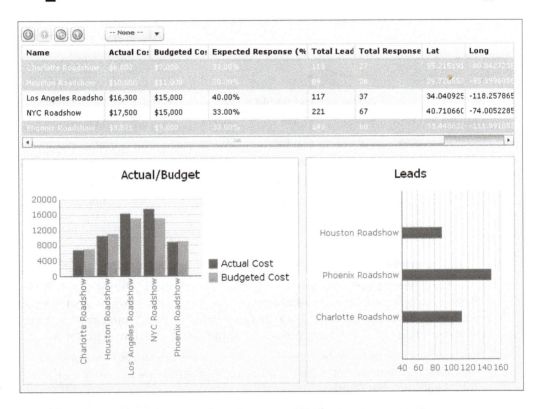

12. Leave the **Preview** mode and add a **Horizontal Slider** component to the canvas.

13. Bind the **Data** field of this component to cell **C1**.

14. Select the **Salesforce.com DataViewer** component again and go to the **Data Output** tab.

15. We want to filter the records based on the value in the **Total Responses** column. To do this, select the correct column from the **Prompt Column** selector and bind the **Prompt Value** field to cell **C1**. For the **Prompt Operator** selector, we select **greaterOrEqual**.

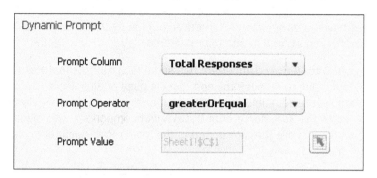

16. Preview the dashboard once more.

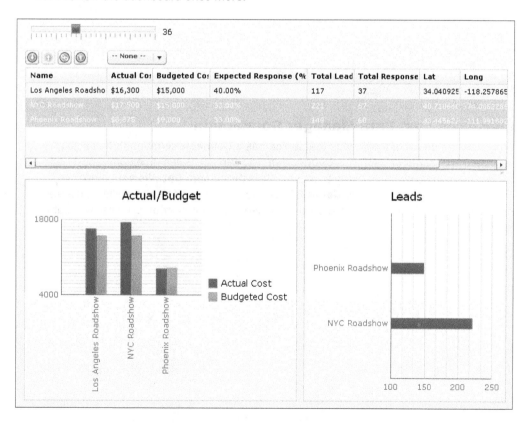

How it works...

The **Salesforce.com DataViewer** component does most of the work for us. As you have seen, we only had to enter our Salesforce.com credentials, select a report, and preview the dashboard to see how the data will be returned. After binding the fields of the **Data Output** tab, we can reuse the report data in other components.

The **Salesforce.com DataViewer** component has some nice runtime features to drill down or up in the report data, open the Salesforce.com details page of all selected items, set filters, and aggregate data by a certain field. With these options, you can dynamically change the data being retrieved by the **Salesforce.com DataViewer** component. This also means that the values in spreadsheet cells that are bound to the Main result destination field in the **Data Output** tab change as well.

There's more...

To conclude this recipe, we will discuss two more options: the **Data Manager Connection** and **Working Mode** settings.

Salesforce.com Data Manager Connection

A very nice feature of this add-on is that it also has a **Connection** option that is available from the **Data Manager**. With this **Connection**, you can use Salesforce.com report data in your dashboards without having to use the **Salesforce.com DataViewer** component. Another important feature of the **Connection** option is that it offers the ability to constantly refresh data from Salesforce.com reports—just like other **Connection** options—without being prompted for credentials.

Except for the **Usage** tab, most settings are similar to those of the **Salesforce.com DataViewer** component.

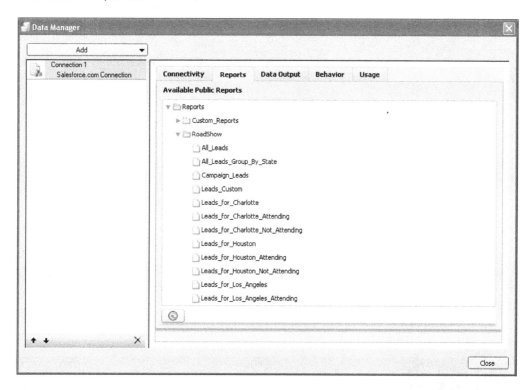

Working Mode settings

In the **Behavior** tab of the component and **Data Manager Connection**, you can find the **Working Mode** setting, as seen in the following screenshot. In the default **Online** setting, an Internet connection is required to use the component to connect to Salesforce.com. In **Offline** mode, the (first level of) report data is embedded within the dashboard.

The third **Online/ fallback to Offline** mode is a combination of the online and offline modes and will try to retrieve live data first; but if this fails, it uses the embedded data.

Presenting micro charts in a Tree Grid

The **Micro Chart Suite** is an extensive set of small charting components by Inovista. It includes a micro version of most of the chart types that are part of the standard SAP BusinessObjects Dashboards components: **Bar Chart**, **Area Chart**, **Stacked Bar Chart**, **Bullet Chart**, **Column Chart**, **Line Chart**, and **Pie Chart**. In addition, there are components to show micro versions of a plot chart, win/lose chart, shape alerts, a traffic light, and a text/number indicator.

While you can use these components separately, a nice feature by Inovista is the **Tree Grid** component in which we can present micro charts in a hierarchical format. This recipe shows you how to set up the **Tree Grid** component with a few micro charts.

Getting ready

Go to the Inovista website (`http://www.inovista.com/`), browse for the trial downloads section, and download the **Micro Chart Suite**. Install the components with the **Add-On Manager**.

How to do it...

1. First, we need to add some data to the spreadsheet. Open a new SAP BusinessObjects Dashboards file and add some data, as shown in the following screenshot:

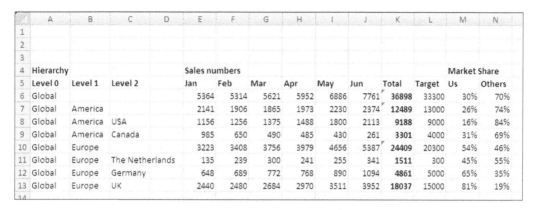

	Hierarchy			Sales numbers								Market Share	
	Level 0	Level 1	Level 2	Jan	Feb	Mar	Apr	May	Jun	Total	Target	Us	Others
6	Global			5364	5314	5621	5952	6886	7761	36898	33300	30%	70%
7	Global	America		2141	1906	1865	1973	2230	2374	12489	13000	26%	74%
8	Global	America	USA	1156	1256	1375	1488	1800	2113	9188	9000	16%	84%
9	Global	America	Canada	985	650	490	485	430	261	3301	4000	31%	69%
10	Global	Europe		3223	3408	3756	3979	4656	5387	24409	20300	54%	46%
11	Global	Europe	The Netherlands	135	239	300	241	255	341	1511	300	45%	55%
12	Global	Europe	Germany	648	689	772	768	890	1094	4861	5000	65%	35%
13	Global	Europe	UK	2440	2480	2684	2970	3511	3952	18037	15000	81%	19%

2. Add a **MicroChart Tree Grid** component to the canvas.
3. Click on the **insert** button in the properties pane.
4. Select **MicroTrafficLight** as **Chart Type**.

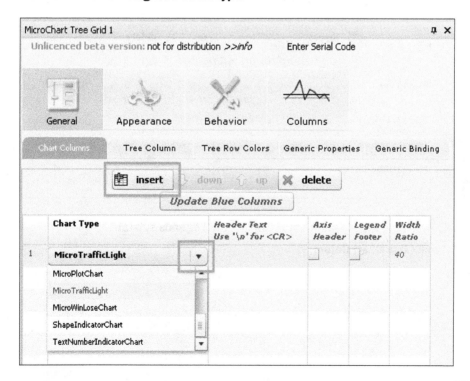

5. In the **Header Text** column, enter Status as a title for this chart and set the **Width Ratio** to 10.

6. In the **Data Source for Column: 1** section, bind the **Chart Data** field to cell range **K6:K13**. Bind the **Target Data** field to cell range **L6:L13**.

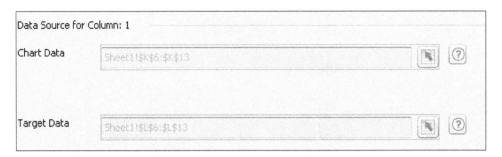

7. Insert a **MicroLineChart** into the **Tree Grid** and enter Monthly sales trend in the **Header Text** column. Also set the **Width Ratio** to 40.

8. Bind this chart to cell range **E6:J13**.

9. Insert a **Micro100BarChart** into the **Tree Grid**. Enter Market Share as the title for this column. Also set the **Width Ratio** to 40.

10. Bind this chart to cell range **M6:M13**.

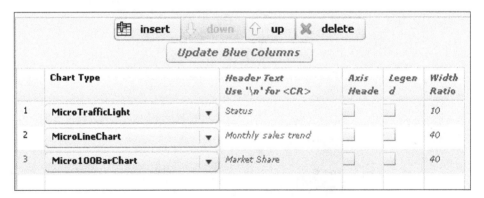

11. Click on the **Edit Column** button. Select the **Legends** sub-tab.

12. Select **Use Chart Colors**.

13. Select a dark color for the first value and a light color for the second.

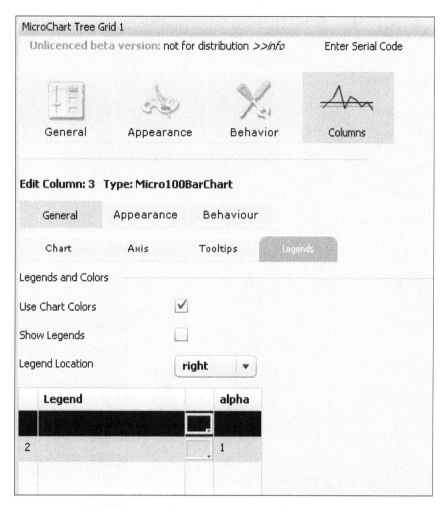

14. Now return to the **General** tab and select the **Tree Column** sub-tab.

15. Bind the **Source Data** field to cell range **A6:C13**.

16. Also set the **Column Width** to 250 and the **Opening Indentation** to 0.

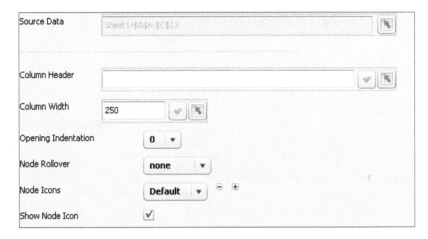

17. Preview the dashboard and try to navigate through the hierarchy tree.

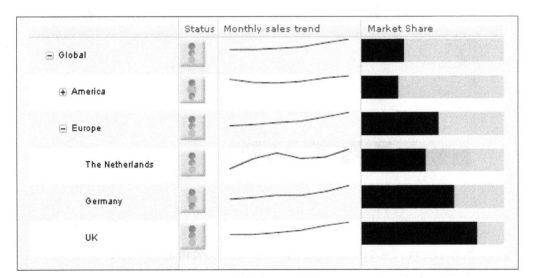

How it works...

As we have seen in this recipe, the Inovista **Micro Chart Suite** offers a good solution to present numerous data visualizations in a compact way. The **MicroChart Tree Grid** component gives us a framework to display these micro charts in a structured and hierarchical way.

To use the **MicroChart Tree Grid** component, we have to define the spreadsheet in the right way. We first created a hierarchical structure with three levels—global, continents, and countries. Next, we added all the data for the graphs in the columns, where each node has its own row of data.

There's more...

If you don't want or don't need to show a hierarchical structure in your dashboard, you can use the **MicroChart Table** component as another container to present the micro charts in. The only difference is that this component doesn't have the **Tree Column** and **Tree Row Colors** sub-tabs.

 As the **MicroChart Table** component doesn't have **Tree Column** to display the row headers, you could use a **TextNumberIndicatorChart** chart type to add these.

The following screenshot shows the **MicroChart Table** component:

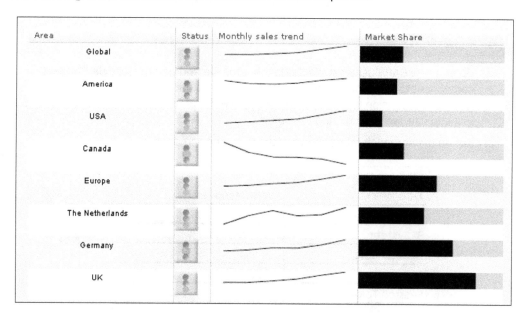

 Visit the Inovista website (http://www.inovista.com/) for more information on the **Tree** and **Data Grid** components and the individual components in the **Micro Chart Suite**. Here you can also find the other add-ons Inovista offers.

Integrating Web Intelligence with Antivia XWIS Advantage Express

Antivia XWIS Advantage Express is an add-on by Antivia that lets us connect to Web Intelligence documents, Crystal Reports, and even SQL databases and OLAP cubes. Also, it comes with a large set of components to display and analyze the retrieved data.

As we have seen in *Chapter 8*, *Dashboard Data Connectivity*, SAP BusinessObjects Dashboards is already able to connect to a number of data sources. This recipe will show you some of the capabilities of Antivia XWIS Advantage Express and the advantages it has over the standard connection types.

Getting ready

Go to the Antivia website (`http://www.antivia.com/xwis-advantage-express/`) and download the free 50-name user license. This recipe won't discuss the server-side installations for the Antivia framework that are required to run Antivia XWIS Advantage Express.

How to do it...

1. Open a new SAP BusinessObjects Dashboards file and add the **Antivia Connect** component to the canvas. This component controls the user authentication and generates a session token. In every **Antivia XWIS** data component that we are going to use, we need to bind this token.

2. Set up the spreadsheet as shown in the following screenshot:

	A	B
1	Title	XWIS Dashboard
2	Antivia Server URL	https://xwis.yourserver.com
3	BI System	systemname
4	BI Username	username@yourserver.com
5	BI Password	password
6	Session Token	

3. Bind the five fields of the **General** tab of the properties pane to the corresponding cells in the spreadsheet.

4. Fill in your **Username** and **Password** in the **Design time connection** section and click on **Connect**.

5. Add an **XWIS Table** component to the canvas.

6. First bind the **Session Token** field to cell **B6**.

7. Select a dataset from the **Dataset Picker**.

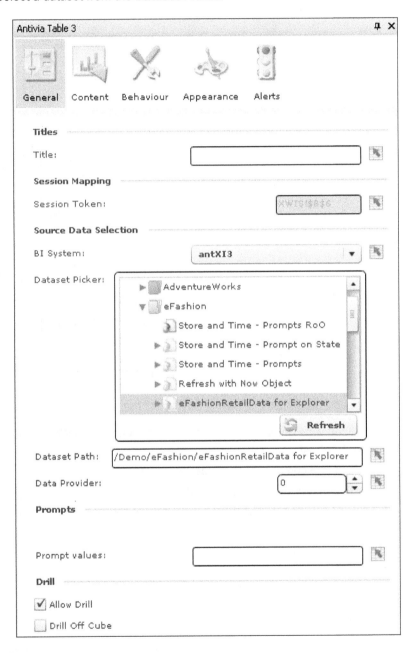

8. Now go to the **Content** tab. Here you can define the layout of the table.
   Drag the objects you want to show in the table from the **Available Objects** area
   to the **Result Objects** area. For this example, select **Year**, **Category**, **Quantity sold**,
   and **Sales revenue**.

9. Preview the dashboard, click on the **Connect** button, and check out what you just configured.

10. Click on a value in the **Year** column to drill down to quarterly data. You can sort a column by clicking on its label. Now leave the **Preview** mode.

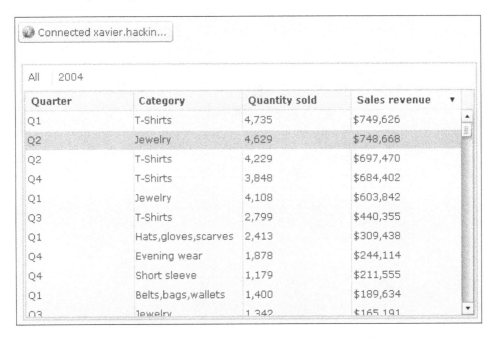

Quarter	Category	Quantity sold	Sales revenue ▼
Q1	T-Shirts	4,735	$749,626
Q2	Jewelry	4,629	$748,668
Q2	T-Shirts	4,229	$697,470
Q4	T-Shirts	3,848	$684,402
Q1	Jewelry	4,108	$603,842
Q3	T-Shirts	2,799	$440,355
Q1	Hats,gloves,scarves	2,413	$309,438
Q4	Evening wear	1,878	$244,114
Q4	Short sleeve	1,179	$211,555
Q1	Belts,bags,wallets	1,400	$189,634
Q3	Jewelry	1,342	$165,191

11. Add a **Pie Chart** and a **Line Chart** component to the canvas.

12. Return to the **Content** tab of the **XWIS Table** component. Select the **AutoWire** sub-tab.

13. Select both the **Enable AutoWire** and **Manage layout** options.

14. Also select **AutoWire** for these charts only.

15. Select the **Bind** option for both chart components and also select the **Layout** option for the **Pie Chart** component.

16. Preview the dashboard to see what happens.

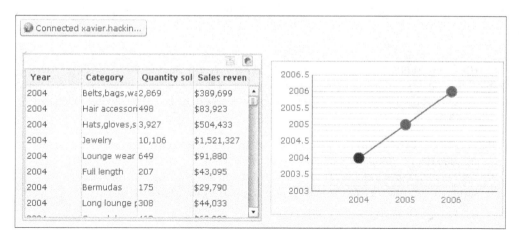

17. As you can see, the **XWIS Table** component now has two little symbols in its upper right-hand side. If you click on the pie chart symbol, the table will be replaced with the **Pie Chart** component. Click on this symbol.

18. Click on a slice of the pie chart to drill down.

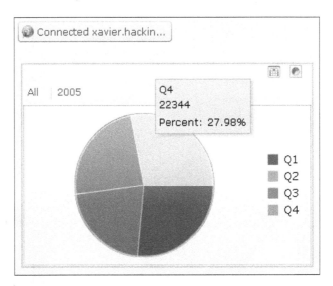

How it works...

In this recipe, we showed you only a few of the possibilities of Antivia XWIS Advantage Express. One thing should be clear already: setting up an interactive dashboard that is capable of displaying and drilling through a large set of data is made very easy with this add-on.

The Antivia Service URL, username, password, and session token need to be bound to the spreadsheet; the BI System can be selected or bound. When connecting to a SAP BusinessObjects environment, your username and password are your SAP BusinessObjects credentials.

The **XWIS Table** component enables us to analyze a very large set of data (30,000+ rows) from within a dashboard, without the need to configure multiple data connections with QaaWS or Live Office, set up the spreadsheet, and define the bindings to a component. This is a huge efficiency gain!

We demonstrated the **AutoWire** feature that makes dashboard development even easier and faster because it completely takes care of the binding of data to standard SAP BusinessObjects Dashboards chart components. If you still want to bind the data to the spreadsheet, Antivia XWIS Advantage Express also provides this feature.

There's more...

Antivia XWIS Advantage Express comes with a large number of components, which we will discuss in this section.

XWIS Slice and Dice component

The **XWIS Slice and Dice** component lets the dashboard user create their own report layout. The user can use drag-and-drop to configure the report from a set of available objects. The following screenshot shows the interface where the user gets to do this:

XWIS Export component

The **XWIS Export** component enables us to export data from the dashboard to MS Excel files, which is an extremely powerful option. The button gives us two options—exporting the complete dataset or exporting the data as shown in the components.

Alerts

In all data-based Antivia XWIS components, alerts can be used to highlight cells when a certain condition is met. A nice feature here is that these alert definitions are stored in the Antivia XWIS repository, so they can be reused in other components or even in other dashboards.

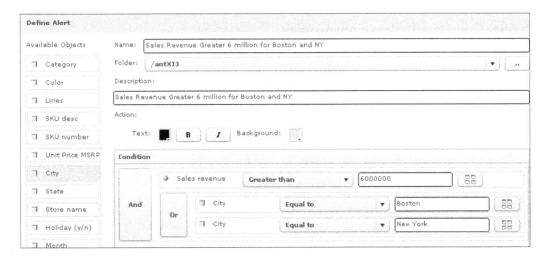

Antivia Timer component

The **Antivia Timer** component is the only component that can work independently and does not need a session token to run. It writes the current time to a cell at a defined interval. This component can be useful to trigger components with the **Refresh on change** option or in combination with **Dynamic Visibility**.

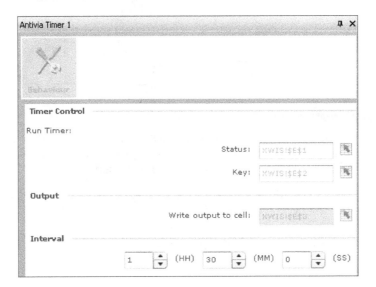

Visit the Antivia XWIS Advantage website at `http://www.antivia.com/xwis-advantage-express/` for a complete overview of all Antivia XWIS Advantage add-on features and to check out some demo videos.

Advanced printing with Xcelsius Dashboard Printer

The standard **Print Button** component in SAP BusinessObjects Dashboards has pretty basic functionality: it prints your dashboard as it is displayed on the screen. It's all or nothing; you can't select a specific part of the dashboard. The only setting you can make is whether the dashboard should be scaled to fit the page or to a certain percentage. When you click the button, the default Windows **Print** window appears and you can start printing.

The Xcelsius Dashboard Printer add-on by DataSavvyTools has a lot more options. It lets the user select a portion of the dashboard, queue up multiple snapshots before printing, format the output, and add annotations. Instead of printing, it can also send the screenshot to the clipboard or save as a file.

Getting ready

You can find the Xcelsius Dashboard Printer add-on at the DataSavvyTools website, `http://www.datasavvytools.com/`.

How to do it...

1. Open an existing SAP BusinessObjects Dashboards file.

2. Add the **Xcelsius Dashboard Printer** component to the dashboard. Actually, you're pretty much done setting up the component right now.

3. Hit the **Preview** button or export the dashboard to an SWF file.

4. Run the dashboard and click on the **Printer** button.

5. A selection cursor is activated. Select a part of the dashboard.

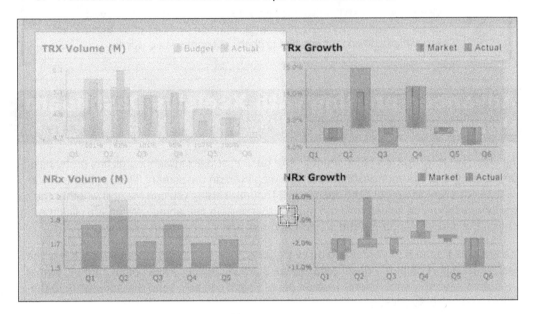

6. Click on the **Capture** button to save the selection. The screenshot is now added to the **Capture Queue**.

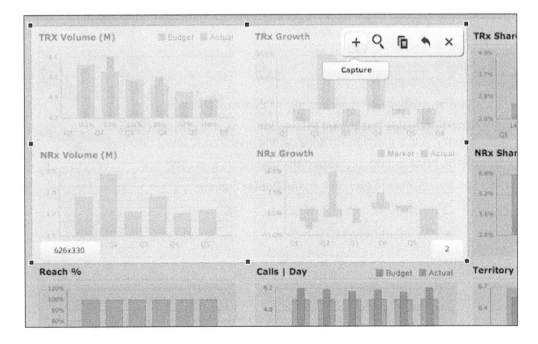

7. Repeat steps 5 and 6 to add some more screenshots.

8. Click on the **Preview** button to show the **Preview Overview**. Here you can adjust your screenshots and prepare them before you save them.

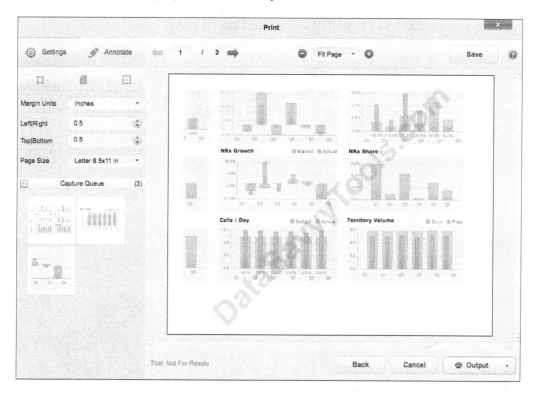

9. Select a screenshot from the **Capture Queue** and click on the **Output** button. Choose **Image** to export to a JPG, PNG, or GIF file. Enter a file name and click on **OK** to save the file.

How it works...

In this recipe, we demonstrated some of the advanced printer features that the Xcelsius Dashboard Printer add-on delivers. The beauty of this component is that it doesn't need any setup to work. Just add it to your dashboard and start printing!

There's more...

Besides adding a queue of screenshots and saving them to local files or directly sending them to a printer, the component also allows you to make annotations to the screenshots before saving or printing them.

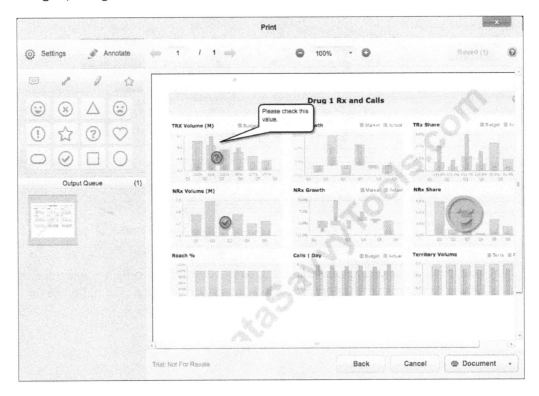

SUCCESS with graphomate charts

The charts in the graphomate add-on are based on the SUCCESS rules for data visualization and business communication, compiled by Rolf Hichert. A known pitfall when developing dashboards is that a dashboard can consist of colorful and shiny pie charts that are nice to look at but not always that effective to use. A dashboard should present data in such a way that the users can perform effective analysis, compare values, and quickly see what is good or bad. For more information on the SUCCESS principle by Hichert, check `http://www.hichert.com/en/success`.

The graphomate add-on charts include six charts: Bar & Column, Needle, Deviation, Line, Stacked, and Waterfall. Compared to the standard charts in SAP BusinessObjects Dashboards, these charts tend to look a bit minimalistic and clean with no axes and little color, but they can help you to create really useful dashboards.

Getting ready

Go to the graphomate website and request a trial at `http://www.graphomate.com/en/contact_trial/`. We will use a very simple dataset for this recipe, as shown in the following screenshot:

	A	B	C	D	E	F	G	H
1								
2								
3								
4								
5	2013				2014			
6	Q1	Q2	Q3	Q4	Q1	Q2	Q3	Q4
7	50	125	105	55	85	65	110	95
8	75	95	105	85	75	95	105	85

How to do it...

1. Open a new empty SAP BusinessObjects Dashboards file.
2. Add the **graphomate Chart** component to the canvas.
3. Go to the properties pane and enter the serial number you got when requesting the trial. This will activate the component and you'll see a chart appearing.

4. Now go back to the **General** tab and select the **Data** sub-tab. Here we can bind the data from the spreadsheet to the component. Bind the **Measures** field to cell range **A7:H7**.

5. Bind the **Basic values** field to cell range **A8:H8**.

6. Bind the first **Category labels** field to cell range **A6:H6** and bind the second field to cell range **A5:H5**.

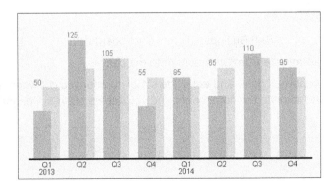

7. Go back to the **General** tab and select **Chart type** as **Deviation**.

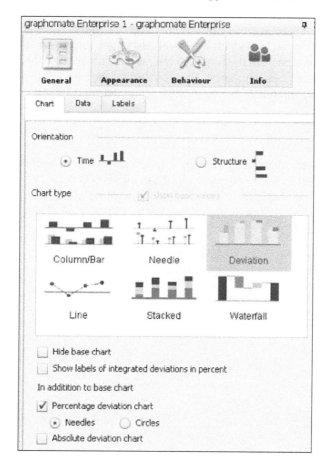

8. Finally, check **Percentage deviation chart.**

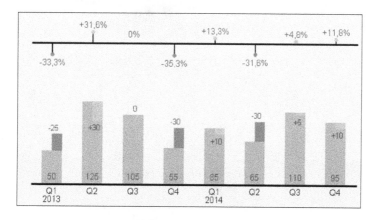

How it works...

In this recipe, we quickly set up a **Deviation** chart from the graphomate charts add-on. We compared data over two years with their quarterly target values. The final chart provides both the nominal deviation from the target as well as the percentage. This makes it easy to find out which period did best and worst. The double category label option made it easy to add years to the x-axis without cluttering it with a lot of recurring values.

There's more...

This recipe only showed a very basic setup of a graphomate charts add-on chart. As we have seen, there are in total six chart types that can be used in both a horizontal and vertical orientation. The charts can be completely customized to the finest details. Visit the graphomate website (`http://www.graphomate.com/`) for a list of all the features.

11
Performance Tuning

In this chapter, we will cover the following recipes:

- ▶ Improving Excel spreadsheet performance
- ▶ Using scheduled Webis to save on querying time
- ▶ Running connections after loading the dashboard
- ▶ Checking master data loading performance of connections
- ▶ Optimizing BEx Query performance
- ▶ Using Fiddler to identify the cause of performance issues

Introduction

When we create a dashboard, we want users to have the best experience possible. The faster the dashboard starts up, the better it is. When a selection is made and data needs to be refreshed, we want the charts and tables in the dashboard to change as soon as possible. A dashboard that performs poorly usually gets discarded by users because they consider it slow and unusable. As a general rule, we would say that a dashboard needs to load and refresh in a maximum time of 8 seconds.

It can be a difficult job to fix a slow dashboard since a lot of different factors can influence performance. The fact is that a lower number of the following points will result in better performance:

- ▶ Number of data manager connections and queries
- ▶ Number of used spreadsheet cells
- ▶ Amount of data that is loaded into the spreadsheet from the connections
- ▶ Number of Excel formulas

▸ Number of components used and the levels of container nesting (Canvas, Panel, Tab Set)

▸ Number of bindings from components to the spreadsheet

▸ Size of the XLF file

In this chapter, we will look into several topics that can help you optimize the usability of your dashboard.

Improving Excel spreadsheet performance

Excel is an extremely powerful tool containing many useful calculation functions. However, some of these functions consume a lot of CPU power, thus slowing down the performance of a dashboard.

If you are a user who works with a lot of complicated Excel reports, you will most likely experience that some Excel reports take a very long time to recalculate whenever any data is changed within any of the spreadsheets.

How to do it...

Here are some tips with workarounds to improve Excel performance:

▸ **Work from left to right**: By default, Excel will first calculate expressions at the top-left corner of the spreadsheet and then continue to the right and downwards. Because of this, it is best to put expressions that are referencing to values in other cells to the right or to the bottom of those referenced cells. This is called **forward referencing**. With a small worksheet it won't make much of a difference, but for very large worksheets it will.

▸ **Avoid using volatile functions**: Some examples of volatile functions are RAND(), RANDBETWEEN(), NOW(), TODAY(), OFFSET(), CELL(), and INDIRECT(). The issue with using volatile functions is that they will recalculate every time a change is made in a worksheet. For example, if you change cell **A1** from X to Y, the RAND() function in cell **A2** will recalculate and display another value. Note that some of these functions such as RANDBETWEEN() don't even work with SAP BusinessObjects Dashboards during runtime.

▶ **Avoid array formulas**: Formulas such as SUMIF(), COUNTIF(), AVERAGEIF(), VLOOKUP, and HLOOKUP are memory hogs especially when the arrays are very large. If possible, replace SUMIF(), COUNTIF(), and AVERAGEIF() with regular formulas. VLOOKUP() and HLOOKUP() can be replaced with the Filtered rows component found in *Chapter 3*, *From a Static to an Interactive Dashboard*, or with a combination of MATCH() and INDEX().

▶ **Avoid giant formulas**: Complex formulas that are very large should either be completed on the database side, or in a Web Intelligence (Webi) report (see the following recipe), or a BEx query when possible. This puts the load on the server, which has a lot more horsepower than the client machine.

Using scheduled Webis to save on querying time

As mentioned in *Chapter 8*, *Dashboard Data Connectivity*, being able to schedule Web Intelligence (Webi) reports instead of running live queries for each and every query will help improve performance drastically.

Let's take an example where it takes two minutes to execute a query. If we were to have the dataset prescheduled instead of running live, we could retrieve the data in seconds rather than minutes.

There will be people who complain that your database architecture or query strategy is incorrect if it takes two minutes to execute a query. However, a lot of times it is impossible to speed up a query due to the sheer size of data or the amount of work it would take to re-architect the entire data warehouse.

Getting ready

Create a Webi document. In our example, we will create a simple Webi from the eFashion Universe that contains a crosstab with months as columns and stores as rows. Also, make sure that you have a Live Office connection as well as a BI Web Services connection created based on the Webi document.

How to do it...

1. Create a schedule for your Webi to execute from BI Launchpad. In our example, we will have the Webi refresh daily at 8 a.m.

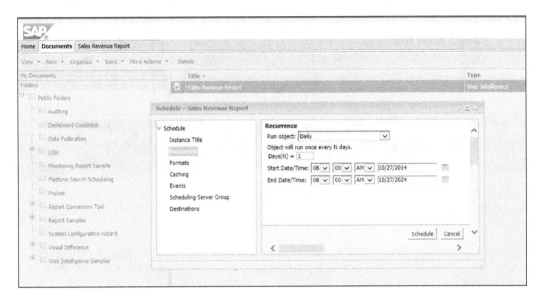

2. In the Live Office connection, modify the properties so that we refresh based on the latest instance.

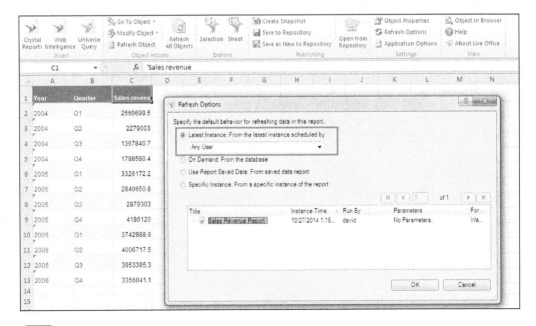

3. On the BI Web Services connection from the **Data Manager**, set the **getFromLatestDocumentInstance** property to **1**.

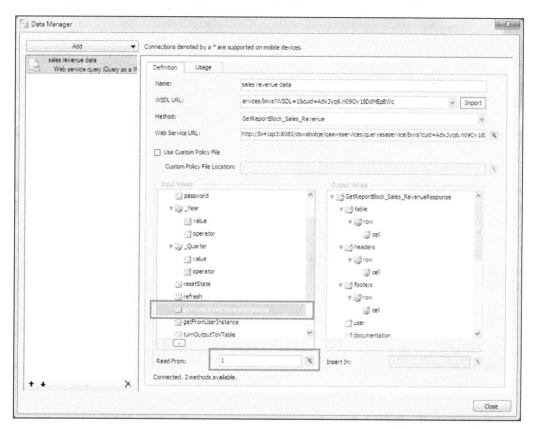

 When you test the BI Web Service, the boolean properties work based on TRUE/FALSE. However, in the SAP BusinessObjects Dashboards **Data Manager**, you need to use **1/0**, otherwise it will not work.

How it works...

As you can see, all we need to do to use scheduled Webis is to first schedule the Webi document, and then set the refresh on the latest instance properties of either your Live Office or BI Web Services connection to true.

Running connections after loading the dashboard

When you run a dashboard, the initialization message and a loading bar is shown. When initialization is finished the message disappears and the dashboard is presented and made available for usage.

During initialization, all dashboard connections and queries are loaded by default when the **Refresh Before Components Are Loaded** option in the **Usage** tab of the **Data Manager** is set. This means that when you have one or more connections that require some time to load, the whole dashboard has to wait for them to finish. Only when all data is loaded is the initialization message removed and the dashboard can be used. Why not let users see the dashboard immediately and let it fill with data as soon as a connection has finished loading? Luckily, there is a workaround for this issue, as we will see in this recipe.

Getting ready

Use a dashboard with one or more **Data Manager** connections or **Queries Browser** queries.

How to do it...

1. For the connection, go to the **Data Manager**, select the connection, and choose the **Usage** tab.

2. For the query, select the query in the **Query Browser**, select **Edit**, and go to the **Usage Options**.

Uncheck **Refresh Before Components Are Loaded** in the **Data Manager**...

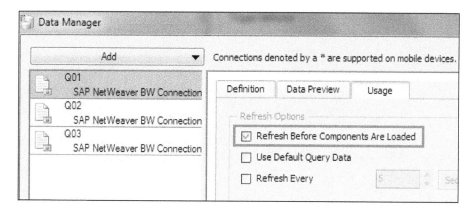

...or in the **Query Browser**:

3. Now add a **Refresh** button. Add a **Connection Refresh Button** component for the connection or a **Query Refresh Button** component for the query to the canvas.

4. In the **General** tab of the **Refresh** button, select the connections or queries you want to load.

5. Now go to the **Behavior** tab and check the **Refresh After Components Are Loaded** option.

 You can also bind the **Trigger Cell** to a spreadsheet cell here to refresh the connections or queries when the bound cell value changes.

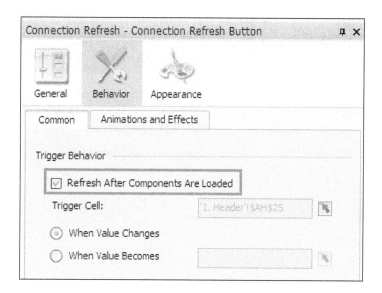

6. Since we only use this component to initially load the data after the dashboard components are loaded, we want to hide this component. Go to the **Appearance** tab and uncheck the **Show Button Background** option.

7. Go to the **Text** tab and uncheck the **Label** option.

We set up the **Connection Refresh Button** and **Query Refresh Button** components here as automated background components, as we actually don't need the dashboard user to click and activate it. When the user accidentally moves over the component, the cursor will turn into a hand symbol, indicating a clickable action. To avoid this you could minimize the size of the component and locate it behind a logo or another part of the dashboard that is unlikely to be clicked.

How it works...

With this option, the dashboard components load and show up before the data loading is finished. This is more appealing to the user as they can see something happening instead of watching the dull initialization message. We can also use this to initially load only the data that is required for the first or initial screen of the dashboard, while the other data (that even might require some more time to load) is loaded in the background or only after a user triggers it.

Checking master data loading performance of connections

When data is loaded or refreshed, the associated connections are executed in parallel by default. This is a great feature because it dramatically reduces the total loading time of the dashboard.

To check the loading state of all your connections, it is a good practice to create a custom debug mode that lets you monitor how the connections are performing.

Getting ready

Use a dashboard with multiple connections.

How to do it...

1. Add a **Spreadsheet Table** component to the canvas.

2. Set up the spreadsheet as shown in the following screenshot:

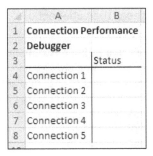

3. Go to the **Data Manager** and select the **Usage** tab. Here you'll find a section called **Load Status**. For each connection, bind the **Insert In** field to the corresponding spreadsheet cell.

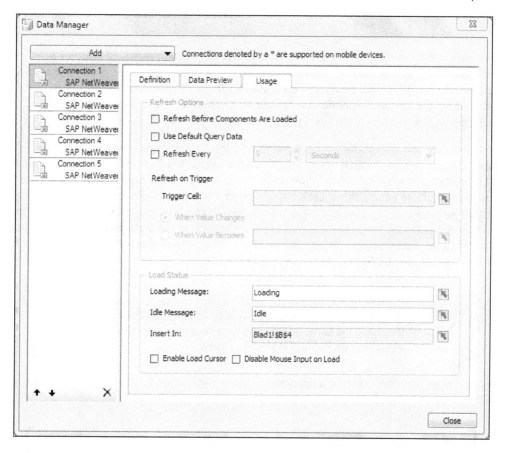

4. Bind the **Spreadsheet Table** component to the spreadsheet area.

5. Publish and Launch the dashboard and see what happens while the connections are executed.

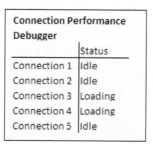

Connection Performance Debugger	
	Status
Connection 1	Idle
Connection 2	Idle
Connection 3	Loading
Connection 4	Loading
Connection 5	Idle

You can use Dynamic Visibility to make the **Spreadsheet Table** component appear and disappear when required. Read _Chapter 4, Dynamic Visibility_, to learn more about this feature.

There's more...

As we have seen in the *Using the SAP NetWeaver BW Connection* recipe in *Chapter 8, Dashboard Data Connectivity*, we can use the same BEx query that provides the transaction data (the result set) to load the master data values. These master data values are mostly used to fill up the labels of selection components. A connection with such a setup has, of course, a longer execution time, since more data has to be loaded.

If you are using only one of the connections to load the master data values for multiple characteristics, this connection could slow down the overall loading performance in case of a lot of available master data. A solution would be to divide the loading of the master data values over multiple connections. Let's say you need to load all values for the characteristics, calendar year, country, and project into your dashboard spreadsheet, to fill the labels for three selection components. You also have multiple connections in the **Data Manager** that all use the same dataset as a source. You then could load the calendar year values from connection 1, the values for country from connection 2, and the values for project from connection 3.

 Make sure that the connection that you use can functionally deliver the same master data values. This is, for example, the case when they have the same source and they have the same master data value settings defined in the BEx Query.

You could even consider creating a specific, separate connection for the loading of (a part of the) master data values.

 Experiment with different scenarios to find out which setup gives the best overall performance results.

Optimizing BEx Query performance

In this recipe, we will give you some specific performance optimization recommendations when using BEx Queries as a data source for your data connection. Standard SAP BW optimization practices like InfoCube design, using aggregates, OLAP caching, and so on have not been covered here, as it is too general and out of the scope of this book.

How to do it...

We will discuss three topics here.

Use dashboard specific queries

Do not reuse existing queries that are used for reporting with analysis tools, such as BEx Analyzer, SAP BusinessObjects Web Intelligence, or SAP BusinessObjects Analysis. These queries tend to have a broad setup with lots of (free) characteristics and key figures, whereas for a dashboard, extremely specific queries are required. The dashboard queries should provide a result set with only the data that is required, and nothing more.

Also, do not use BEx Query Views. Instead, if you want to reuse an initial query and change its structure, make use of the **Data Preview** tab of the **Data Manager**.

Use the BEx Query Designer features

The SAP BW environment is highly optimized for query execution, so make sure you do all calculation and summarization in the query and not in the dashboard. Avoid using an Excel formula whenever you can create the same outcome in the BEx Query. So, if you need a column total or average, use the features of the **BEx Query Designer** to add a total row or an additional formula or selection to your output. If you need a specific, complex key figure calculation, let the BEx Query take care of that. Do not make these calculations with Excel formulas, as this will increase the size of your dashboard and decrease its loading performance greatly.

Also, for data filtering options you can use the **BEx Query Designer**. It has tons of options for custom input variables, with offsets and even user and default SAP exits, which let the SAP BW system do the complex calculations of the required values. An example is the selection of the year-to-date period range until the previous month. In addition to this, you can use Text variables to create dynamic labels.

Only use and reload necessary (master) data

It sounds pretty obvious, but you do not want to reload all connections every time a selection is made. Try to set up a smart system to reload only those connections that provide data for parts of the dashboard that are used and displayed at the time of data refreshment. Use trigger cells to set this up.

Make sure you only bind the master data values for the characteristics that you actually are using in the dashboard (for example, to fill the labels of selection component). Only for those characteristics that have **Output Values** from the **Value Help** section bound to a spreadsheet cell range are the values retrieved.

We can reduce the amount of master data values by making smart selections in the BEx Query. In case you only need the last five years of data, add a (variable) selection on the year characteristic in the **Global Filter** in the **BEx Query Designer**. Now for the time characteristics only master data values for the last five years will show up in the dashboard.

Also, if the master data values that are provided by the BEx Query are static, it doesn't make sense to load them each time the connection is refreshed. If this negatively influences the loading performance too much, you could consider the creation of a separate connection to load these master data values only once.

Using Fiddler to identify the cause of performance issues

Dashboards can become quite complex as it is very common to have multiple queries executing at once, especially during the initial load. When we encounter performance issues, it is very difficult to pinpoint exactly where the issue is coming from. Fortunately, we can use the Fiddler tool to help us identify the root cause of a performance-related issue.

Getting ready

Download **Fiddler** from `http://www.telerik.com/download/fiddler`. Create a simple dashboard that contains one query and one chart. In our example, we created a query that contains the **Calendar Year** dimension and **Sales Amount** measure. The data is then plotted on a **Column Chart**.

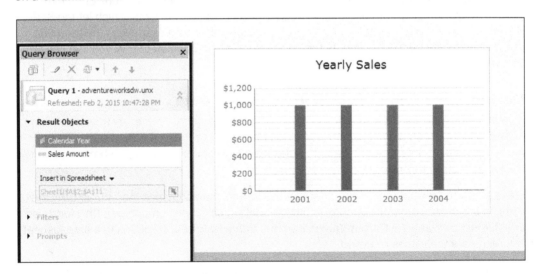

How to do it...

1. Make sure Fiddler is running and then **Preview** your dashboard.

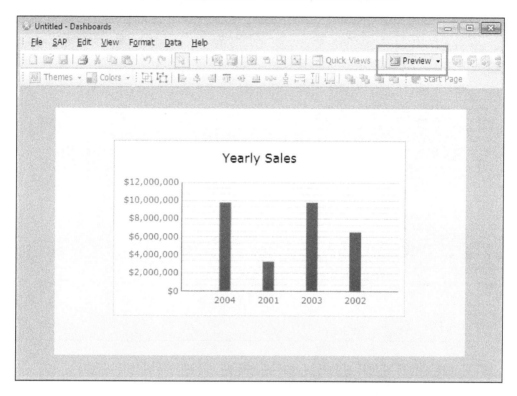

2. In Fiddler you will notice that there are three lines on the left-hand side window. The first line and last line are session initialization and session ending items. The second line is our query process. The way we can tell this is that query requests have the URL /dswsbobje/services/XcelsiusWebServices.

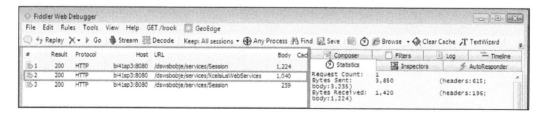

3. Now let's analyze the query. Click on the **Statistics** tab on the right-hand side window. Here you can see the performance of the query being executed. In our example, the query executes in 0.389 seconds. In a real-life scenario, you would have to go through each of your queries and figure out which query is performing poorly.

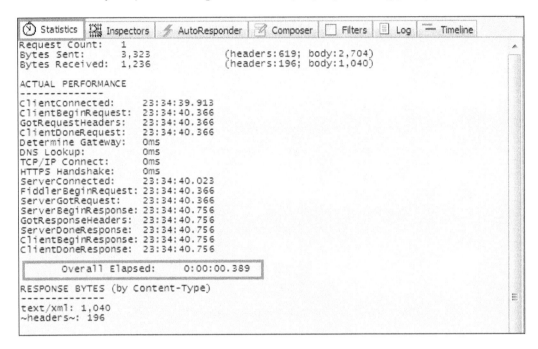

```
Statistics    Inspectors    AutoResponder    Composer    Filters    Log    Timeline
Request Count:      1
Bytes Sent:         3,323              (headers:619; body:2,704)
Bytes Received:     1,236              (headers:196; body:1,040)

ACTUAL PERFORMANCE
--------------
ClientConnected:       23:34:39.913
ClientBeginRequest:    23:34:40.366
GotRequestHeaders:     23:34:40.366
ClientDoneRequest:     23:34:40.366
Determine Gateway:     0ms
DNS Lookup:            0ms
TCP/IP Connect:        0ms
HTTPS Handshake:       0ms
ServerConnected:       23:34:40.023
FiddlerBeginRequest:   23:34:40.366
ServerGotRequest:      23:34:40.366
ServerBeginResponse:   23:34:40.756
GotResponseHeaders:    23:34:40.756
ServerDoneResponse:    23:34:40.756
ClientBeginResponse:   23:34:40.756
ClientDoneResponse:    23:34:40.756

        Overall Elapsed:      0:00:00.389

RESPONSE BYTES (by Content-Type)
--------------
text/xml: 1,040
~headers~: 196
```

4. Now let's learn how to retrieve some more useful information about this query request. Click on the **Inspectors** tab and you will notice a top window and bottom window. The top window is the request and the bottom window is the response. We are interested in the response. Generally, it is preferable to look at the XML result in **WebView**. Click on **WebView** and then click on the bar above, which says **Response is encoded ... Click here to transform**.

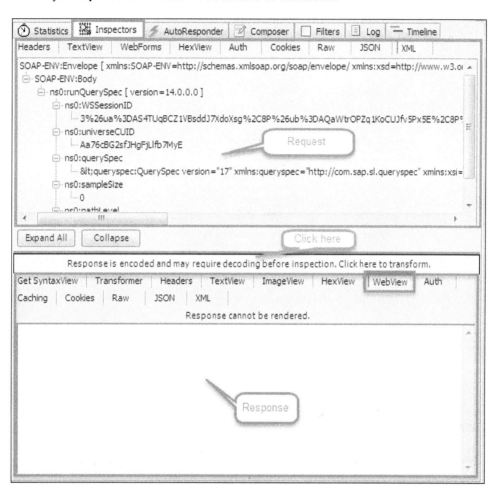

5. We can see some interesting information about the query now. First, if you look at the highlighted area at the bottom, you will see that it is the query that returns the result containing the **Calendar Year** dimension and **Amount** measure. The highlighted area on the top contains the SQL statement from the query being executed. Using this information, we can figure out if a bad query has been caused by inefficient SQL query generation.

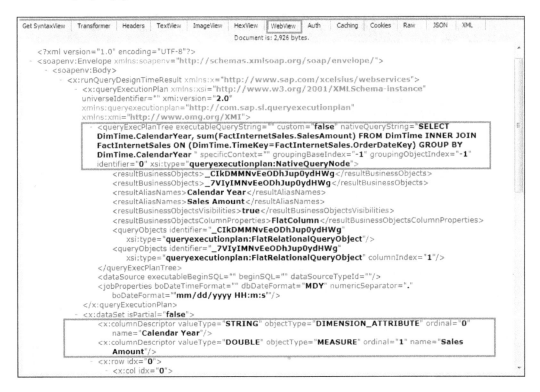

How it works...

Fiddler helps capture all the HTTP(S) traffic between the user running the dashboard and the SAP BusinessObjects server that we are communicating with. In our example, we perform some analysis on the communication between the server and client when a query is executed. We track performance by looking at the **Statistics** and when we want to dive deeper, we can look at the **Request** and **Response** in detail.

There's more...

Not only can we monitor performance of our dashboards with Fiddler, we can see in detail if there are any web server errors such as the common 404 not found error.

We can even modify and manipulate requests and responses by setting break points during runtime. For example, we can compose our own HTTP request, run it through Fiddler, and then receive a response from the server.

Finally, Fiddler has a rich extensibility model that ranges from a simple FiddlerScript to powerful extensions, which can be developed using any .NET language.

See also

▶ For full documentation on what you can do with Fiddler, visit `http://docs.telerik.com/fiddler`.

12

Increasing Productivity

In this chapter, we will cover the following recipes:

- Using the Spreadsheet Table component to debug
- Time-saving tips during dashboard development
- Fixing corrupt XLF files

Introduction

Developing a dashboard with SAP BusinessObjects Dashboards can be fun at times, but it is important to work efficiently. Doing unnecessary and repetitive tasks can be very frustrating.

In this chapter, we will go through a bunch of tips and tricks to increase your productivity when developing a dashboard. We will show you how to debug a dashboard and how you can recover your work in the unfortunate case your XLF file gets corrupted.

Using the Spreadsheet Table component to debug

When developing dashboards, there will always come a time when you are totally stumped on why something is not working correctly. Refer to `spreadsheet debugger.xlf` to follow the example.

Getting ready

In our example, we will illustrate a simple bug and how to find its cause. Our example contains a drop-down control that populates a chart with preloaded data.

We've purposely populated the data area incorrectly ahead of time where we've accidentally forgotten to map an extra column on the row output. In reality, we won't know that the data has been incorrectly populated.

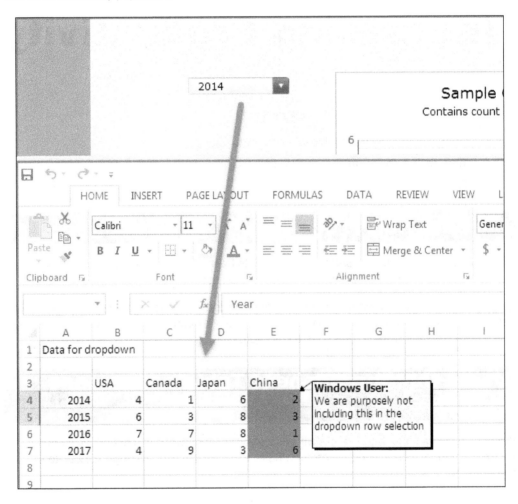

How to do it...

1. Execute the dashboard. You will notice that the data looks off on the dropdown and the chart.

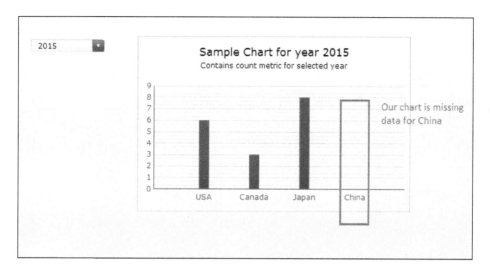

2. Insert a **Spreadsheet Table** component anywhere on the dashboard.
3. Map the spreadsheet to the area that is populated by the data.

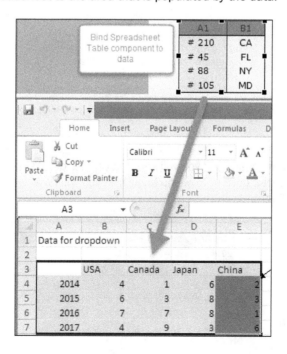

4. Execute the dashboard. You will see that the data looks okay. There's data under **China**. So let's see what the output of the drop-down selector is.

	USA	Canada	Japan	China
2014	4	1	6	2
2015	6	3	8	3
2016	7	7	8	1
2017	4	9	3	6

5. Bind the spreadsheet table to the output area of the drop-down selector.

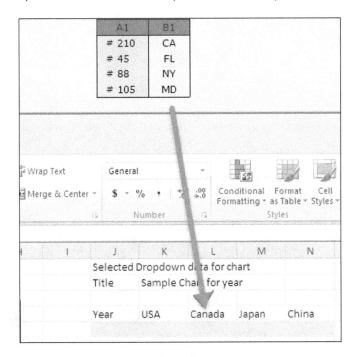

6. Execute the dashboard and you will see that China's data is missing from the dropdown selector output. Now you know that you will have to fix the dropdown selector binding.

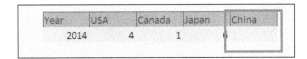

How it works...

As you can see, using the **Spreadsheet Table** component is very helpful in seeing what is happening under the hood. In this example, you can easily oversee a large area of data. If we were to try to debug by figuring out which component is causing the issue, it would take much longer as we would have to go through the **Dropdown** component, **Chart** component, and **Data Connection** in order to find the culprit. This is a simple example, but just imagine if there were a lot more components involved.

Time-saving tips during dashboard development

Developing dashboards can be very tedious. So we wanted to provide you with a set of time-saving tips that will make your life a lot easier.

How to do it...

In this big *How to do it...* section we will cover all tips for this recipe.

Global Fonts

1. It is always a best practice to use a Global Font. This way, the font is consistent throughout the dashboard. Each time a component is inserted into the dashboard, it will use the font set in the Global Fonts setting.

2. To set a Global Font, click on **File | Document Properties...**.

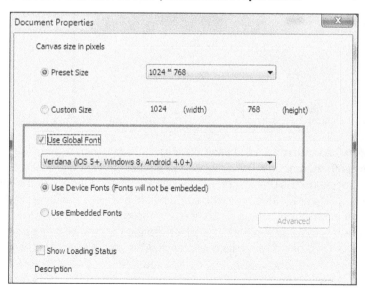

> Note that the font should be available on the local machine of each dashboard user, otherwise the developer will need to embed the font. This is unadvisable due to size and resolution issues with Adobe Flash. Thus, try not to use exotic fonts.

Grouping from the Object Browser versus grouping with a Canvas Container

When grouping components, you can either group directly from the **Object Browser** or you can insert a **Canvas Container** and then drop the objects you want grouped inside the **Canvas Container**.

Here are some pros and cons of both:

> ▶ **Grouping objects directly**: This is the quickest and easiest way to group objects. However, if you want to move or resize objects within the group, you will need to ungroup everything, adjust the position/size of the objects, and then regroup the objects. You will also need to rename the group again. In addition, if you want to add objects to a group that has **Dynamic Visibility** set, you will need to manually add **Dynamic Visibility** onto the new object in the grouping. Finally, when you ungroup and then regroup objects, you will risk running into human errors (setting **Dynamic Visibility**, layering, and so on).

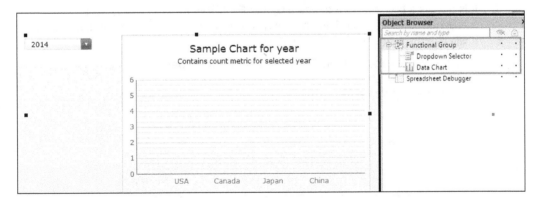

> ▶ **Grouping objects using a Canvas Container**: This method requires that a user inserts a **Canvas Container** onto the dashboard, and then drops the grouped objects into it. The benefit here is that you do not have to worry about setting **Dynamic Visibility** when dropping new objects into the container. In addition, you do not have to ungroup the objects when you want to move or resize the objects. A minor issue with Canvas Containers is that you see the dotted lines around the canvas in the development screen, which is only a minor inconvenience. Also, you will see that the inside of the canvas is shaded so you will not be able to see what the true color looks like during runtime. Finally, using Canvas Containers may increase the file size of your dashboard.

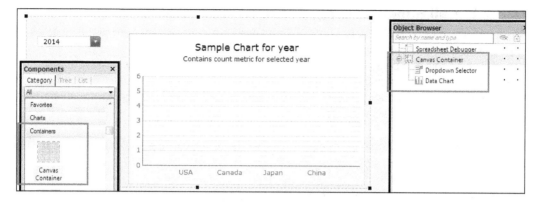

Editing multiple components at once

This is a very useful feature. For example, you may have three bar charts and want to resize all the title fonts. Instead of resizing each one individually, you can select each one by holding *Ctrl* and clicking on each chart from the dashboard canvas, or holding *Ctrl* and clicking on each chart from the **Object Browser**. You will now be able to edit items that are common to all the charts (such as the **Appearance** tab).

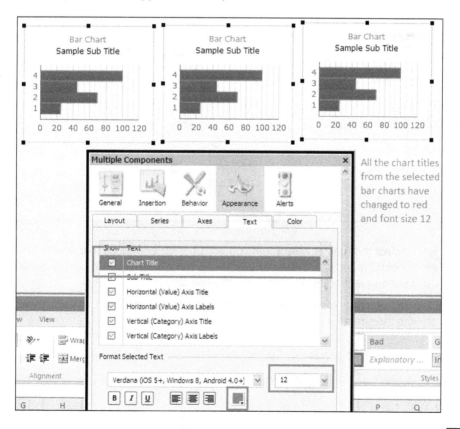

Using the alignment, sizing, and spacing buttons

As mentioned in *Chapter 7, Dashboard Look and Feel*, creating a dashboard that is neatly aligned with charts and components of similar sizing provides a cleaner user experience. Accomplishing this can be a very tedious task when there are many objects involved. Just imagine slowly resizing, aligning, and spacing each and every object manually. Fortunately, we can resize, space, and align objects easily using some of the helpful toolbar functions as shown in the following screenshot:

For example, if you wanted to resize the following bar chart to be exactly the same as the line chart and align the top so that it is equal as well, you would do the following:

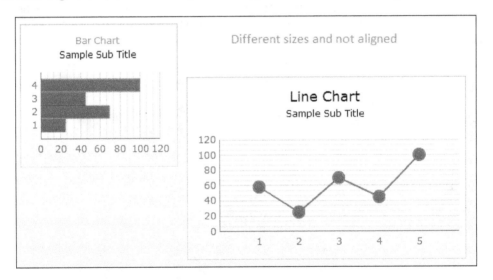

1. First, select the master object that you want the other objects to follow. In this case, hold *Ctrl* and select the bar chart first. Then, keep holding *Ctrl* and select each subsequent object (in this case, the line chart).

2. Click on the equal make same size icon. Sometimes, you might want to make objects the same height or width, but in our case, it's both.

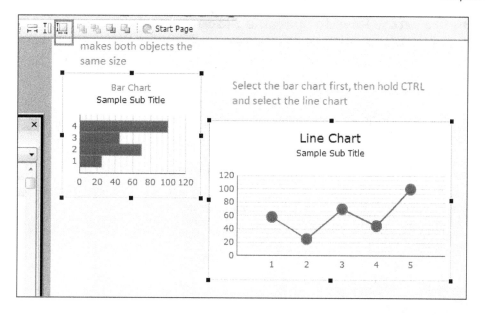

3. Click on the **Align Top** icon so that the bar chart becomes aligned with the line chart on the left.

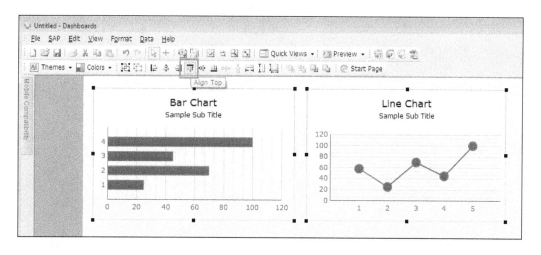

 Always remember that the first object selected controls the sizing and alignment of subsequent objects.

Using the arrow keys for precise placement of components

The alignment functions are great for moving components so that they are exactly aligned with one another. However, there are cases when we may want to move a particular object to an exact location. In most cases, we can drag with the mouse, but it is difficult to drag a component to the exact pixel for pinpoint accuracy.

Thus, what a user can do is first drag the component close to the exact position of choice. Then, they can use the arrow keys to slowly move the object to the exact pixel.

Using the Grid to help with relative positioning

The **Grid** is a helpful mechanism to visually aid developers on the exact pixel location of components. To turn on the **Grid**, navigate to **View | Grid**.

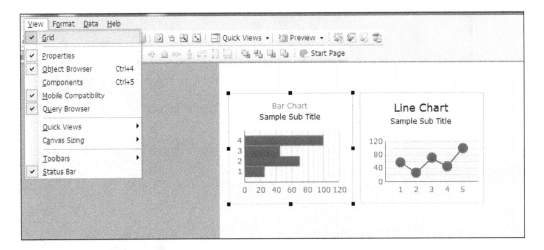

You can also set the sizing of each Grid as well as the option to snap objects to the Grid when moving objects around. To set the **Grid** options, click on **File | Preferences | Grid**.

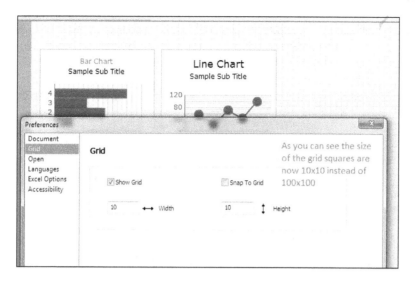

Copying objects from another dashboard

Templates are a great way of reusing components such as headers, footers, and color schemes over and over without having to recreate them on every dashboard. However, there are cases where certain charts, selectors, and buttons may be needed in some dashboards.

One neat feature that SAP BusinessObjects Dashboards has is the ability to have another SAP BusinessObjects Dashboards instance open, and then copy the objects from that dashboard to another dashboard currently in development. This is useful if there is formatting and cell binding that can be reused. If there were 20 reusable objects, for example, this would save us a great deal of time by copying and pasting the components instead of recreating each one.

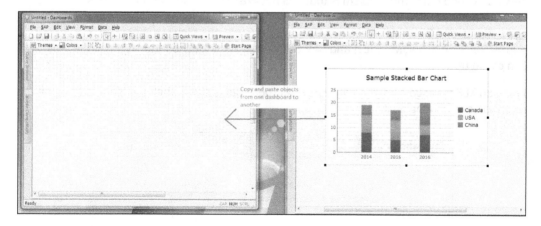

If you want to copy the cell binding of the objects from one dashboard to another, make sure that you also copy the worksheet; otherwise, you will lose all the cell bindings.

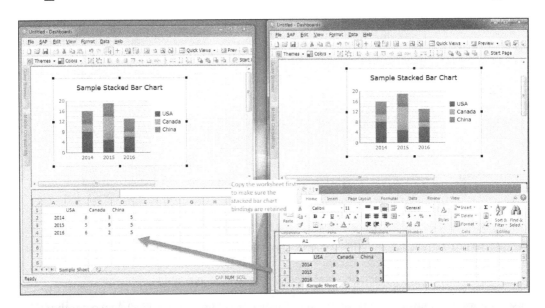

Fixing corrupt XLF files

Unfortunately, sometimes the XLF file gets corrupted, and when this happens, it is obviously never at a good time. The problem is that it is not exactly clear why and when this happens, so it is hard to prevent this from happening at all. The only thing we know is that the more components and Excel logic used in a dashboard model, the higher the chance is of this happening. Also, using MS Excel and SAP BusinessObjects Dashboards at the same time can cause trouble.

When an XLF file is corrupt, the following error message is given when the file is loading or when you are working on it:

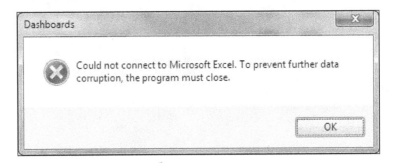

Older versions of SAP BusinessObjects Dashboards (Xcelsius) show the following message: **An error occurred while communicating with Microsoft Excel. To prevent further data corruption, Xcelsius must close**. After clicking the **OK** button, SAP BusinessObjects Dashboards exits.

A best practice is to create a lot of (local) backups of the dashboard you are working on. Try to save a copy for every 30 or 60 minutes of work, or after making a bunch of changes. Do this consistently! You can use a simple incremental file name strategy to tell the files apart. For example, use the date and time of the backup at the end of the file name (`dashboard_name_201411201556.xlf`, `dashboard_name_201411201623.xlf`), or just use an incremental number with each backup file (`dashboard_name_001.xlf`, `dashboard_name_002.xlf`).

When a corruption error occurs, you can revert to the last working backup. If this doesn't work or isn't possible, you can try this recipe where we will try to replace the corrupt Excel file.

Getting ready

We need a corrupt XLF file.

How to do it...

1. Make a copy of the corrupted XLF file.

2. Rename the extension (`.xlf`) of the file as `.zip`. You will get a Windows message about changing the extension, which could cause the file to be unusable. Click **Yes**.

db_corrupt.xlf   db_corrupt.zip

3. Open the ZIP file. Here you will see a folder and two documents. In the folder, the images of the dashboard model are saved. If you don't use images, you won't see this folder. In the `document.xml` file, the dashboard model properties are stored (component size, position, and so on). The `xldoc` file is the spreadsheet model.

Name	Type	Compressed size	Password ...	Size
2003384500-10987-04579-150-068-1712461080047061134	File folder			
document.xml	XML Document	63 KB	No	1,288 KB
xldoc	File	28 KB	No	168 KB

4. Drag the `xldoc` file out of the ZIP file.

5. Rename the `xldoc` file as `xldoc.xls`.

6. Open `xldoc.xls` in MS Excel. As you can see in the following screenshot, there are a lot of **#VALUE** errors in the spreadsheet file.

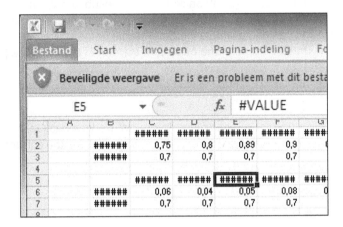

7. Save the file as an Excel Workbook file (`xldoc.xlsx`). Close MS Excel.

8. Now reopen MS Excel and load the XLSX file you just created. Save it as an Excel 97-2003 Workbook file (`xldoc.xls`).

9. Rename `xldoc.xls` back to `xldoc`.

10. Go back to the ZIP file and delete the `xldoc` file from it.

11. Drag your edited `xldoc` file into the ZIP file.

12. Rename the `ZIP` file back to `XLF`.

13. Open the dashboard model in SAP BusinessObjects Dashboards.

You might need to repair some cells in the spreadsheet, but at least you can access your dashboard model again.

How it works...

Corrupt files are a big frustration among SAP BusinessObjects Dashboards developers. This unofficial workaround might solve the issue by hacking into the XLF file and replacing the spreadsheet source file. Use this method only when necessary.

There's more...

Instead of using the `xldoc` file from the corrupted XLF file, you can also replace it with the `xldoc` file from a recent backup XLF file. When you do this, make sure that there aren't too many changes to your spreadsheet or bindings with the dashboard components.

Real-world Dashboard Case Studies

In order to take advantage of the full range of features and include various techniques that could be implemented while working through these chapters, we'll discuss two examples of commonly used dashboards. This approach will help you streamline some of the actions that you have been undertaking.

The following are real-world dashboard examples explained in the form of recipes:

- ▶ What-if scenario – Mortgage Calculator
- ▶ Sales/Profit dashboard example

 Please find the respective example XLF source files
(`Mortgage_Calculator.xlf` and `Sales_Profit.xlf`)
in the code bundle of this book.

What-if scenario – Mortgage Calculator

In this recipe, we will create a what-if scenario dashboard. The purpose of the dashboard is to calculate and show the monthly payments and the total cost of a mortgage, based on a set of adjustable variables.

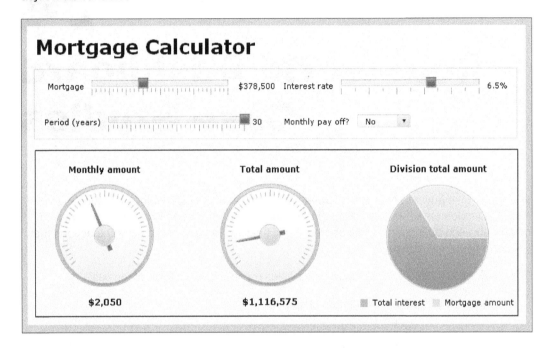

We will use techniques from the following chapters and recipes:

- *Chapter 1, Staying in Control*
- The *Using sliders to create a what-if scenario* recipe from *Chapter 3, From a Static to an Interactive Dashboard*
- The *Selecting your data from a list* recipe from *Chapter 3, From a Static to an Interactive Dashboard*
- The *Illustrating single values* recipe from *Chapter 2, Data Visualization*
- The *Using a pie chart* recipe from *Chapter 2, Data Visualization*
- *Chapter 7, Dashboard Look and Feel*

Getting ready

As we are starting from scratch, you only have to open a new SAP BusinessObjects Dashboard file.

How to do it...

1. The dashboard will contain four variables: **Mortgage amount, Mortgage term in years, Yearly interest rate**, and a variable that states whether the mortgage will be paid off by equal monthly payments (annuity) or just at the end of the mortgage term, which is the **Monthly interest rate**.

2. First, set up the spreadsheet. Make sure your spreadsheet looks like the following screenshot:

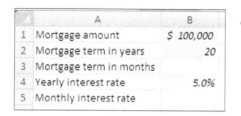

3. To calculate the monthly and total payments, we need the mortgage term in months, which is the number of years multiplied by 12. Add this Excel formula to cell **B3**: =B2*12.

4. To calculate the monthly interest rate, we need the formula = (1+B4)^(1/12)-1. Enter it into cell **B5**.

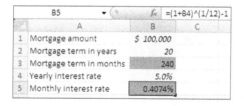

 Instead of using the ^ operator, you can also use the POWER Excel formula: =POWER(1+B4,1/12)-1.

5. Now drag three **Horizontal Slider** components to the canvas.

6. Bind the **Data** field of the first **Horizontal Slider** component to cell **B1**. Also set the **Maximum Limit** to 1,000,000. Enter Mortgage as the **Title**.

7. Select the second **Horizontal Slider** component and bind its **Data** field to cell **B4**. Set the **Maximum Limit** to 0.1. As we are dealing with percentages, the maximum limit is now 10% due to this setting. Enter Interest rate as the **Title**.

8. Go to the **Behavior** tab, and in the **Slider Movement** section, change the **Increment** to 0.001.

9. Select the third **Horizontal Slider** component and bind the **Data** field of this one to cell **B2**. Set the **Maximum Limit** to 30 and enter Period (years) as the **Title**.

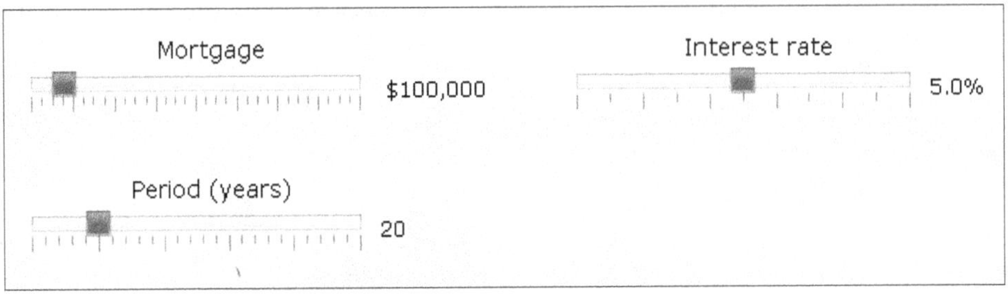

10. Now we need to add some more logic to our spreadsheet to calculate the monthly payments. Adjust your spreadsheet as shown in the following screenshot:

	A	B	C
1	Mortgage amount	$ 100,000	
2	Mortgage term in years	20	
3	Mortgage term in months	240	
4	Yearly interest rate	5.0%	
5	Monthly interest rate	0.4074%	
6			
7	**Monthly pay-off?**	Yes	No
8	Monthly amount		
9	Total amount		
10	Total interest		
11	Mortgage amount		

11. Enter the following formula in cell **B8** to calculate the monthly annuity:

```
=B1*(B5/(1-(1+B5)^(-B3)))
```

12. Enter the formula =B3*B8 in cell **B9** to calculate the total amount.

13. Enter the formula =B9-B1 in cell **B10** to calculate the total interest amount.

14. In cell **C8**, enter the formula =B1*(B4^1/12) to calculate the monthly amount, which is only the interest.

15. Enter formula =B3*C8 in cell **C10** and enter formula =B1+C10 in cell **C9**.

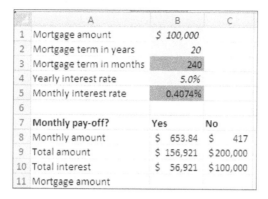

16. Add a **Combo Box** component to the canvas. We will use this component to determine whether the mortgage will be paid off in monthly installments. Bind the **Labels** field to cells **B7** and **C7**. Go to the **Behavior** tab and set **Item** to Label 1.

17. Return to the **General** tab, and in the **Data Insertion** section, set the **Insertion Type** to **Column**. Bind the **Source Data** field to cell range **B8:C10**. Bind the **Destination** field to cell range **D8:D10**.

18. Finally, enter Monthly pay off? as the **Title**.

19. Go back to the spreadsheet and enter the formula =B1 into cell **D11**.

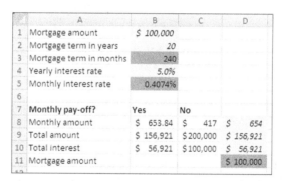

20. Now that the spreadsheet and all the selectors are set up, it is time to show some data in the dashboard. Add a **Gauge** component to the canvas.

21. Bind its **By Range** field to cell **D8** and set the **Maximum Limit** field to 5000. Enter Monthly amount as the **Title**.

22. Add another **Gauge** component to the canvas and bind its **By Range** field to cell **D9**. Set its **Maximum Limit** field to 10,000,000. Enter Total amount as the **Title**.

23. Drag a **Pie Chart** component to the canvas. Bind its **Values** field to cells **D10** and **D11**. Next, bind the **Labels** field to cells **A10** and **A11**. Enter Division total amount as the **Title**.

24. Go to the **Appearance** tab and deselect **Show Chart Background**. Set the position of the legend to **Bottom**.

25. All right! The what-if section of the dashboard is now in place and ready to be tested. Preview the dashboard and play around with the sliders and selectors to see if everything works.

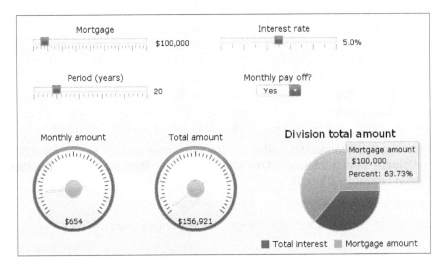

26. Leave the **Preview** mode. We will now adjust the layout of the dashboard so it looks a bit smoother.

27. First select the **Phase** theme from the **Theme** selector in the **Format** menu.

28. Use the **Alignment** options from the **Format** menu to adjust the placement of the three sliders and the selector.

 You can also use the **Grid** to help with alignment and positioning. You can activate the **Grid** in **Preferences** in the **File** menu.

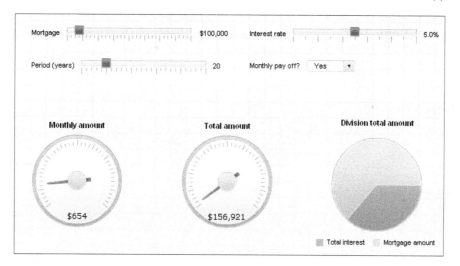

29. Add a **Rectangular** component and resize it so it will fit over the sliders and selector. Change the **Border Color** into a lighter color; for example, gray.

30. Add a **Label** component to the canvas and enter `Mortgage Calculator` in the **Enter Text** field. Select the **Appearance** tab and go to the **Text** sub-tab. Select **Bold** and set the **Text Size** to `28`. Make sure you resize the **Label** component if the text doesn't fit anymore.

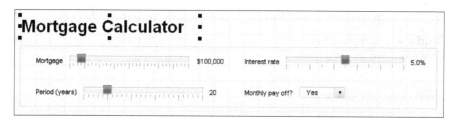

31. Select the **Pie Chart** and the **Gauge** components. Align them by **Middle and Space Evenly Across**.

32. As you can see, the title of the **Pie Chart** is placed a bit higher than the titles of the **Gauge** components. Select both **Gauge** components. Go to the **Appearance** tab and select the **Text** sub-tab. Now adjust the **Y Offset** so all titles will have the same height.

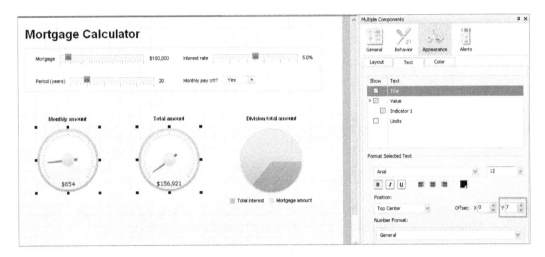

33. Select **Value**. In the **Format Selected Text** section, select **Bold** and adjust the **Y Offset** so the values of the **Gauge** components will be at the same height as the legend of the **Pie Chart** component.

34. Go to the **Behavior** tab and deselect the **Enable Interaction** option.

35. Add another **Rectangular** component to the canvas and place it over the **Gauge** components and **Pie Chart**.

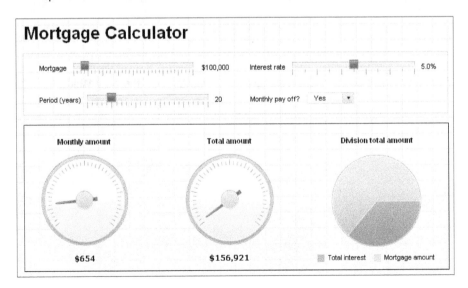

36. Select **Fit the Canvas to Components** from the **Canvas Sizing** options in the **View** menu. You can also use the buttons from the **Standard Toolbar**. Select the **Increase Canvas** option twice.

37. Your what-if dashboard is complete!

How it works...

▶ In steps 1-4, 10-15, and 19, we utilized what we learned in recipes from *Chapter 1, Staying in Control*, to properly set up the spreadsheet

▶ In steps 5-9, we set up the sliders like we did in the *Using sliders to create a what-if scenario* recipe from *Chapter 3, From a Static to an Interactive Dashboard*

▶ In steps 16-18, we used the *Selecting your data from a list* recipe from *Chapter 3, From a Static to an Interactive Dashboard*, to define the **Combo Box** component to determine whether the mortgage is paid off or not

▶ Steps 20-24 used recipes *Illustrating single values* and *Using a pie chart* from *Chapter 2, Data Visualization*, to show the data in two gauges and a pie chart

▶ In the final steps, we used what we have learned from recipes in *Chapter 7, Dashboard Look and Feel*, to implement a different dashboard theme and fine-tune the look of the dashboard

Sales/Profit dashboard example

In this example, we will utilize many techniques that we have learned in the previous recipes to create a Sales/Profit dashboard.

The Sales/Profit dashboard displays the sales or profit of each state on the map. From the map, a user can select a state and then view year-to-date (YTD) sales/profit information for products that are sold from the bar chart in the top right. The user can then drill down further by clicking on a product bar.

A detailed scorecard and trend chart at the bottom right will then be shown for the selected state and product.

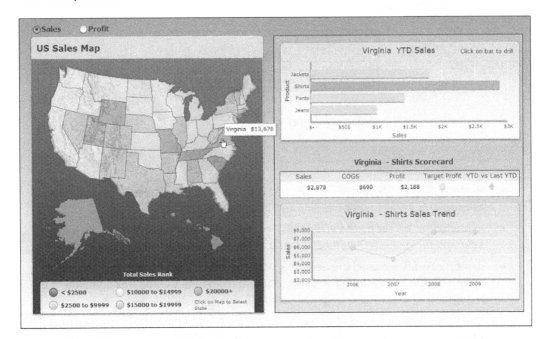

Techniques from the following chapters and recipes were used for this example:

▸ *Chapter 1, Staying in Control*

▸ The *Adding a line chart to your dashboard* recipe from *Chapter 2, Data Visualization*

▸ The *Drilling down from a chart* recipe from *Chapter 3, From a Static to an Interactive Dashboard*

▸ The *Using Filtered Rows* recipe from *Chapter 3, From a Static to an Interactive Dashboard*

▸ The *Selecting your data from a list* recipe from *Chapter 3, From a Static to an Interactive Dashboard*

▸ The *Using maps to select data of an area or country* recipe of *Chapter 3, From a Static to an Interactive Dashboard*

▸ The *Using alerts in a Scorecard* recipe from *Chapter 5, Using Alerts*

▸ The *Displaying alerts on a map* recipe from *Chapter 5, Using Alerts*

Getting ready

It is important that you have the `Sales_Profit.xlf` file as a reference. Please open it before proceeding to the next section as the spreadsheet layout has already been completed for your convenience.

How to do it...

1. Drag the **Map – USA** component onto the canvas.
2. Bind the **Region Keys** to the **State Keys** on the **Control Sheet** tab.
3. In the **Data Insertion** section, select **Row** as the **Insertion Type**. The **Source Data** will be the keys that we selected in step 2. The **Destination** will be cell **E1**.

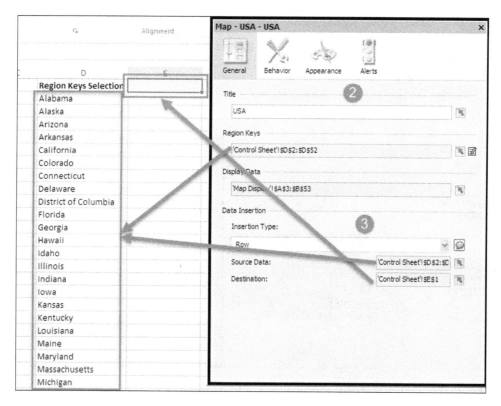

4. Bind **Display Data** to the key-value pair items in the **Map Display** worksheet.

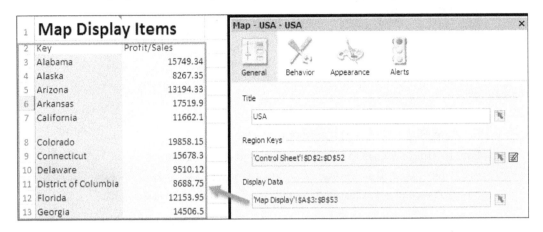

5. Go to the **Alerts** properties, check the **Enable Alerts** checkbox, select **By Value**, check the **Use a Range** checkbox, and bind to the range section in the **Map Display** worksheet. It is important that you bind starting at 2500, otherwise it will add another range starting from minimum to 0.

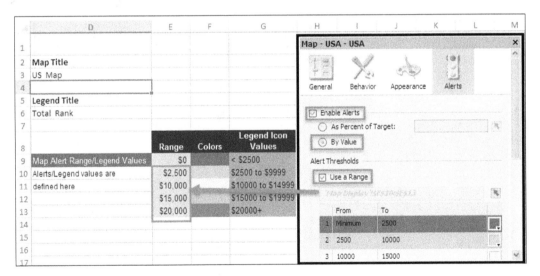

6. The next step is to complete the YTD chart in the top right-hand corner. Drag a **Bar Chart** component and place it in the top right-hand corner of the canvas.

7. Bind the **Titles** to the appropriate cells in column **T** of the **State and Drilldown Display** worksheet. Then bind the **Data** to the cells **V3:W7**. The data in **V4:W7** is populated depending on whether a user selects **Sales** or **Profit**. Note that the cells are pre-populated with test data.

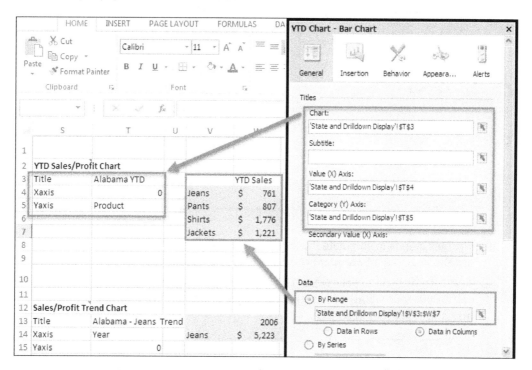

8. Go to the **Insertion** properties of the **YTD Chart**. Check the **Enable Data Insertion** checkbox and select **Row** as the **Insertion Type**. Bind the **Source Data** to cells **A4:Q7** of the **State and Drilldown Display** worksheet. Bind the **Destination** to cells **A14:Q14**. Note that the cells are pre-populated with test data.

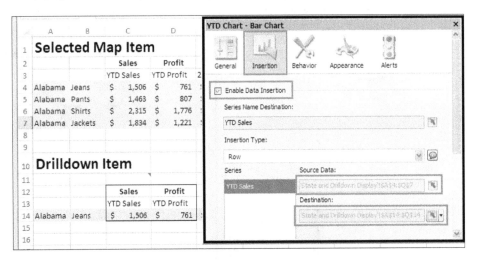

9. The next step is to complete the scorecard in the middle right-hand side of the dashboard. Drag a **Scorecard** component onto the canvas.

10. Bind **Display Data** to cells **M13:Q14** of the **Drilldown Scorecard** section in the **State and Drilldown Display** worksheet. These cells are the drilldown values populated from the **YTD Chart** in step 8.

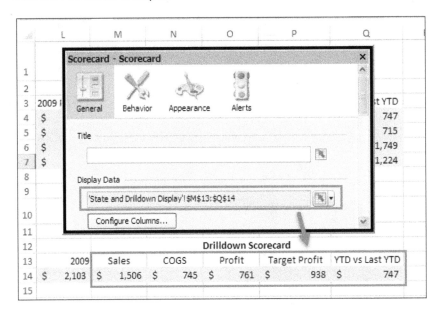

11. Go to the **Appearance** properties of the **Scorecard** and click on the **Text** tab. Unselect the **Target Profit** and **YTD vs Last YTD** checkboxes. The reason is that we only want to see alert shapes on these cells and not the text value.

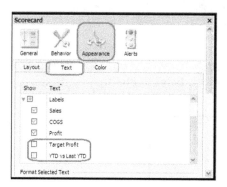

12. Go to the **Alerts** properties of the **Scorecard**. Check the **Target Profit** and **YTD vs Last YTD** checkboxes. In both cases, the **Alert Values** will be bound to cell **O14** of the **State and Drilldown Display** worksheet. In both cases, make sure to have **As Percent of Target** selected. Bind **Target Profit** to cell **P14** and **YTD vs Last YTD** to cell **Q14**. In the **Alert Thresholds** section, we want `Min/70%/85%/Max` for **Target Profit**. Set the alert threshold for the **YTD vs Last YTD** to `Min/99.999%/100%/Max`.

[

The reason why we have 99.999% is so that the yellow arrow symbolizes anything that has YTD equal to Last YTD.
]

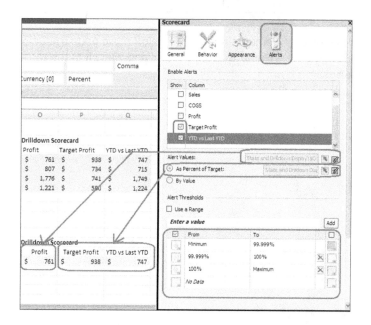

13. Next, we will complete the trend line chart in the bottom right-hand corner of the dashboard. Drag a **Line Chart** component and place it in the bottom right-hand corner of the canvas.

14. Bind **Titles** and **Data Range** to the appropriate section in the **State and Drilldown Display** worksheet.

 Note that the purple section is populated depending on whether a user selects **Sales** or **Profit**.

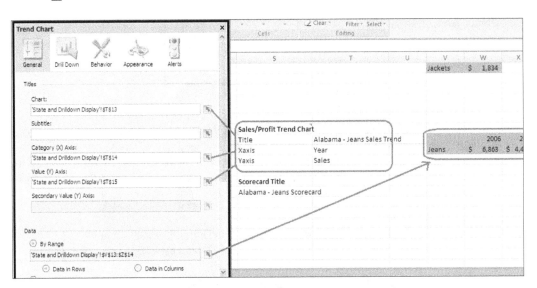

15. Now that the display elements are in place, we'll move on to the Sales/Profit Radio selector. Drag a **Radio Button** selector and place it in the top left section of the canvas.

16. There are two sets of data bindings here. First, we will select **Label** as **Insertion Type** and then bind the data to the selected label (Sales or Profit) cell **B1**. The data is found in columns **A** and **B** of the **Control Sheet** worksheet.

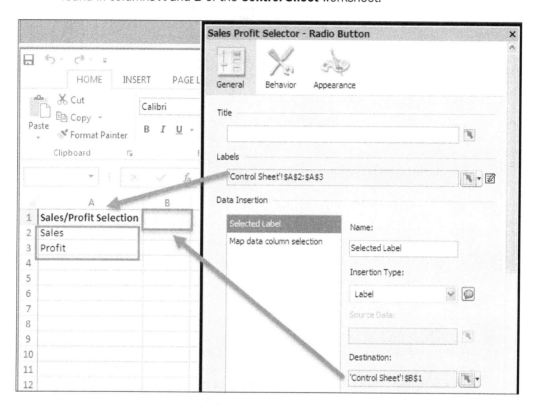

17. For the next data binding, **Map data column selection**, select **Column** as the **Insertion Type**. Bind **Source Data** to columns **B** and **C**.

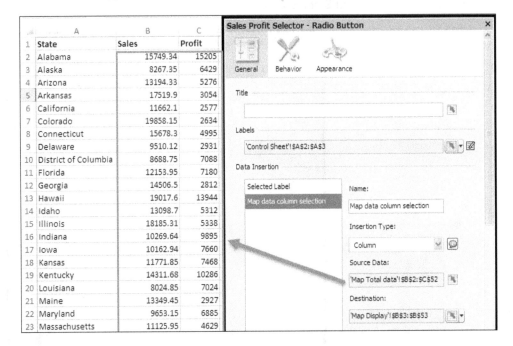

	A	B	C
1	State	Sales	Profit
2	Alabama	15749.34	15205
3	Alaska	8267.35	6429
4	Arizona	13194.33	5276
5	Arkansas	17519.9	3054
6	California	11662.1	2577
7	Colorado	19858.15	2634
8	Connecticut	15678.3	4995
9	Delaware	9510.12	2931
10	District of Columbia	8688.75	7088
11	Florida	12153.95	7180
12	Georgia	14506.5	2812
13	Hawaii	19017.6	13944
14	Idaho	13098.7	5312
15	Illinois	18185.31	5338
16	Indiana	10269.64	9895
17	Iowa	10162.94	7660
18	Kansas	11771.85	7468
19	Kentucky	14311.68	10286
20	Louisiana	8024.85	7024
21	Maine	13349.45	2927
22	Maryland	9653.15	6885
23	Massachusetts	11125.95	4629

Within the panel (Sales Profit Selector - Radio Button):

- General, Behavior, Appearance
- Title
- Labels: 'Control Sheet'!$A$2:$A$3
- Data Insertion
  - Selected Label / Map data column selection
  - Name: Map data column selection
  - Insertion Type: Column
  - Source Data: 'Map Total data'!$B$2:$C$52
  - Destination: 'Map Display'!$B$3:$B$53

18. The final interactive component is the hidden **State** filter, which will select the appropriate data for the State and Product details. Insert a **Combo Box** selector into the canvas and make sure it is underneath all of the backgrounds. To make sure it is underneath, right-click on the **Combo Box** selector on the **Object Browser** and select **Send To Back**.

19. Now we will bind the data from the **Product Data** worksheet. The labels will be bound to column **B**, since we are collecting all rows that belong to a state when clicking on a state from the map. Select **Filtered Rows** as **Insertion Type** and bind the **Source Data** to cells **B2:R205**. The **Destination** cells will be the peach area in the **State and Drilldown Display** worksheet.

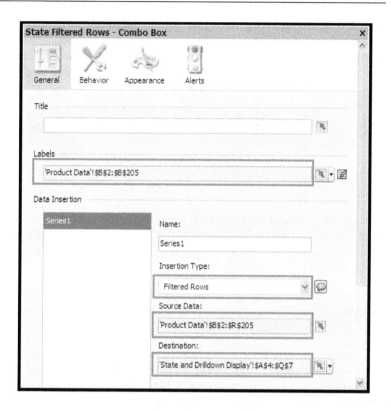

20. Go to the **Behavior** section of the hidden filter and bind **Selected Item** to the selected Map item on cell **E1** from the **Control Sheet** worksheet.

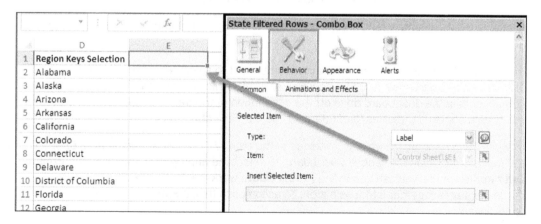

21. Now that the dashboard is complete, we want to improve the look a bit. As you can see, there are several layers of background objects that add depth to the dashboard components. Drag a variety of **Background** and **Rectangle** components onto the canvas and play around with the look until it becomes something that you desire.

 Refer to the source code on the type of layering that we have accomplished with the **Background** and **Rectangle** components.

How it works...

In steps 1–3, you utilize what you learned in the *Using maps to select data of an area or country* recipe of *Chapter 3, From a Static to an Interactive Dashboard*, to set up your map display and data on the left-hand side of the dashboard. From your map selection, you then drive the right-hand side of the dashboard.

Steps 4–5 used the *Displaying alerts on a map* recipe from *Chapter 5, Using Alerts*, to display the different colored states on the map representing the amount of sales/profit each state produced.

In steps 6-8, you use what you learned in the recipes *Adding a line chart to your dashboard* from *Chapter 2, Data Visualization*, and *Drilling down from a chart* from *Chapter 3, From a Static to an Interactive Dashboard*, to create a YTD Sales/Profit chart that allows a user to drill down from the data values to a particular product.

In steps 9-12, you will use the *Using alerts in a Scorecard* recipe from *Chapter 5, Using Alerts*, to show a product's details and threshold for a selected state.

In steps 13-14, we simply built a **Line Chart** that takes the trend data from a selected product and state.

In steps 15-17, we used a **Combo Selector** component to select from two sets of data. The first set of data consists of the label **Sales/Profit**, which is important because other components in the dashboard drive off the destination of the **Sales/Profit** label. The second set of data contains the sales/profit data for the map object.

In steps 18-20, you utilize what you learned in the *Using Filtered Rows* recipe from *Chapter 3, From a Static to an Interactive Dashboard*, to select the appropriate data from the **Product Data** worksheet. As you can see in the **Product Data** worksheet, you need to somehow group the states together into a selection. To accomplish this, a **Filtered Rows** selection is necessary.

The final steps consisted of adding backgrounds and providing a uniform aligned look and feel, recipes of which can be found in *Chapter 1, Staying in Control*.

B

Additional Resources – Supported Excel Functions and System/ Software Requirements

This appendix can be used as a great reference for developers. We have provided a list of online resources that are very useful for problem solving and additional knowledge. We have also provided the necessary Excel functions that users can print out and keep handy on their desk. In addition, during installation and planning, users can refer to the *System and software requirements* section found at the end of the appendix.

Online resources

The following is a list of online resources:

- ▶ SAP Community Network (SCN): The SAP BusinessObjects Dashboards section at `http://scn.sap.com/community/businessobjects-dashboards`.

  The Official SAP Community Network provides a wealth of knowledge on SAP products, forums to help developers overcome any problems, blogs to learn new tips and tricks, and much more.

▸ BusinessObjects Board: `http://www.forumtopics.com/busobj/`.

Before SAP bought BusinessObjects, this was the largest support forum that developers would go to. Even after the acquisition of BusinessObjects, the forum still remains very active.

▸ SAP Help: SAP BusinessObjects Dashboards 4.1 page: `http://help.sap.com/bodash/`.

This is the official SAP help page where you can find information on new releases, known issues, fixed issues, an error message guide, documentation on the SDK and SAP installation, and user guides. Also, documentation on older versions of SAP BusinessObjects Dashboards is available here.

▸ EverythingXcelsius.com: Xcelsius Gurus Network: `http://www.everythingxcelsius.com`.

This is a website for all your SAP BusinessObjects Dashboards (Xcelsius) news, tips, tricks, templates, consulting, and training.

▸ MyXcelsius.com: `http://www.myxcelsius.com`.

This is a blog that contains a huge amount of tips, tricks, and best practices for SAP BusinessObjects Dashboards.

▸ Interactive Data Visualization by Ryan Goodman: `http://ryangoodman.net/blog/`.

This is Ryan Goodman's blog on data visualization, location intelligence, and dashboard creation with SAP BusinessObjects Dashboards.

▸ Visual Business Intelligence by Stephen Few: `http://www.perceptualedge.com/blog/`.

Stephen Few is a well-recognized author and trainer on the topic of data visualization. In this blog, he shows and explains his ideas on how to create proper visualizations of data.

▸ Data Ink by Josh Tapley: `http://data-ink.com/`.

Josh Tapley's blog provides a lot of interesting ideas and examples of dashboards created with SAP BusinessObjects Dashboards.

▸ HackingSAP.com: `http://www.hackingsap.com/`.

This is Xavier Hacking's blog that provides a wealth of information on SAP-related products, focusing mainly on the Business Intelligence realm.

- David Lai's Business Intelligence Blog: `http://www.davidlai101.com/blog`.

  David Lai's blog provides a great number of tips, tricks, and best practices mainly on SAP BusinessObjects-related products. He also provides insight into other Business Intelligence toolsets.

- Colorbrewer: `http://colorbrewer2.org`.

  Colorbrewer is a very useful online tool that can help you to choose good color sets for your charts and maps.

- DashboardSpy: `http://www.dashboardspy.com/`.

  At the DashboardSpy website, you can find a lot of dashboard examples.

Supported Excel functions

The following is a table of supported Microsoft Excel functions:

ABS	ACOS	ACOSH	AND
ASIN	ASINH	ASSIGN	ATAN
ATAN2	ATANH	AVEDEV	AVERAGE
AVERAGEA	AVERAGEIF	BETADIST	CEILING
CHOOSE	CEILING	CHOOSE	COMBIN
CONCATENATE	COS	COSH	COUNT
COUNTA	COUNTIF	DATE	DATEVALUE
DAVERAGE	DAY	DAYS360	DB
DCOUNT	DCOUNTA	DDB	DEGREES
DEVSQ	DGET	DIVIDE	DMAX
DMIN	DOLLAR	DPRODUCT	DSTDEV
DSSTDEVP	DSUM	DVAR	DVARP
EDATE	EFFECT	EOMONTH	EVEN
EXACT	EXP	EXPONDIST	GE
GEOMEAN	GT	HARMEAN	HLOOKUP
HOUR	IF	INDEX	INT
INTERCEPT	IPMT	IRR	ISBLANK
ISERR	ISERROR	ISEVEN	ISLOGICAL
ISNA	ISNONTEXT	ISNUMBER	ISODD
ISTEXT	KURT	LARGE	LE

LEFT	LEN	LN	LOG
LOG10	LOOKUP	LOWER	MATCH
MAX	MEDIAN	MID	MIN
MINUS	MINUTE	MIRR	MOD
MODE	MONTH	N	NE
NETWORKDAYS	NORMDIST	NORMINV	NORMSINV
NOT	NOW	NPER	NPV
ODD	OFFSET	OR	PI
PMT	POWER	PPMT	PRODUCT
PV	QUARTILE	QUOTIENT	RADIANS
RAND	RANGE_COLON	RANK	RATE
REPLACE	REPT	RIGHT	ROUND
ROUNDDOWN	ROUNDUP	SECOND	SIGN
SIN	SINH	SLN	SMALL
SQRT	STANDARDIZE	STDEV	SUM
SUMIF	SUMPRODUCT	SUMSQ	SUMX2MY2
SUMX2PY2	SUMXMY2	SYD	TAN
TANH	TEXT	TIME	TIMEVALUE
TODAY	TRUE	TRUNC	TYPE
UPPER	VALUE	VAR	VDB
VLOOKUP	WEEKDAY	WEEKNUM	WORKDAY
YEAR	YEARFRAC		

System and software requirements

This section will show the minimum hardware/software requirements, as well as supported software that works in conjunction with SAP BusinessObjects Dashboards 4.1.

The minimum hardware requirements for SAP BusinessObjects Dashboards and for viewing SWFs are listed as follows:

- Minimum screen resolution of 1024 x 768 is recommended
- SAP BusinessObjects Dashboards:
    - 1.8 GHz processor
    - 2 GB RAM
    - 900 MB available hard drive space (installer files)
    - 350 MB available hard drive space (installed)

- Dashboard SWF:

    - 1.8 GHz processor

    - 1 GB RAM

The list of supported software that work in conjunction with SAP BusinessObjects Dashboards is as follows:

- Supported operating systems:

    - Windows Server 2008

    - Windows Server 2008 R2

    - Windows Server 2012

    - Windows Server R2

    - Windows 7 SP1

    - Windows 8

    - Windows 8.1

- Supported browsers:

    - Microsoft Internet Explorer 8+

    - Mozilla Firefox 24.x+

    - Google Chrome

    - Safari 7+

- Supported Flash players:

    - Adobe Flash Player 11 and above

- Supported Microsoft Office versions:

    - Microsoft Office 2007 SP3+

    - Microsoft Office 2010 SP1+

    - Microsoft Office 2013

- SAP BusinessObjects BI Platform connectivity: For optimal performance, it is recommended to update all the versions of SAP BusinessObjects BI Platform, Query as a Web Service, and Live Office to the current support pack available.

- SAP BusinessObjects BI Platform:

    - SAP BusinessObjects BI 4.1

    - SAP BusinessObjects Enterprise XI 3.1

    - SAP BusinessObjects Enterprise XI R2 SP5

- ▸ SAP BusinessObjects Live Office:
    - ❑ Live Office BI 4.1 connected to SAP BusinessObjects BI 4.1
    - ❑ Live Office XI 3.1 connected to SAP BusinessObjects Enterprise XI 3.1
    - ❑ Live Office XI R2 connected to SAP BusinessObjects Enterprise XI R2

- ▸ Query as a Web Service (QaaWS) for SAP BusinessObjects Enterprise:
    - ❑ QaaWS BI 4 connected to SAP BusinessObjects BI 4
    - ❑ QaaWS for SAP BusinessObjects Enterprise XI 3.1
    - ❑ QaaWS for SAP BusinessObjects Enterprise XI R2

- ▸ Supported SAP NetWeaver BW:
    - ❑ SAP NetWeaver BW 7.0 Enhancement Pack 1 Service Pack 5 or higher

- ▸ SAP Application Servers: The BusinessObjects XI 3.1 Integration for SAP Solutions must be installed in order to use an SAP application server as a data source. For the latest information on SAP platforms required by BusinessObjects XI 3.1 Integration for SAP Solutions, visit the support section of the SAP website at `http://help.sap.com`.

C The Future of Dashboarding with SAP Design Studio

When the first edition of this book was published back in 2011, SAP BusinessObjects Dashboards served as the only and premier dashboarding solution within the SAP BusinessObjects BI portfolio. A lot has changed since then. In 2012, SAP released the first version of **SAP BusinessObjects Design Studio**. This new tool has been built from scratch and lets you create interactive applications and dashboards that are fully HTML5-compatible and support direct connectivity to SAP HANA, SAP NetWeaver BW, and SAP BusinessObjects Universe (UNX) sources.

In this appendix, we will discuss the following topics:

- What is SAP BusinessObjects Design Studio?
- SAP BusinessObjects Dashboards versus SAP BusinessObjects Design Studio
- What is the SAP roadmap for dashboarding?

What is SAP BusinessObjects Design Studio?

Design Studio is a fresh new tool within the SAP BusinessObjects BI portfolio to create dashboards and interactive applications.

Design Studio tackles two of the biggest problem areas of SAP BusinessObjects Dashboards:

▸ Connectivity to SAP source systems

▸ Compatibility with mobile devices without any dependency on Adobe Flash

Design Studio fully supports SAP HANA, SAP NetWeaver BW, and SAP BusinessObjects Universe (UNX) sources. Since the tool is HTML5-compatible, we can run the applications we make on any device, whether it is a personal computer with a browser or a mobile device such as an iPad or iPhone.

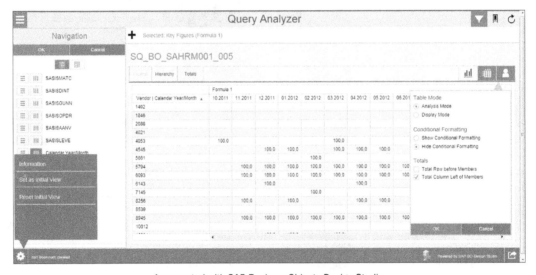

App created with SAP BusinessObjects Design Studio

Just as in SAP BusinessObjects Dashboards, the Design Studio development environment lets you drag and drop components you want to use in a dashboard into a canvas and position them exactly as you want. A wide set of such components is available within Design Studio. Analytical components such as tables and charts can be used to visualize and display the data. Also, several filter, button, text, image and drop-down box components are present to facilitate interactive options. To facilitate the grouping of components, a set of container components is available. In addition, developers can create their own Design Studio components using the Design Studio SDK.

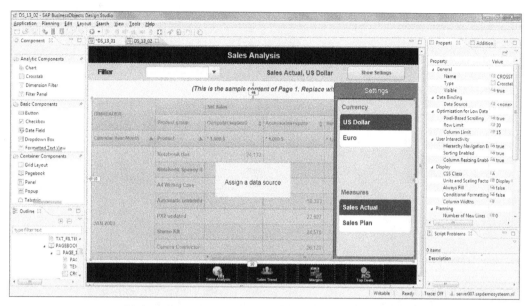

SAP BusinessObjects Design Studio Integrated Development Environment

To create interactivity between components, Design Studio uses scripting with JavaScript. For example, if a user selects a filter value from a drop-down box component, the datasource has to execute that filter and refresh the chart or table that displays the result. To make this work, a script has to be added to the drop-down box component so it will be executed each time the component is used. A wizard is included to support the developer in writing these scripts.

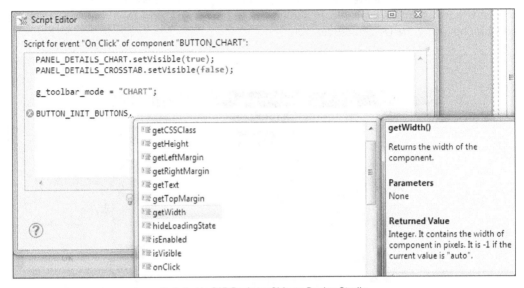

Scripting in SAP BusinessObjects Design Studio

Design Studio offers the option to fully take control of the look and feel of a dashboard or an application by using Cascading Style Sheets (CSS). In CSS, the specific look of a component can be defined, such as its background color and its font size. Such a piece of CSS code can be used throughout the application for multiple components, while the CSS definition remains in a single location. These CSS files can be stored on a central server location and even be reused by multiple applications.

Design Studio applications can be deployed in three types of SAP environments: SAP BusinessObjects BI Platform, SAP NetWeaver BW, and SAP HANA.

SAP BusinessObjects Dashboards versus SAP BusinessObjects Design Studio

SAP BusinessObjects Dashboards is an extremely flexible tool. It supports a wide range of different data sources and offers the integrated spreadsheet to tie everything together. Also, there is a very wide range of components (standard and third-party) available, which have detailed property settings to make specific adjustments.

Design Studio, on the other hand, has a more robust setup. The spreadsheet layer is gone and only datasources via SAP systems are supported. Also, web standards such as JavaScript and CSS are incorporated. The export functionality to create standalone SWF files is also gone and the deployment of Design Studio apps is only available through SAP environments.

The following table lists some key differences and similarities between SAP BusinessObjects Dashboards and Design Studio:

	Design Studio	Dashboards
Platform	SAP BW JAVA Portal	SAP BW JAVA Portal
	SAP BusinessObjects BI Launchpad	SAP BusinessObjects BI Launchpad
	SAP HANA	SWF (Flash) file (standalone or embedded in MS Office / PDF)
Output format	HTML5	SWF (Flash)
		HTML5 (limited number of components and connection types)
Mobile	100 percent compatible through the SAP BusinessObjects Mobile app or through the direct URL in a browser	Limited compatibility through the SAP BusinessObjects Mobile app
Components	High number of chart and table components	Very high number of chart, table, buttons, selection, and miscellaneous graphical components
	Limited number of buttons, selection (sliders), and miscellaneous graphical components (gauges)	

	Design Studio	Dashboards
Development flexibility	High flexibility; drag and drop supported, including relative positioning of components Interactivity enabled through JavaScript and CSS can be used for visual adjustments	High flexibility; drag and drop supported Integrated spreadsheet can be used to set up interactivity
Connectivity	SAP NetWeaver BW SAP HANA SAP BusinessObjects Universes (UNX)	SAP NetWeaver BW SAP BusinessObjects Universes (UNX) Web Service Query XML SAP BusinessObjects Live Office
Data input	SAP NetWeaver BW Integrated Planning supported	Not supported
SDK	Eclipse IDE	Adobe Flex

What is the SAP roadmap for dashboarding?

When we take a look at the SAP product roadmap for SAP BusinessObjects Dashboards, we see that there are almost no more planned innovations and future directions named. On the other hand, the product roadmap for Design Studio is packed with new features. Also, Design Studio has quite a steady release schedule with a new version every six months.

You can find the most recent versions of the SAP product roadmaps at http://service.sap.com/roadmap.

SAP BusinessObjects Design Studio Roadmap

Drag and drop in navigation panel & navigation panel usability	Offline click-through apps	Export to Microsoft PPT & Word
Context menu in crosstab	Export data to PDF	Pre-calculation & broadcasting
Cell locking (for planning apps)	Unmerge variables (performance)	Adhoc exceptions & conditions
Report to Report Interface	Improved designer experience	BW variants
Script API extensions & global functions	Geomaps	Dynamic Analysis Office & Lumira export
Multi language support	Lumira interoperability	Local calculations
Enhanced standard analysis template	Multi-selection in crosstab & charts	Additional hierarchical filter components
Online composition of apps & bookmarking	Enhancements: mobile, charting, scripting, online composition	Copy & paste variable values
Data source SDK	Better commentary handling (based on new BW 7.40 SP8 capabilities)	Call RFC modules from DS scripts
Lumira (CVOM) SDK		Lumira interoperability
Real-time streaming		
Fiori / sFin integration		
Today	**Planned Innovations**	**Future Direction**
(Release 1.4) Planned Nov 2014		This is the current state of planning and may be changed by SAP at any time.

This is in line with the statement of direction for dashboarding that was published by SAP in 2012. Eventually, the goal is to integrate SAP BusinessObjects and Design Studio into a single dashboarding tool.

> To read the statement of direction, visit `http://blogs.sap.com/analytics/2012/04/17/the-future-of-dashboards-strategy-and-direction/`.

Although there are no concrete timelines set as yet, we can expect SAP to support SAP BusinessObjects Dashboards for a very long time as it has done so in the past. But it definitely would be a good idea to start looking at Design Studio and to stay up to date with the ongoing developments.

Index

password protection, for
    dashboard 135-139
pop-up screen, building 125-128

E

Excel Concatenate function 258
Excel spreadsheet performance
  improving 346, 347
  tips, for improving 346, 347
Excel XML Maps
  Connection Refresh Button 229
  Usage tab 228
  used, for creating news ticker 222-228

F

Fiddler
  URL 358
  used, for identifying cause of performance
    issues 358-363
filled radar chart 49
Filtered Rows
  about 84
  using 84-87
filters
  using 257-259
Filter selector component
  using, for hierarchies 73-76
Fisheye Picture Menu selector
  using 92-95
Flash Variables
  used, for passing values from one dashboard
    to another 268-273
format
  copying, from one cell to another cell 18
forward referencing 346

G

gauges
  used, for illustrating single values 64, 65
Google Maps
  integrating, with CMaps plugin 307-314
graphomate website
  URL 341
Grid component
  using 173, 174

versus List View component 173
versus Spreadsheet Table component 173

H

heat map. *See* **tree map**
Hierarchical Table
  using 79-84
hierarchy selection
  alternative method 76-79
History component
  using 181-183

I

IdeaCrop
  URL 316
image component
  used, for making selections from custom
    image 96-100
Infoview 110
Inovista
  URL 322

L

line chart
  about 24
  adding, to dashboard 24-28
  data, binding manually 28
  series, displaying 29
  series, hiding 29
List View component 64
Live Office Connection
  about 237
  using 237-240
  working 241

M

Mac OS X-looking dock
  adding, to dashboard 92-95
map
  about 88
  alerts, displaying 151-154
  alerts, displaying of different
    thresholds 154-156
  using 88-91

X

Xcelsius Dashboard Printer
  used, for advanced printing 337-340
XWIS Export component 335
XWIS Slice and Dice component 335

Y

y axis, charts
  Allow Zoom Out Only option 59
  scaling 57, 58
  variable maximum limits 59

Z

zooming, charts
  about 55
  range slider option, using 55, 56

About Packt Publishing

Packt, pronounced 'packed', published its first book, *Mastering phpMyAdmin for Effective MySQL Management*, in April 2004, and subsequently continued to specialize in publishing highly focused books on specific technologies and solutions.

Our books and publications share the experiences of your fellow IT professionals in adapting and customizing today's systems, applications, and frameworks. Our solution-based books give you the knowledge and power to customize the software and technologies you're using to get the job done. Packt books are more specific and less general than the IT books you have seen in the past. Our unique business model allows us to bring you more focused information, giving you more of what you need to know, and less of what you don't.

Packt is a modern yet unique publishing company that focuses on producing quality, cutting-edge books for communities of developers, administrators, and newbies alike. For more information, please visit our website at www.PacktPub.com.

About Packt Enterprise

In 2010, Packt launched two new brands, Packt Enterprise and Packt Open Source, in order to continue its focus on specialization. This book is part of the Packt Enterprise brand, home to books published on enterprise software – software created by major vendors, including (but not limited to) IBM, Microsoft, and Oracle, often for use in other corporations. Its titles will offer information relevant to a range of users of this software, including administrators, developers, architects, and end users.

Writing for Packt

We welcome all inquiries from people who are interested in authoring. Book proposals should be sent to author@packtpub.com. If your book idea is still at an early stage and you would like to discuss it first before writing a formal book proposal, then please contact us; one of our commissioning editors will get in touch with you.

We're not just looking for published authors; if you have strong technical skills but no writing experience, our experienced editors can help you develop a writing career, or simply get some additional reward for your expertise.

Creating Universes with SAP BusinessObjects

Create and maintain powerful SAP BusinessObjects Universes with the SAP Information Design Tool

Taha M. Mahmoud

Creating Universes with SAP BusinessObjects

ISBN: 978-1-78217-090-7   Paperback: 310 pages

Create and maintain powerful SAP BusinessObjects Universes with the SAP Information Design Tool

1. Gain all the skills needed to achieve your business intelligence goals by linking your business, data, and people using SAP BusinessObjects.

2. Master the SAP Information Design Tool to create a universe and explore its resources such as the connection, data foundation layer, and business layer.

3. Learn to use a business case supported with illustrated diagrams that will help you to build robust universes.

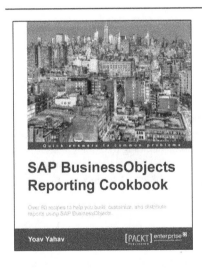

SAP BusinessObjects Reporting Cookbook

Over 80 recipes to help you build, customize, and distribute reports using SAP BusinessObjects.

Yoav Yahav

SAP BusinessObjects Reporting Cookbook

ISBN: 978-1-78217-243-7   Paperback: 380 pages

Over 80 recipes to help you build, customize, and distribute reports using SAP BusinessObjects

1. Discover how to master different business solutions which will help you deliver high quality reports to your organization and clients.

2. Work efficiently in a BI environment while keeping your data accurate, secured, and easily shared.

3. Learn how to build and format reports that will enable you to get the most useful insights from your data.

Please check **www.PacktPub.com** for information on our titles

SAP HCM - A Complete Tutorial

ISBN: 978-1-78217-220-8   Paperback: 380 pages

Deploy and implement the diverse functionalities of SAP HCM

1. Delve into the SAP HCM system and the multitude of features it provides.

2. Explore the various infotypes related to numerous business processes in order to manage human resources better.

3. A practical guide filled with real life scenarios, screenshots, and useful tips and tricks.

SAP HANA Starter

ISBN: 978-1-84968-868-0   Paperback: 60 pages

Everything you need to know to be able to build your first SAP HANA standalone application!

1. Learn something new in an Instant! A short, fast, focused guide delivering immediate results.

2. Understand key principles behind SAP HANA.

3. Discover the main features of the SAP HANA Studio for application design.

4. Create a reporting application on the SAP HANA platform.

5. Visualize your reporting data in Microsoft Excel.

Please check **www.PacktPub.com** for information on our titles